UNITED THEOLOGICAL SEMINARY OF THE TWIN CITIES

An Ecumenical Venture

UNITED THEOLOGICAL SEMINARY OF THE TWIN CITIES

An Ecumenical Venture

Arthur L. Merrill

The Edwin Mellen Press
Lewiston/Queenston/Lampeter

Library of Congress Cataloging-in-Publication Data

Merrill, Arthur L.
United Theological Seminary of the Twin Cities : an ecumenical venture / Arthur L. Merrill.
p. cm.
Includes bibliographical references.
ISBN 0-7734-9201-1
1. United Theological Seminary of the Twin Cities--History. 2. Theological seminaries--Minnesota--New Brighton. 3. United Church of Christ--Education. I. Title.
BV4070.U69M47 1993
207'.776579--dc20 92-41819
CIP

A CIP catalog record for this book is available from The British Library.

The Edwin Mellen Press
P.O. Box 450
Lewiston, NY 14092
USA

The Edwin Mellen Press
Box 67
Queenston, Ontario
CANADA L0S 1L0

The Edwin Mellen Press, Ltd.
Lampeter, Dyfed, Wales
UNITED KINGDOM SA48 7DY

Printed in the United States of America

To the Memory of
Louis H. Gunnemann
Dean, 1953-1974
and all those who
have gone before.

TABLE OF CONTENTS

LIST OF ILLUSTRATIONS

56. Mary Potter Engel, Historical Theology, 1983-91.
57. Valerie DeMarinis, Theology and Psychology, 1984-86.
58. Mary B. McMillan, Interim President, 1982-83, and Chair of Board of Tustees.
59. Howard M. Mills, President, 1983-87.
60. Clyde J. Steckel, Academic Vice President, 1979-89.
61. Helen A. Archibald, Christian Education, 1987-91.
62. Benjamin T. Griffin, President, 1987- , Liturgics, 1988-.
63. John W. Bodwell, III, Vice President for Development, 1990-.
64. H. Wilson Yates, Dean, 1989-.
65. Marilyn Salmon, New Testament Theology, 1989-.
66. Carolyn J. Pressler, Old Testament Theology, 1990-.
67. Christine M. Smith, Preaching and Worship, 1991-.
68. Barbara Anne Keely, Educational Ministries, 1991-.
69. Christine Cozad Neuger, Theology and Psychology, 1992-.
70. Paul E. Capetz, Historical Theology, 1992-.

1. United Theological Seminary of the Twin Cities

PREFACE

It is no doubt premature to write the story of United Theological Seminary of the Twin Cities. Thirty years is but a moment in time from the point of view of history. Those who have had an influential part in that story and claim it for their own still live and look over the shoulder of the author. Not all will agree on the course of events, the causes and outcomes, the motivations and meanings. Strong emotions and sharp experiences will be evoked by the mere recitation of the events. At times one can despair of saying anything at all clearly about the recent past.

However the telling of the story of United is an important task. As the years pass the edges blur, the memories dull, the distinctions fade. In many ways that is most fortunate. But the church and those who are concerned with theological education need to know this story and preserve the memory of those who struggled to shape a new vision of theological education and committed their lives to bring that vision to reality. It is not just an institutional history, though certainly that is the focus of the story. At the same time it is also a window into theological education in America in the latter part of the twentieth century. It reveals, we hope, the dynamics of turbulent times and the possibilities which those times engendered.

The contemporary era is a time of great changes in theology, the church, the ministry and in the society generally. Some have identified the situation in terms of "crisis", the crisis in theology, the crisis in the church, the crisis in the ministry, the crisis in society.[1] If "crisis" is understood in the biblical sense as a time of repentance and change it connotes opportunity and promise rather than negative judgment. This is the perspective from which this story is told. We have been given an unusual opportunity and this is the story of that opportunity. It is for the reader, and ultimately history itself, to judge whether that story is a story of success or failure.

I have tried to catch the excitement and challenge of these times and the persons who were deeply involved in the processes. This is not the story of saints but of human beings, who sought to be faithful to the vision as they discerned it. There will be those who will look for certain incidents or particular persons. Some will be disappointed in the choices made and the stories remembered. No one knows better than I the judgments that had to be made and the choices exercised. I take full responsibility for those judgments and decisions. Fairness in recording facts and interpreting their meaning is obviously a responsibility to be taken seriously. Objectivity is clearly not possible. The story is itself an interpretation.

If there is a "hero" it is the seminary itself. It is the embodiment of those who have given their commitment to an institution for the sake of an understanding of theological education in and for the church. I offer this story and this interpretation in the hope that the memory might be kept alive and the vision renewed and reformed.

---

[1]See, respectively, Theodore W. Jennings, *The Vocation of the Theologian*, Philadelphia: Fortress, 1985; Wade Clark Roof and William McKinney, *American Mainline Religion*, New Brunswick: Rutgers University Press, 1987; Leonard F. Sweet, "The Ladder or the Cross: The Plover Report," Nashville: United Methodist Board of Ministry, 1987; and Robert Bellah, et al., *Habits of the Heart*, Berkeley: University of California Press, 1985.

ACKNOWLEDGEMENTS

This book is dedicated to the memory of Louis H. Gunnemann, Dean of the Mission House Theological Seminary and United Theological Seminary of the Twin Cities. Louis had been asked to write the history of the Seminary but had been unable to complete the job before his untimely death on October 31, 1989. On his death bed he asked that I complete the task. This book is not the book that Louis would have written, but the first section is indebted to his work, and the appendices include a portion of his original manuscript. His vision and commitment to the Seminary have given us an institution with a story worthy of being told. The Seminary and the Church have lost a great churchman, educator, and human person.

Others who have also gone before to join the great communion of saints have each made their own contribution to the existence of this school. We name them here in special memory: Edward Sayler, Thomas C. Campbell, Theophilus G. F. Hilgeman, Roland G. Kley, Emil J. Naef, Christine Bryant, Barbara Jean Merrill.

I wish to thank my colleagues for their interest in this project and their willingness to spend time with me, sharing memories, recalling times of pain and joy. They have helped me balance the story and recall events which needed to be told. Especially I want to thank Ruben H. Huenemann, the first President of United Theological Seminary, for reading the manuscript of the early days, responding with criticism and support, and offering his time in conversation and reflection. Without him the story of the early days would suffer from serious omissions, though any interpretations of those days remain mine for correction or change. I am also grateful to President Benjamin Griffin and Dean Wilson Yates who have given great support and encouragement in this task. They have read the manuscript and responded appropriately. They have provided me freedom to do the work and to express my own viewpoints. My friend and colleague, Clyde Steckel, has read and commented on the whole document. Without their help I would have written a much less satisfactory story. The errors and interpretations are my own.

I wish to thank Willis and Katherine Hutchinson for the generous financial support which helped to get this book published. Anne Hage and Susan Ebbers have been of special help in editing and proof-reading the manuscript.

This is not strictly history, it is my story of United Theological Seminary and its vision and commitment to ecumenical theological education in and for the Church. It is written with affection and from a particular point of view. It could not be otherwise for I have spent my career in teaching at this school and its antecedents for the past 35 years. I hope it will help others see this school as a noble experiment in theological education.

24 May 1992
Arthur L. Merrill
New Brighton, Minnesota

PART ONE

BACKGROUNDS AND BEGINNINGS

CHAPTER 1

NEW LIFE IN OLD TRADITIONS

When United Theological Seminary of the Twin Cities began its life as a school of the United Church of Christ on September 27, 1972, it represented a bold venture in theological education. With fifty students and ten faculty members its intent was to find a new way to educate persons for ministry in a changing world. Housed in a new contemporary building, set on a 63 acre campus in the northern suburbs of Minneapolis and St. Paul; it was the first seminary with an ecumenical charter in mainline Protestantism in the current era.

Even as it began the debate was joined whether it was merely the merger and relocation of two previous seminaries or a new creation as the institutional expression of the United Church of Christ. The two schools were Mission House Theological Seminary of Plymouth, Wisconsin and the School of Theology of Yankton College, Yankton, South Dakota. The United Church of Christ was a merger of the Congregational Christian Churches and the Evangelical and Reformed Church. Those who wanted to stress the continuities and maintain the constituencies place the emphasis on the notion of merger and relocation. From this perspective the development of United Theological Seminary was the consequence of the maturing immigrant churches. Those who wished to express a new venture or challenge pushed the idea of the uniqueness of this new school. It represented an institutional reorganization that not only matched the developing framework of the United Church of Christ but also was a minor revolution in theological education.

To understand this development, in which two seminaries of neighboring states, both established in the nineteenth century by German immigrant churches, came together to form one of the most liberal and innovative seminaries in the country, one needs to look at both the context and the tradition.

The first half of the Twentieth Century had passed into history. The world had survived the unprecedented destruction of two World Wars and the demoralizing bitterness of a great depression. By the 1950's the storms had at least partially subsided. Powerful and weak nations had agreed to resolve their differences and plan their future together under the untested guidance of the United Nations. The hope was that the Twentieth Century would finally become a Century of Progress. Technical advances in transportation and communication would quickly shrink the world into a global village. Peacetime applications of nuclear power, developed in wartime, were to solve the threatened energy shortage. The hope of many rested in the quest for the larger unities of life, in both the structures of society and the mind.

In the American churches statistical advances were being recorded. Local congregations were growing. New educational and youth programs prospered. The mass media gave promise of becoming an effective tool in the proclamation of the Gospel. The missionary outreach of the denominations was transformed into channels of cooperation with overseas partner churches. The formation of the National and World Councils of Churches gave tangible expression to the ecumenical dream. The churches in the mission fields led the way in ecumenical action by organizing national united churches. In the United States local, state and national councils of churches influenced the ecclesiastical climate.

There were reasons for optimism in both church and state. As Louis Gunnemann, the first dean of United Theological Seminary, observed, this was a time of euphoria for the churches. The ecumenical vision was shining brightly. The seminaries were growing in size, though perhaps not in influence. The church's enterprise possessed an air of self-confidence.

Yet there were signs that all was not well. Two vastly different philosophical and economic systems were struggling for world domination. One claimed to govern society in freedom and democracy, the other with central planning and regulation. The dominant political concern became the struggle between communism and democracy. "The Wall" became the visible symbol of the Cold War. The churches on both sides were soon involved in the struggle. Some capitulated to the dominant political climate and proclaimed divine sanction for a new parochialism. Others sought ways to be the church in and for, but not of, society. Particularly for the churches in the East it was a difficult period as they found themselves a church in the *Diaspora*.

In the churches of America there was the increasing search for ways to be agents of peace and of a more just social order. The optimism of previous decades had faded, but the struggle for justice remained. The hunger for peace and the horror of an atomic war spurred a growing anti-war movement, that included the resistance to civil defense exercises. The restrictive covenants known as "Gentlemen's Agreements" had been ruled unenforceable. Brown v. the Board of Education had mandated school desegregation. Yet discrimination continued. In 1946 the first freedom ride had been initiated by the Council on Racial Equality. The struggle for the rights of minorities was joined, but few anticipated the turbulence that would mark that struggle in the Sixties.[1] For many in the churches the Fifties could be characterized as the silent generation. Those who reflected on the time theologically recognized that peace and tranquillity could not rest on raw power and submerged injustice.

One expression of the ecumenical spirit in that optimistic time was the formation of the United Church of Christ. The Congregational Christian Churches, rooted in British Separatism and Puritanism, and the Evangelical and Reformed Church, an American counterpart to German and Swiss Protestantism, both originated in a modified Calvinism. However, in their history they had developed individual theological trends and differing

---

[1]Roger G. Betsworth, *The Radical Movement of the 1960's*, ATLA Monograph Series, No. 14, Metuchen, NJ: Scarecrow Press, 1980.

concepts of church polity. The formation of the United Church of Christ was hailed in ecclesiastical circles as a breakthrough in church union because it represented a merger that transcended differences and acknowledged and celebrated diversity. An immediate byproduct of the formation of the United Church of Christ was the merging of Mission House Theological Seminary and Yankton School of Theology to create the United Theological Seminary of the Twin Cities. The planning initiated in the Fifties led to the formation of the school in the Sixties.[2]

There were reasons to take a fresh look at the theological enterprise in America.[3] Those outside could observe the theological discussions and assume that they were debates over outmoded speculations. Theology appeared to serve as a defense for a fortress on a rocky island of dogma or justification for the slippery slopes of confessional isolation. The more sophisticated thought theology was a subheading under philosophy, or psychology, or sociology, or some other discipline. Consequently its appropriate location would be in a university department of religion. Higher education in America was largely under the influence of a pragmatic rationalism, hardly sympathetic to theological reflection. The program of theological education as it developed at United Theological Seminary challenged the use of theology either as an instrument of sectarian or denominational justification or as an impersonal, intellectual reflection on the history of religion.

Those who founded and shaped United Theological Seminary had to deal with both the problems of institutional development and the issues of theological meaning and purpose. Often these problems were so deeply intertwined that the debate was difficult to follow and the issues remained clouded and confused. The founders perceived theology as the task of the whole church as it reflected upon its message and mission. For them it was

---

[2]Other parallel accounts of this period can be found in E.C. Jaberg, et al., *A History of Mission House-Lakeland*, Philadelphia: Christian Education Press, 1962 and in Roland G. Kley: *United Theological Seminary: The First Ten Years*, New Brighton, MN: United Theological Seminary, 1972.

[3]One such important study was that by H. Richard Niebuhr, Daniel D. Williams and James Gustafson, *The Advancement of Theological Education*, New York: Harper & Brothers, 1957.

by definition ecumenical. There was little interest in a comparative religion approach to theological studies, not because of an inherent opposition to such studies, but because it was their conviction that the church needed to reflect theologically on its primary purpose and mission as well as on the issues that were foremost in the society.

This awareness was heightened by the fact that during the formative years of the United Church of Christ the distinctly theological issues were frequently subordinated to pragmatic decisions. Those deeper implications were often conveniently ignored or postponed. Questions concerning the general theological stance of the United Church of Christ were resolved in part by the acceptance of "The Statement of Faith" in 1959. These divisions over the structure of the church, debates over the nature and application of autonomy, and discussions about the meaning and character of covenantal relationships continued to be a source of ferment.[4] Other questions related to the preparation for pastoral leadership and the structures that the denomination would provide for such preparation.

Both merging bodies had a strong tradition of establishing institutions of higher education that included seminaries. Among Congregationalists these schools had been encouraged to achieve independence, and in some cases they eventually dropped virtually all denominational affiliation, or acknowledged the connection only to their historical beginnings. The Evangelical and Reformed seminaries, on the other hand, while operating in a climate of academic freedom, were structurally linked to and supported by the denomination. Indeed in 1959 the Evangelical and Reformed Church authorized a two million dollar fund raising campaign to support the three church-related seminaries, Eden, Lancaster and Mission House. At the same time this act signaled to the merging church the importance of theological education in the life of the church.

The ecumenical vision of United Theological Seminary could become a reality only if the new school continued to serve the constituencies of the two merging schools. It is therefore appropriate to provide a brief historical

---

[4]Louis H. Gunnemann, *The Shaping of the United Church of Christ*, New York: United Church Press, 1977, especially chapter 2.

sketch of the two schools and the theological heritage and attitudes that characterized their graduates and supporting churches. Without the loyal support of the local congregations and the intense interest of faithful alumni the venture could not have come to fruition.

The School of Theology of Yankton College, as it was formally known, was an important symbol and unifying center for the German Congregational Churches. These churches were the products of the faith and life of immigrants who had settled in the Dakotas and Nebraska during the latter half of the nineteenth century. More than a century earlier the Russian government had invited their ancestors to settle in the Ukraine and the Volga Valley to develop the agricultural potential of the regions. They came originally from Lutheran and Reformed areas of Germany where they had been strongly influenced by the pietist movement. Maintaining those traditions in Russia, they resisted the impact of the Russian Orthodox Church and the formal Lutheranism of the German state church. Instead there was a basic anti-clericalism that was expressed through the *Bruedergemeinschaft* (The Brotherhood) which focused on biblical study and private devotions.

When the Russian government broke its original agreement to exempt their young men from military service the so-called German-Russians migrated in large numbers to the United States. There they diligently worked the prairie soil or labored to expand the railroad system. They stretched from the prairies of South Dakota and Nebraska, through Colorado and the mountain states, and on to the northern Pacific coast of Oregon and Washington. The Church was the center of their religious and cultural existence. A simple worship service, weekly prayer meetings and a conservative theology characterized the pioneer congregations. The openness and autonomy of the congregational polity were attractive to them. Financial support from the Board for Home Missions of the Congregational Christian Churches helped to make the extension of their churches across the western states possible. Through this connection this immigrant church was drawn into the process that ultimately led to the United Church of Christ.

The various associations were soon organized as the German General Conference of Congregational Churches.[5]

Soon discovering that they could not depend on clergy from Russia or Germany to supply their leadership the *Bruedergemeinschaft* established in 1978 a pro-seminary in Crete, Nebraska to prepare pastors for German-speaking congregations. In 1882 the school was incorporated into the Chicago Theological Seminary as the German Department. The geographical and cultural distances between Chicago and the western prairies proved to be insurmountable. In 1916 the German Theological Department moved to Redfield College in Redfield, South Dakota. The merger of Redfield and Yankton colleges in 1932, both Congregational schools, resulted in another relocation, this time to Yankton, South Dakota. Here the school received space on the campus and provided the college with a department of religion although the ownership and supervision of the school remained with the German General Conference. On the campus of Yankton the School of Theology was located in Ward Hall, named for the founder of Yankton. There was no separate library for the theological department and housing was provided by the college for theological students.

By 1945 students received training in English as well as German, and the graduates were serving both English- and German-speaking Congregational churches. Several state conferences acknowledged the value of this service by providing modest support from conference and local church budgets. A five year program offered graduates both a B.A. and a B.Th. degree, though increasingly students were enrolling for further study in accredited three-year seminaries elsewhere. A leadership crisis was developing among the German background churches because many Yankton students were accepting calls to congregations affiliated with the English speaking state conferences. Although many General Conference churches were now bilingual, the younger pastors did not feel qualified to conduct a worship service in German.

---

[5]George J. Eisenach, *The History of the German Congregational Churches*, Yankton, SD: Pioneer Press, 1938, and *Pietism and the Russian Germans in the United States*, Berne, IN: Berne Publishers, 1948.

The need for more adequately trained clergy, who could serve bilingual congregations, was urgent and obviously difficult to meet. Under the leadership of Dean Edward Sayler the faculty addressed itself to the task. That faculty included the noted historian George J. Eisenach whose studies of the German Congregational Church are seminal; Howard Bozarth, professor of theology and James H. Cobb, professor of biblical studies. Ralph Hoffmann, Conference Minister of South Dakota and later chair of the Board of Trustees at United, had been the professor in the English section of the school and supported the changes of the school. The faculty deliberations issued in a plan for a new curriculum called the "Seven Year Plan" for its suggestion that the school offer along with the B.A. degree, a three-year seminary program leading to the B.D. degree. The B.D. degree was the accepted ministerial degree then. When the proposal was presented to the Board of Home Missions in 1957 the Board was reluctant to support the ambitious, expanded program at the Yankton location. It suggested instead that the General Conference consider joining with Mission House Seminary to form a new school in a different setting.

This new recommendation confronted the General Conference with a critical decision. Although it provided a viable opportunity to realize some of the advantages of the seven year plan there were also undeniable limitations. Some feared that it would dilute the pietistic practices dear to many lay members. Some wanted to maintain a rural location and focus. Others were convinced that the intimate sense of fellowship that characterized the Conference would be jeopardized. Still others deplored the loss of Conference control over the school. Some of the more cautious members feared the attenuation of their religious and cultural heritage. More forward-looking clergy and laity sensed an opportunity to enter into the mainstream of American Protestantism from which they could gain benefits and make a contribution. General Conference superintendents Benjamin Kissler of Denver, Colorado, and Edward Grauman of Portland, Oregon, provided enthusiastic support because they were convinced that the churches would benefit from the wider association. They were also aware that the General Conference alone could not provide the resources for the expanded

2. Joseph Ward of Yankton

3. Ward Hall, Yankton College

program that was projected. A new venture in theological education was required and it needed to be an ecumenical enterprise.

In a similar manner the origins of Mission House Theological Seminary lay in the immigrations of the nineteenth century. German immigrants from Westphalia arrived in Sheboygan County, Wisconsin, in the summer of 1847. There was discontent in the German church because rationalistic tendencies had increased. The economic plight of the people led to a precarious existence. Rumors of political turmoil and revolution abounded and America beckoned as a land of unlimited potential.

By the summer of 1854 three pastors, J. A. Muehlmeier, H. A. Winter and Jakob J. Bossard, together with lay representatives, organized the Sheboygan Classis of the German Reformed Church. A primary concern was to secure pastoral leadership for the many unchurched settlements. Only a few clergy were available from the homeland. In 1858 Pastors Bossard and Muehlmeier had instituted an informal tutorial program in their parsonages for several carefully selected candidates. By 1859 the Sheboygan Classis was prepared to establish a Mission House, named after the pastoral and missionary training schools they had known in Germany and Switzerland. In the rural environs of Town Herman, in eastern Wisconsin, the Mission House was established. The venture soon received the support of German and Swiss background churches in Wisconsin and Iowa, as well as more distant states, including Indiana and Ohio.

In less than twenty years this modest start had become a recognized college and graduate seminary. Because of the scarcity of high schools in the farming communities of early Wisconsin, a preparatory department, which later became a four year academy, was added. For many decades it was possible to pursue eleven years of academic work on the campus, largely at the expense of the church. It is not surprising that a strong sense of comradeship and loyalty to their alma mater developed among the clergy graduates.

4. H.A. Muehlmeier, Founder and President of Mission House

5. Mission House in the early years

Uncertainty about the location of both the college and the seminary continued to mark the passing years. Some looked upon the rural setting as an ideal place to study, others deplored its relative isolation. At various times suggestions were made to relocate, but after the original frame buildings were replaced with brick structures, the question of location would seem to be settled.

However the issue did not disappear. Suggestions to move to Milwaukee, or Chicago, or merge with Central Seminary in Dayton, Ohio, were heard and rejected. Even a move into Sheboygan itself was proposed though never realized.

The question of the location of the seminary was tied to not only the relationship of the seminary with the college but also to the educational expectations and policies of the Evangelical and Reformed Church. It had become evident by the early 1950's that if the United Church of Christ should come into being, it would largely accept the congregational polity for structuring the state conferences and national boards.[6] The signs were clear that the former close structural relationship between the denomination and the seminaries would not prevail. In Evangelical and Reformed circles it was generally assumed that Lancaster and Eden would continue and find a basis for support. The future of Mission House was less secure. As early as 1954 the General Council of the Evangelical and Reformed Church appointed a committee "in order to secure an adequate basis of facts for judgment on the long range policy" that would shape the future of Mission House College and Seminary.[7] Two ministers, John R.C. Haas and Ruben H. Huenemann, and two laymen, Fred Diehl and John Lantz, were appointed to make the study.

In September the committee's report was accepted by the General Council. It stated that both the college and the seminary served a definite need in the church, but that to fulfill their purpose they should be

---

[6]Gunnemann, *The Shaping of the United Church of Christ*, pp. 46-47. As Gunnemann points out this was presaged in Cadman v. Kenyon which resulted in an injunction against the proposed merger of the United Church of Christ.

[7]Minutes of the General Council, February 16-18, 1954, pp. 2-3.

administratively separated.[8] Further recommendations for reorganization and increased funding were included in the report. The Committee of Four, as it was known, was enlarged to include three more members, Messrs. Newell, Nelson and Jordan. It held several meetings during the ensuing year at which specific steps leading toward accreditation and expansion were discussed. In this evaluation it was assisted by Sheldon Mackey from the Board of Higher Education, Arthur Krueger, president of Mission House College and Seminary, Louis H. Gunnemann, dean of the seminary and Oscar Hoffman, dean of the college.[9]

The recommendations of the evaluation committee were approved by the General Council at its Winter meeting in Kansas City, Missouri, on February 7, 1956. As a result the newly organized Seminary Board of Trustees and Faculty understood that the Evangelical and Reformed Church was committed to continuing its traditional support of higher education and to bringing its three theological seminaries into the union.

As the planning for the United Church of Christ continued it soon became clear that what appeared to be a straightforward decision would be subject to several years of further negotiation and discussion before it could finally be implemented. However the actions of the General Council formed the basis for the seminary faculty to plan for a future that needed to be shaped considering the changing circumstances.

---

[8]*Report of the Study Committee on Mission House College and Seminary, September 21, 1954.*

[9]Minutes of the Meeting of the Special Committee on Mission House College and Seminary, December 7, 1955.

CHAPTER 2

SHAPING A FUTURE

Internally at Mission House the vision of a new seminary began to take shape in 1953-54. With the arrival of a new generation of faculty a series of discussions led to a comprehensive rethinking of the task of theological education designed to serve the emerging United Church and at the same time express a thoroughly ecumenical stance. This planning was further influenced by the study of theological education in American that was being conducted by H. Richard Niebuhr, Daniel Day Williams and James Gustafson, sponsored by the American Association of Theological Schools. In September of 1955 the Seminary Board of Trustees received a "Development Plan for the Seminary" from the faculty that based its conclusions on the perceived character of theological education and its implications for the life of the school.

The clear ecumenical vision, which had also permeated the AATS study, was not a novelty on the campus. As early as the 1930's Professors Karl J. Ernst and Josias Friedli had published some of Karl Barth's works in English.[1] Ernst and Barth had maintained a regular correspondence and Barth's role in the ecumenical movement that encouraged the formation of the World Council of Churches is well known. Ernst and Friedli together

---

[1]*Come Holy Spirit* (1935), *God in Action* (1935) and *God's Search for Man* (1936) were published by Round Table Press, New York. Prof. George W. Richards of Lancaster Seminary and Dr. Elmer G. Homrighausen (later of Princeton Seminary) also collaborated on the last two books.

with Professors Louis C. Hessert and Ernest Fledderjohn had formed the core of the teaching faculty during the years of Depression and World War II. All had exerted a strong influence on the Mission House constituency and in the wider church, and used their influence to surmount a residual parochialism.

In the early 1950's two crucial appointments to the faculty provided the necessary leadership for shaping the future of the school. The first was the election of Arthur M. Krueger to the presidency of both college and seminary in 1950. A graduate of Heidelberg College, Tiffin, Ohio, and Mission House Seminary, Krueger had served churches in Wisconsin and St. Paul, Minnesota. His courageous commitment together with his understanding of the needs of the church, helped to set the seminary on a new course during the difficult years of transition and transformation.

The other faculty addition was the calling of Louis H. Gunnemann to the chair of practical theology in 1953 and his subsequent appointment as dean in 1954. As a graduate of both Mission House College and Seminary he had been identified by his professors as theologically astute, of deep and genuine piety and committed to the purpose and mission of the church. A native of Indiana he had successfully served pastorates in Tipton, Iowa and Lafayette, Indiana, and done further graduate study at Princeton Theological Seminary. His irenic spirit and natural leadership were to shape the faculty into a coherent whole. Gunnemann would largely supply the guiding ecumenical vision that would mold the theological discussions and the character of the Seminary.

Upon the retirement of Professors Friedli, Hessert and Ernst in the 1950's four new faculty appointments were made. Theophilus F. M. Hilgeman, a Mission House graduate and former missionary to China, succeeded Friedli in Church History. Walter F. Kuentzel, the grandson of a Mission House founder and with a doctorate from Princeton, was called to the chair of New Testament Theology. Frederick L. Herzog assumed the chair of Systematic Theology. He also had a Princeton doctorate, and though born in the United States had resided in Germany throughout his earlier years and had lived in the home of Karl Barth during his graduate study at Basel. With the retirement of Karl J. Ernst, honored teacher of both the Old and New Testament (1926-1954), Brevard S. Childs was called to the Old Testament chair. Childs, a Presbyterian, was the first appointment outside the direct German Reformed tradition.

This "New Faculty," as it became known, recognized its opportunity to evaluate the Mission House tradition and to deal with the larger issues of the tasks and responsibilities of theological education for the ecumenical church. It was an existential issue for them because most of this group of young scholars were without previous seminary teaching experience. How could they move an institution with ninety years of history and tradition into a new age and a new church?

In the process of dealing with such issues the faculty was shaped into a team with singularity of purpose and unity for its task. The immediate product was a statement with the unassuming title of "Theological Studies at Mission House" that appeared from then on in the annual *Announcements* of the Seminary. A key paragraph implied new directions while at the same time preserving continuity in time-honored traditions:

> We believe in the One Holy Catholic Church. There is a unity of the communion of believers throughout all ages and among all people. Jesus Christ is the foundation of this unity. Our theological studies are integrated into this communion on the basis of our unity in Jesus Christ, and therefore intentionally ecumenical as we join the Ecumenical Confessions of our faith.

That declaration was both Christologically centered and tied to the beloved Heidelberg Confession. Here was an ecumenicity that was neither ecclesiastically nor institutionally focused. It was a spirit of openness that permeated both Mission House and later United Theological Seminary, though the basis of that ecumenicity would be modified in time. It reflected among other influences that of Ernst and Friedli especially, for three of the faculty had studied with them and Ernst had shared in the early discussions.

This understanding of the nature and purpose of theological education was to shape all further decisions. In it the faculty reaffirmed its commitment to the task of the school as theological education in and for the Church. The critical juncture was perceived to be located in two primary factors: the revival of biblical studies and the ecumenical understanding of

Christian faith and the Church. This was understood as a call for a radical reorientation of the educational program which focused on the training of ecumenical leadership for the local church. Here was no denial of the seminary's denominational heritage but the logical consequence of its heritage and self-understanding. As the plan stated, the demand is for an "extension and intensification of basic ecumenical understanding in all fields."

This ecumenical understanding was expressed concretely in three aspects of the theological curriculum. It appeared first, in the Key Books Program, a listing of approximately fifty volumes that had shaped the church in its history and tradition. These books reflected the heritage of the Church and were to be used in courses and in the shaping of the theological education of the students. Second, there were Interdepartmental Seminars in which all students and faculty were required to participate. These seminars usually focused on one or more of the Key Books and dealt with issues that transcended what was then the traditional fourfold division of the curriculum. Finally, there was the provision for special courses in ecumenical concerns. Here instructors from other denominations were engaged to enrich the offerings of the school.

The implications of this plan ranged over a wide set of issues. Though the school wished to preserve it's denominational relationship it saw that it needed to develop working relationships with other denominations. This was to be done by recruiting board members and students from other church bodies. The Board of Trustees was to be reorganized to include both lay and ecumenical representation; staff and facilities would need to be expanded. Four additional faculty members were proposed and three new buildings suggested. Lastly, the curriculum would need expansion, including not only the proposed ecumenical courses but also more electives. In-service training for ministry called for new ways of teaching. A course for training missionaries in an ecumenical approach was proposed. And the development of a Master of Theology program was desired.

Here was an ambitious undertaking for a school of five faculty members and some thirty students. Yet the vision of an ecumenical theological school was outlined and the trajectories of the future had been set. It would take five years before that vision was brought to fruition, but the groundwork had been laid.

About the "Development Plan of the Seminary," approved by the Board of Trustees on September 8, 1955, Dr. James E. Wagner, president of the Evangelical and Reformed Church wrote in a letter to Gunnemann, "If it means what it says, it breathes an ecumenical spirit and anticipates an ecumenical program the like of which not many seminary faculties have been bold enough to conceive."[2]

The faculty of Mission House underwent further changes before the practical steps of merger with Yankton and the formation of United Theological Seminary could be achieved. The first quite unanticipated change resulted from the untimely death of Walter Kuentzel, professor of New Testament.[3]

Before the opening of the Fall Term 1958 Paul L. Hammer was elected to replace Walter Kuentzel. Hammer, a native of Nebraska and a member of the Evangelical Covenant Church, represented the first faculty appointment outside the Reformed tradition. He had begun his college work in the Naval Academy at Annapolis, Maryland, but transferred to Wesleyan College in Nebraska for the completion of his B.A. He earned his seminary degree at Yale Divinity School and his doctorate at Heidelberg University in Germany under Guenther Bornkamm. His facility in the German language helped him gain ready acceptance among the German background churches of Mission House, for whom he became a popular teacher and guest speaker.

Early in 1958 Brevard S. Childs announced his resignation to accept an appointment at Yale Divinity School. To fill the vacancy Arthur L. Merrill, a doctoral candidate at the University of Chicago, was invited to teach for a year and then elected to the chair of Exegetical Theology, Old Testament. Merrill was the son of American Baptist missionaries, born while

---

[2]Letter of James E. Wagner to Louis H. Gunnemann, November 3, 1955.

[3]Kuentzel died on August 3, 1957 having just completed his Th.D. degree at Princeton Seminary. The seminary was devastated by his death. As an interim measure Wilhelm Wuellner, a doctoral student at the University of Chicago was secured to cover the academic year 1957-58.

his parents served in northeast India. Before his enrollment at Chicago he had graduated from the College of Wooster in Ohio and what was then Berkeley Baptist Divinity School in California. His ordination was in the American Baptist Churches.

During the same year the faculty was increased by two additional appointments. Because of the separation of the college and the seminary, also of the libraries, the seminary was in urgent need of a qualified librarian. Roland G. Kley, an Evangelical and Reformed pastor in New Holstein, Wisconsin, and a member of the Board of Trustees, was willing to fill the position if he could earn his M.A. in Library Science at the University of Wisconsin in Madison. The Board approved his appointment, moved his family to the campus, and supported his studies at Madison for a year. His organizational skills proved to be invaluable in the immediate reorganization of the library and later in the establishment of a new library at United.

A fourth appointment was Eugene C. Jaberg, professor of Homiletics, a faculty position that had not been filled for a number of years. He was elected in the academic year 1957-58 and began his tenure in the Fall of 1958. Jaberg came from a family that had long been associated with Mission House, for both his father and older brother were graduates before him. Jaberg had graduated from the college and then taken work at Westminster College in Cambridge, England and at Princeton Theological Seminary, before receiving his B.D. from Mission House. At the time of his appointment he was pursuing doctoral studies in speech and communications at the University of Wisconsin in Madison.

In the Fall of 1958 the seven faculty members, Gunnemann, Herzog, Hilgeman, Jaberg, Kley, Hammer and Merrill, constituted a teaching force in which over half of them had not participated in the development plan nor necessarily shared the specific ecumenical vision of the "New Faculty." Yet under the gentle guidance of Dean Gunnemann the faculty was soon brought on board, introduced to the development plan and became strong advocates of the proposal to enhance the school as a theological seminary of the church with an ecumenical vision. All but Herzog, who later went to Duke University, became part of the faculty at United Seminary of the Twin Cities several years later.

6. Arthur M. Krueger,
President of Mission House College and Seminary

7. Edward Sayler, Dean of the School of Theology and First Chair of the Board of Trustees of United Theological Seminary

8. Mission House Seminary Faculty, 1958-1959.
Back row, left to right: Eugene Jaberg, Frederick Herzog, Arthur Merrill, Paul Hammer;
Front row, left to right: Theophilus Hilgeman, Louis Gunnemann, Roland Kley

However, the vision and program of theological education supported by the faculty was not sufficient cause nor inducement for the establishment of United. The rather complex series of studies, discussions, negotiations and actions by committees, conferences and General Synods can best be compared to the movements of a yo-yo, bouncing up and down on a string, except that the yo-yo is controlled by a guiding hand. There was no such definable center of control during the formative years of the United Church of Christ. The moving and guiding force for the seminary was the determination of the faculty, the support of the Board of Trustees and the loyal backing of the constituency, especially the alumni.

From the beginning the task of establishing an ecumenical seminary had to be pursued on three fronts. Most urgent were the negotiations with the agencies of the United Church of Christ, which was itself struggling to become a reality. Also crucial were the efforts to consolidate Mission House and Yankton as a faculty and seminary in such a way as to preserve some of the desirable qualities of both schools. Finally, with the decision to locate in the Twin Cities of Minneapolis and St. Paul, it was important to develop interest and support among the churches and the wider community of the new location.

An important step toward raising the Evangelical and Reformed Church's consciousness about theological education had been taken by the three seminaries in 1954. That summer the faculties of Eden, Lancaster and Mission House initiated a series of annual conferences. These meetings not only dealt with the theological issues facing the denomination but also created a bond of fellowship among the individuals and institutions. It is probable that the initiation of these meetings came from Louis Gunnemann as a result of conversations with Harold Pflug of Eden and Lee Gable of Lancaster at a meeting of the Commission on Higher Education (E&R) at Buck Hill Falls, Pennsylvania, earlier in the year.

Strongly supported by President Wagner, these conferences marked the first time that the three faculties engaged in formal conversation. From the beginning the meetings became a successful forum and greatly improved the position of the seminaries in the structures of the church. That the three seminaries could often present a common position in the councils of the church proved to be very useful in the negotiations about Mission House.

The last meeting of the tri-faculty conference was held in summer of 1962. By that time the Division of Higher Education for the United Church had been created and the seminaries of both traditions had come together under this agency of the church. The logistics of arranging a meeting to include the many seminaries now related to the United Church of Christ were never solved. In succeeding years only the presidents and deans met in connection with the annual meeting of the Division.

The tortuous path of negotiations concerning the future of seminaries in the United Church came into focus in 1956 when the General Synod (E&R), looking toward the denominational merger, took a fateful and potentially fatal step when it authorized a Special Committee on Theological Seminaries, under the chair of Donald Dearborn, Dean of Catawba College. This committee of seven was to study the facilities and programs of the three seminaries of the E&R Church and bring a recommendation to the Synod, regarding their needs in the coming years. The Dearborn Committee, after visiting the three schools and receiving data on the seminaries, reported to the General Council (executive body of the E&R Church between synods) that in its judgment, as it was uneconomical to operate a small seminary, Mission House Seminary should be merged with one or both of the other seminaries. The report was in direct contradiction to positions that the denomination had previously expressed.

When the Board of Trustees of Mission House received word of this report, it petitioned the General Council to set aside the Dearborn Committee's recommendation. A ground for this petition was that in the meantime the Board of Trustees had petitioned the Executive Council of the United Church of Christ to initiate a study to determine how Mission House could best meet the needs of the United Church of Christ. The General Council (E&R) at its meeting in Cleveland, Ohio, on February, 4, 1959, did vote to set aside the Dearborn Committee's recommendation until the results of the United Church authorized study could be known.

However, the *Blue Book for the Spring Meetings of Synods* in 1959 included a recommendation from the Finance Committee of the General

Council that "if this study does not open the way for merger with another theological school or some other practicable alternative, the Study committee's (the committee authorized by the 1956 General Synod) *report having indicated the extremely high cost per student in a small seminary*,...appropriate steps be taken forthwith looking to the discontinuance of Mission House Theological Seminary."[4] This report of the Finance Committee raised profound questions among many as to whether or not it prejudiced the decision in advance. The correspondence of Louis H. Gunnemann for 1959 is thick with letters from alumni, other pastors, consistories, and interested persons who felt that the statement in the Blue Book was unfair.

Gunnemann, as Director of Development, sent out a letter to all alumni, dated April 6, 1959, analyzing the argument of both the actions taken by the seminary and by the church concerning this issue, as well as arguments to refute the Dearborn committee's contention that the training of Mission House students was uneconomical. The cost to the church at the time was a total annual contribution to the seminary of $31,000, resulting in an average cost of $2,314 per student for three years of study!

As the consequence of the work of loyal alumni in the congregations and synods, the General Synod was petitioned to reverse the conclusions of the Dearborn Committee. At the General Synod of July 1959 in Cleveland, Ohio the Dearborn Committee submitted a supplementary report. It recommended that the United Church of Christ study team complete its survey for only a preliminary report had so far appeared. Further Mission House was asked to explore all factors involved in the establishment of a seminary in the Twin Cities and to make this development a joint effort with Yankton School of Theology. The supplementary report also recommended that the new seminary be a project of the United Church of Christ, the matter being referred to the Executive Council and that the recommendation of the General Council regarding the capital funds campaign of $2 million for the three seminaries be adopted. This supplementary report of the Committee was adopted by General Synod. Though the struggle had taken a

---

[4]*Blue Book for the Spring Meetings of Synods*, p. 7.

heavy toll in energy and trust, the outcome meant that the future of the seminary had won approval. The support of the Evangelical and Reformed Church would not be withdrawn either morally or financially.

In the meantime the Development Plan of Mission House Seminary was faced with the second facet of the church and seminary relationship, in consequence of the impending consummation of the union of the Evangelical and Reformed Church with the Congregational Christian Churches, a process that had been initiated in 1938. A delay of five years in those negotiations ended in 1954. In the ensuing three-year interval before the 1957 consummation of the union all the Evangelical and Reformed seminaries had to assess the implications of the union for their own existence. Accustomed to direct support from the denomination, they had to face the fact that the new United Church of Christ structure might not continue that pattern. Mission House Seminary was the most vulnerable in that situation, but also, in many respects, faced unprecedented opportunity. In conceiving a new future for the Seminary the Faculty and Board of Trustees saw the birth of the United Church of Christ as an auspicious moment for launching a new venture in theological education, especially important for the new church in its intention to be a "united and uniting" communion.

With the approval of the reorganization of the Seminary by the General Synod and its promise of support, the faculty moved its discussions to a new level of expectations. In a memo to the Board of Trustees of the Seminary the faculty asked for the consideration of four items: 1. The addition to the faculty of two persons, 2. The development of the areas of Alumni Relations and Public Relations, 3. The study of prospective student recruitment, and 4. A Centennial Advance Program that would provide for new and adequate buildings for the seminary, further addition to the teaching staff and an endowment of adequate size.

By March of 1957 the Committee on Self Study and Development of the Board of Trustees had received this memo and discussed it. Here we find the first reference to the possibility of relocation, though the issue had been discussed informally before this time. In this committee a relocation to Milwaukee appeared favorable, because it offered an urban location, with a strong Council of Churches, an inner city that needed help, hospitals and schools of higher education that could provide teaching resources, and a traditional constituency in the churches. The committee, however, recommended to the Board of Trustees further study and examination of the seminary's program, resources, development plan, and possible relocation using the expertise of Charles Taylor (executive director of the American Association of Theological Schools) or some other qualified person. It was at this point that the Board of Trustees appointed Louis H. Gunnemann Director of the Development Plan and appointed a steering committee to implement the recommendations of the Self-study and Development Committee.

In the Fall of 1957 Gunnemann reported to the trustees that during the summer at General Synod he had met with James Wagner and Fred Hoskins, co-presidents of the United Church of Christ, with the aim of making the relocation and development of Mission House Seminary a concern of the United Church of Christ. He indicated that Wagner and Hoskins had suggested consideration of the Twin Cities, though he had also talked to four other theological educators of whom two had mentioned Seattle as a possible location. Wagner and Hoskins also urged consideration of a relationship to Yankton School of Theology as a strategy to strengthen the support of the wider church for development and relocation.[5] Elsewhere Gunnemann suggests that it was Truman Douglass, executive vice-president of the Board for Home Missions (CC) who suggested that the Mission House proposal would be considerably strengthened if the project were to be made a joint effort with the School of Theology of Yankton College. Gunnemann also reported that he would meet in September with Dean Edward Sayler of Yankton.

---

[5]The source for the proposal that Mission House consider merger with Yankton School of Theology is a matter of some dispute. In the official documents the source is attributed to James Wagner and Fred Hoskins. Gunnemann has suggested that the source was Truman Douglass, Executive Vice-President of the Board of Home Mission. As the participants are now deceased the issue can probably never be decided with certainty. Huenemann, in an interview June 19, 1991, recalled an early conversation with Truman Douglass on the subject.

The Board of Trustees, on August 26, 1957, adopted Gunnemann's recommendation that they petition the Executive Council of the United Church of Christ to make the relocation and development of Mission House Seminary a special project of the United Church of Christ. They also asked the Council to appoint a special committee of theological educators and leading churchmen to review the entire plan and to assist the Seminary in its development and relocation. Thus by the end of 1957 the Development Program had been submitted for study and comment to the Board of Trustees of the Seminary, the American Association of Theological Schools, the Executive Council of the UCC, the Commission on Higher Education (E&R) and the Division of Christian Education (CC) and six theological educators (H. Richard Niebuhr, James Gustafson, Douglas Horton, Paul Lehmann, Otto Piper and Charles Taylor).

The response to the development plan by these consultants was positive. The plan was seen as sound and meriting implementation. The need for re-establishment in a new location was discerned as crucial. The possibility for service to the mainstream Protestant churches in the North Central region of the country was emphasized. The future discussions with Yankton School of Theology now anticipated the development of a new school with an ecumenical vision.

CHAPTER 3

TOWARD A BASIS OF UNION

The first direct conversations between Mission House and Yankton occurred when the two deans, Gunnemann and Sayler, met on September 3, 1957, in Yankton. The purpose of this meeting was to apprise Sayler of the Mission House plan for development and the resultant conversations, negotiations and outcomes that had taken place to that date.

When the General Council of the Congregational Christian Churches met at Buck Hill Falls, Pennsylvania, in January 1958 an ad hoc meeting of Ralph Hoffman, Edward Sayler, Truman Douglass, Philip Widenhouse and Louis Gunnemann was held. Out of this meeting came the creation of what was to be called "The Committee of Four," that was to study the possible joint effort of Mission House and Yankton. The initial members were Widenhouse, Sayler, Gunnemann and one member to be appointed by the Commission on Higher Education (E&R). They also agreed to try to engage H. Richard Niebuhr or James Gustafson to gather additional information to guide the selection of a location.

The next month, on the 18 of February, a series of resolutions was supported by Yankton School of Theology expressing its thanks to the Board of Home Missions (CC) for its support and understanding and its gratitude for the overall evaluation of the prospects of merger for Yankton School of Theology and Mission House Seminary. The Faculty also stated its readiness to cooperate in the formation of a new school and its willingness to defer the Seven Year Plan until such negotiations concluded. These resolutions were signed by the Executive Committee of the General Conference, the Board of Education and others of the school. This action was significant because it marked the official recognition of the conversations between Mission House and Yankton and set the stage for their commitment to the task ahead.

On April 9, 1958, the Committee of Four met in the Hotel Cleveland in Cleveland, Ohio. Otto Gerber had been appointed as the representative from the Commission on Higher Education (E&R), of which he was chair, to complete the membership. Truman Douglass was also in attendance. The outcome of this meeting was to request the Executive Council of the United Church of Christ to appoint representatives of the Division of Higher Education (CC) and the Commission on Higher Education (E&R) for a joint committee to conduct a study of the theological education needs of the UCC in the Great Plains Region and to employ a professional counselor. By September of that year Gunnemann reported that there had been no success in securing technical help for the proposed study. In the meantime Philip Widenhouse had left his position with the Division of Higher Education and had been replaced by Dr. Wesley Hotchkiss. The latter was to suggest in October that Yoshio Fukuyama, Director of Research for the Division of Higher Education, might be available for the study. From the Evangelical and Reformed side it was suggested that Roger Shinn, professor of Ethics at Union Theological Seminary in New York, might also serve on this study. He was in the midst of a professional move to Vanderbilt Divinity School and agreed to undertake the task. Unfortunately he was able to participate in only a few meetings before he had to withdraw.

By January 12, 1959, the research team was organized under the direction of Prof. Victor Obenhaus of Chicago Theological Seminary, with the assistance of Widick Schroeder and Yoshio Fukuyama. The team met with the Committee of Four and with Donald C. Dearborn whose report on theological education in the Evangelical and Reformed Church had recommended that Mission House Seminary be merged with Eden and Lancaster seminaries. Two important actions came out of this meeting. One was the definition of the scope of the study to be carried out by the research team. The study was to:

1. Define and evaluate the roles of Yankton and Mission House as now conceived by the two institutions.

2. Analyze the ministerial needs of the United Church west of Chicago with particular reference to the cultural characteristics of the region.

3. Include in the inquiry a view of the total Protestant strategy for the northern tier of states from Wisconsin to the West Coast.

4. Inquire into the values of integrating the liberal arts program with the theological seminary as is now being tried by the School of Theology of Yankton College.

5. Inquire into the values of placing a theological seminary into a university setting.

6. Make a critical inquiry into whether the theological needs of the United Church may be met through existing institutions, or a union of existing institutions of the United Church, and/or other theological schools of other denominations, or the creation of a totally new institution without reference to existing ones.

The other important consequence of this meeting was the amendment of the Report of Committee to Study the Programs and Facilities of the Seminaries which Dr. Dearborn chaired. This amendment stated that no recommendation would be made at this time regarding the future of Mission House Seminary in view of the study being conducted under the aegis of the Committee of Four.

The presence in the Blue Book of the recommendations of the Dearborn Committee and of the General Finance Committee appears to have prompted the Committee of Four to meet again in Chicago on June 18, 1959. Unfortunately the urgency of this meeting dictated a scheduling decision which did not permit all the members to attend. Those present included Gunnemann, Gerber, Roger Shinn as consultant, and from the research team Obenhaus and Schroeder. Sayler of Yankton and Hotchkiss of the Division of Higher Education were absent. The two major questions discussed at that meeting were: Does the United Church of Christ wish to establish one or more new seminaries? And what does the UCC want in terms of type or types of seminaries? It was recognized that the answers to these questions would assist in answering the questions about Mission House and Yankton. However the United Church of Christ was just coming into being and it would be some time before answers would emerge in a form that would be useful to the two schools.

The discussion turned to the implications of the study regarding the future of the two schools. The first question was about the future of Mission House in the light of the study material. It could be argued, the report noted, that the Twin Cities could be the location for Mission House both to serve its present constituency and to expand its mission in a metropolitan area. If the question is about Yankton and Mission House in a union effort the report noted that again a good case could be made for the Twin Cities location. However the committee asked the research team to delay any further work until after the upcoming General Synod of the Evangelical and Reformed Church and to await further instructions from the Committee of Four.

On June 30, 1959, the Board of Trustees of Mission House Theological Seminary met in Cleveland, Ohio, at the same time and place as the General Synod. Gunnemann reported to the Board the outcomes of the meetings of the Committee of Four with the research team and stated that the Twin Cities was a favorable spot for relocation in terms of the constituency of Mission House. He therefore requested that the Board propose to the Dearborn Committee the relocation of the Mission House Seminary in the Twin Cities area. On the same day Ruben H. Huenemann, chair of the Mission House Board of Trustees, appeared before the Dearborn committee and proposed that: 1. Mission House Seminary be relocated in the area of St. Paul-Minneapolis since this is a cultural, educational and economic center in an area in which there are over a thousand congregations of the United Church without an ecumenically oriented seminary in their midst; 2. Authorization be given to the seminary to explore immediately the possibility of making a relocation a joint effort with the Yankton School of Theology; 3. The seminary be granted the privilege to change its charter to broaden the scope of its services to united Protestantism in the North Central area of the country; and, 4. The General Synod authorize a plan for financial support that would insure the success of this program, such a plan to include the proposed seminary "thrust" during the current biennium and concurrent and subsequent efforts for adequate financial undergirding.

At the General Synod a supplementary report was submitted by the Committee to Study the Programs and Facilities of the Seminaries (the Dearborn Committee) that recommended to the General Synod:

1. That the study team be asked to complete its survey;

2. That the Mission House trustees explore all factors involved in the establishment of a new seminary in the Twin Cities;

3. That the seminary be authorized to explore the possibilities of making this development a joint effort with the Yankton School of Theology; and

4. That because of the conviction of the Committee that a new seminary must be a project of the United Church of Christ, the results of these studies and explorations be referred to the Executive Council of the United Church of Christ.

The General Council adopted the report of the committee, saying "General Synod approves in substance the Supplementary Report of the Special Committee to study the Programs and Facilities of the Seminaries and authorizes the General Council, together with the Board of Trustees of Mission House Theological Seminary, to take such actions as are necessary to implement the recommendations of said report."[1]

What had started out as a mutual conversation and study of the possibility of union and relocation was seen by some in the General Conference as a unilateral action by General Synod to relocate Mission House in the Twin Cities. As the General Synod (E&R) had noted the Obenhaus study was not yet complete. Only the initial data had been presented to the Committee of Four. And at that meeting of the Committee in June Sayler of Yankton had not been present, nor had the representative of the Congregational Christian Churches, Wesley Hotchkiss. Sayler later indicated that the actions of the General Synod had put the Yankton School of Theology into a very difficult position concerning its proposals.

---

[1]*Acts and Proceedings of the Eleventh Meeting of the General Synod of the Evangelical and Reformed Church, July 1-5, 1959, pp. 342-343.*

Nonetheless the School and the General Conference were concerned to strengthen Yankton for its service and to expand its program.

On the positive side the proposal clearly provided a strategic opening in a highly complex situation. Both schools, with uncertain futures in the institutional and ecclesial climate of that time, were able to gain not only denominational support but also recognition as a venture of the United Church of Christ. Following the formation of the denomination itself the new seminary was a "first" institutional venture of the new denomination. Although its recognition by the United Church was gained only with difficulty such recognition was crucial to the aims and hopes of the merging schools.

At the same time, the union of the two schools clearly introduced factors, that, by their very nature, would not automatically contribute to the implementation of the ecumenical vision. At times implementing that vision had to take second place as the two institutions encountered significant differences in articulating the nature and meaning of theological education, the nature of a theological seminary, the nature of the church and its role in theological education, and the goals and aims of ministerial training. Those differences reflected the special histories of the schools. Though both had a German heritage there was considerable diversity in understanding the issues in theological education.

Yankton's plan naturally focussed on maintaining an institution considered essential for training ministerial leadership for General Conference churches. Its own faculty was in a state of transition. Dean Sayler had been at Yankton since 1941 and had carried the school through some very difficult times.[2] George Eisenach had taught at Yankton for many years as a productive scholar but was now in ill health.[3] Howard Bozarth,

---

[2]Sayler had his theological training at Chicago Theological Seminary and had served churches in Nebraska and Illinois. Prior to his teaching at Yankton he had taught at Talladega College in Alabama.

[3]Eisenach has also graduated from Chicago Theological Seminary and had taken his doctorate at the University of Chicago. He had served churches in Wisconsin and South Dakota prior to starting teaching at Yankton in 1939. He died in Yankton on March 28, 1969.

9. Howard P. Bozarth,
Theology

10. James H. Cobb,
Biblical Studies

11. George J. Eisenach,
Church History

12. Ernest Sprenger,
Practical Theology

professor of theology, was approaching retirement.[4] James H. Cobb, in biblical studies, would leave in the school year 1959-60 and be replaced by Allan R. McAllaster. Two other additions were made in 1960. One was Ernest Sprenger in practical theology and the other was W. Robert Strobel, who was completing his doctoral work in Christian education at Union Seminary and Columbia University. Strobel had been a student at Yankton College and as a son of a General Conference pastor was well acquainted with the School of Theology. He had earned his B.D. and S.T.M. at Yale Divinity School.

For some at Yankton the moves of Mission House to get support from the Evangelical and Reformed Church for development and relocation were seen as a unilateral action. The values that it held dear, the relationship to the liberal arts as represented by the College, and the relationship to the General Conference were crucial to its self-understanding. The actions which Mission House had taken were seen as not taking these concerns sufficiently into consideration. From the point of view of Mission House its very existence was being threatened by forces within the Evangelical and Reformed Church and even by persons of power in the Congregational Christian Churches who saw the development of a seminary in the Upper Midwest as a threat to other schools and institutions in the area. Unless it acted with dispatch its future was seemingly jeopardized. So the Summer of 1959 was for Mission House a crucial turning point when definitive decisions needed to be made.

Following the actions of the 1959 General Synod events moved rapidly toward the establishment of a basis of union. On August 26, 1959, a consultation was called at the Protestant Center in Minneapolis to discuss the possible seminary relocation and merger. Present were church officials from Minnesota, Wisconsin, Iowa, South Dakota, North Dakota, Nebraska and Montana representing the Congregational conferences, the German Congregational Conference and the Evangelical and Reformed Synods. Also

---

[4]Bozarth had also attended Chicago Theological Seminary for his theological training. He had served churches in Illinois, Massachusetts, and North Carolina before teaching at Yankton, beginning in 1954. He died in Falls Church, Virginia, on July 1, 1971.

present were lay people and pastors from churches in the area. The Rev. Dr. Wesley A. Hotchkiss presided.

Following introductions and a preliminary statement of purpose by Dr. Hotchkiss, Gunnemann reported on the progress of the Obenhaus Study. Dr. Huenemann then reported on the actions of the General Synod in July. Dr. Sayler reviewed the history of Yankton College School of Theology and the actions that the General Conference of German Congregational Churches had taken concerning the development of a seven year program at Yankton, noting that all actions were postponed pending the outcome of the present survey and discussions.

That afternoon the group formulated a resolution that would shape the ultimate outcome of the attempt to merge the two schools. The resolution was as follows:

> Whereas Mission House Theological Seminary has proposed a relocation in the Twin Cities, and
>
> Whereas Yankton School of Theology has a special interest in the North Central area states and is planning to expand its program to a standard B.D. Degree program, and
>
> Whereas there is in the Twin City (sic) area a great opportunity to act in such a way so as to show the reality of the United Church, and
>
> Whereas the establishment of a United Church Seminary in the Twin Cities would contribute to the latter end,
>
> Be it therefore resolved that the consultant group petition the Executive Council of the United Church to appoint an Implementing Committee, including representatives of Mission House Seminary, Yankton School of Theology, the German Congregational Conference, the Twin Cities, and the United Church, to make whatever plans are necessary to establish the seminary there.

This resolution was adopted without a dissenting vote.

On the 6 of October the Committee of Four, without Hotchkiss of the CC churches and Gerber of the E&R Church, met to hear the second part of the Obenhaus Study. Also present were Huenemann for Mission House and Howard Haemmelmann, Wilbert Hiller, Harry Bernhard and Ralph Hoffman for Yankton. The outcome of this meeting was a set of recommendations to the Executive Council of the United Church of Christ, a copy of the Obenhaus Report, and a statement of reservations defining the position of the representatives of the School of Theology of Yankton College. The latter pointed to the great discrepancies between these recommendations and the earlier plans of Yankton and reserved the right to proceed with their earlier plans if the merger and relocation did not reach consummation.

The recommendation to the Executive Council was that they "approve the efforts of Yankton School of Theology and Mission House Theological Seminary to reestablish themselves as one United Church seminary in the North Central States area - it being understood that in this way the United Church will be serving Protestant churches in general and will be advancing theological education in the United States - and that the Executive Council authorize a consultant group composed of such educators as Dr. H. Richard Niebuhr, Dr. Charles Taylor and Dr. Roger Shinn to aid in the establishment of the new seminary and that the Executive Council give consideration to securing the means for carrying through this project, it being understood that the resources of Yankton School of Theology and Mission House Theological Seminary will be available." This report was joined with an action by the Mission House Board of Trustees in support of the proposal.

When the Executive Council (UCC) met on October 8 it received the report from the Committee of Four and took two actions. The first was a statement that it was impressed with the report and looked to the Commission and Division for further recommendations. The second was to refer the report to the Commission on Higher Education (E&R) and Division of Higher Education (CC) for consideration and further report to the Executive Council.[5] In the memorandum in which Hotchkiss, as General Secretary of the Division of Higher Education, reported this action to the Committee of Four the emphasized phrase was "to continue the study." On this basis Hotchkiss proposed a plan to form a new committee, identify its task, suggest areas of study, and formulate procedures for the committee.[6] The crucial dimension of his proposal was that the task of the committee be

---

[5]These two actions are identified as 59 10EC 16 and 59 10EC 17, in the official minutes of the Executive Council.

[6]Memorandum to the Committee of Four, from Wesley A. Hotchkiss, October 28, 1959.

broadened to include "a total appraisal of existing institutions in comparison to total needs in theological education."

This proposal was not favorably received by Gunnemann and others at Mission House. All the planning to date seemed to be set aside in favor of an expanded study that would investigate theological education throughout the United Church of Christ. Such a study would require intensive work for a number of years. Any hopes of proceeding with the merger and relocation appeared to revert to the beginning. Again it appeared that there were persons and groups that felt that the merger and relocation of the schools would infringe on their turf or at best be an unnecessary creation. There were also voices calling for the creation of a theological school in either the Denver or Seattle areas, possible locations mentioned in the Obenhaus report.

During that Winter of 1959-60 there were discussions, phone calls and meetings to find ways to let the process of merger and relocation continue. Gunnemann appears to have taken the lead by drawing on his relationship to such persons as James Wagner, President of the Evangelical and Reformed Church, Truman Douglass, Executive vice-president of the Board of Home Missions (CC), Hotchkiss and others. The outcome was an action by the Executive Committee of the Board of Home Missions that called for the creation of yet another committee to explore the merger and relocation plans, to make an evaluation of the requirements of the new institution in terms of site, buildings, and operational budget, and to hold further consultations in the Twin Cities.

On that basis a Committee of Six was formed to explore the merger and relocation issues.[7] They met in Minneapolis at the Minnesota Protestant Center on February 23, 1960, to draw up an initial basis of union for Yankton and Mission House. In addition they acted to have Ruben H. Huenemann serve as interim leader beginning in June until the new school was organized and regular leadership could be appointed. Additional funds for the

[7]Representing Yankton were Sayler, Wilber W. Hiller and Howard Haemelmann, while the Mission House representatives were Ruben H. Huenemann, Gunnemann and Walter Odenbach. At the first meeting Dr. Robert Spike of the Board of Home Mission was present in place of Hotchkiss. Gunnemann was elected chair and Sayler secretary.

planning committee and preliminary work were requested from the Board for Home Missions. Theological educators were sought as consultants. A meeting of this committee was called for May 4-5, 1960 to discuss the proposed basis of union. In the minutes it was noted that some discussion was devoted to the name for the new seminary but no consensus was reached.

At the historic May meeting a Basis of Union was approved by the Committee of Six,[8] in consultation with representatives of the Board of Home Missions, the General Council of the Evangelical Reformed Church, and of the General Conference, the Minnesota Congregational Christian Conference, and the E&R Northern Synod. That both the Evangelical and Reformed General Council and the General Conference of Congregational Churches were able to approve the document without delay in June of that year indicated that the basis of union expressed a consensus beyond what might have been expected. Three affirmations stand out among others as a charter of responsibility for the new school: "the uniting of two schools into an effective, ecumenically oriented seminary;" "the seminary...shall affirm its responsibility to the United Church of Christ...and shall be organically related to the United Church of Christ;" and the seminary shall prepare "men and women for the whole ministry of the church in the fulfillment of his (Christ's) mission..."

The first two affirmations link the ecumenical commitment of the seminary to its responsibility and relationship to the United Church of Christ. It was a clear statement that "ecumenical" was not to be understood as "interdenominational" nor "non-denominational" but as recognition of a specific ecclesial understanding of the nature of Christian unity. The third affirmation exhibited the commitment to the church to prepare leadership for the church's mission. All three mark the abandonment of any of the parochialism that had been a limiting factor for both of the merging schools. In that respect they were at least partially prepared for the impact of the emerging pluralism and secularism that were to mark the succeeding decades. An equally noteworthy emphasis is conveyed in the words "men and

---

[8]The Basis of Union is included as an appendix in this volume because of the importance of this document as the defining reality for United Theological Seminary.

women" students to be prepared for the "whole ministry of the church." In view of the small number of women students in all seminaries at that time, such a declaration of intent had a distinctly prophetic note.

Approval of the Basis of Union marks the beginning of an ecumenical venture but did not ensure the existence and establishment of the new seminary. Before the doors of the school could open in September of 1962 there were many hurdles still to be overcome. That period of transition will be the focus of discussion in the following chapters.

PART TWO

TIMES OF TRANSITION

CHAPTER 4

ONE SCHOOL IN THREE LOCATIONS

In the period between May 1960 and September 1962, when United Theological Seminary of the Twin Cities was chartered, built and opened to students, the ecumenical atmosphere was charged with an electric sense of new possibilities. Three major events occurred in the biennium that firmly established ecumenism's major themes for decades to come: the birth of the Consultation on Church Union in the United States, 1960; the Third Assembly of the World Council of Churches in New Delhi, India, 1961; and the beginning of Vatican II in Rome, 1962. Each of these in different way represented the growing dimensions of the conciliar mode of ecumenical relationships and endeavors. The Christian community often seems to have little awareness of the import of these events, yet the themes have been woven into the fabric of the life of the churches, influencing in part their responses to the dramatic changes of the post World War II era.

On December 4, 1960, Eugene Carson Blake, stated clerk of the United Presbyterian Church in the U.S.A., preached at Grace Cathedral (Episcopal) in San Francisco a sermon at the invitation of his friend, Bishop James Pike. The sermon entitled "A Proposal Toward the Reunion of Christ's Church[1] urged the Presbyterian, Methodist, United Church of Christ and Episcopalian denominations to assume leadership in the search for a

[1]Dean K. Thompson, "Eugene Carson Blake and COCU," *The Presbyterian Outlook* Dec.17-24-31,1990, p. 11.

unity that would be expressive of the common claim that Jesus Christ is Lord. Blake had served as a president of the National Council of Churches, 1954-57, and his sermon preceded the opening of the Fifth General Assembly of the National Council of Churches. He opened with the stirring plea, "Led, I pray by the Holy Spirit, I propose to the Protestant Episcopal Church that it together with the United Presbyterian Church in the U.S.A. invite the Methodist Church and the United Church of Christ to form with us a plan of church union both catholic and reformed..."[2] It was a vision of the ecumenical church whose time had come. It was based on the theological conviction that there needed to be only one body of Christ and that unity needed to be expressed visibly to the world. Blake was also aware of the experience of American Christians whose allegiance to specific denominational forms of Christianity was waning. Not only did the four denominations accept the challenge but they were also joined by two others who gathered in April of 1962 in Washington, D.C. They called themselves the "Consultation on Church Union." Although the outcome of the consultation is yet to be determined, and the expectations have changed, the vision of an ecumenical church continues to challenge the patterns and behaviors of the denominations. As Blake said, "This does not mean that this Church must be uniform, authoritarian or a single mammoth organization. But it does mean that our separate organizations...present a tragically divided church to a tragically divided world."[3]

In New Delhi, India, the Third World Council of Churches met under the theme "Jesus Christ the Light of the World." Innocuous as that theme might sound it represented significant changes in the way the Christian church would henceforth understand itself. At this meeting the International Missionary Council united with the World Council of Churches. Five Roman Catholic priests attended as observers. The influence of the Orthodox church manifested itself. Most significantly the so-called "Third World" began to exert a powerful impact upon the awareness of the West. Under

---

[2]David W. A. Taylor, "The Consultation on Church Union - Thirty Years in Progress toward the Reunion of Christ's Church," *Presbyterian Outlook* Dec. 17-24-31,1990, pp. 9-10.

[3]Thompson, *ibid.*, p. 11.

the influence of the Orthodox churches the requirement for membership was changed to strengthen the Trinitarian structure of the faith claim. Moreover strong statements were formulated to express the Church's witness, service and unity in the world. Pronouncements to halt the arms race and to work for peace with justice were promulgated. Whereas earlier assemblies had been concerned with inner Christian dialogue this assembly began the turn outward to demonstrate that the Church needed to be in dialogue with a world that was severely fragmented.

The third great ecumenical event of that time was the beginning of the Vatican Council under Pope John XXIII. Opening up the windows of the Roman Catholic Church by Pope John was an astonishing event both inside and outside the church. This Pope had been expected to be a caretaker pope considering his age. He would not live to see the outcome of the council for he died in 1963. But he had set in motion forces that would radically change the face of the church. Within the church great changes were made in terms of its life and worship. In particular the use of the vernacular in the Mass and of the participation of lay people in the worship of the church was approved. There were also significant changes in the relationship of the Roman Church to other religious groups. Fraternal understanding instead of heretical denunciation was extended to other churches. To the Jews the concern for reconciliation and regret was expressed, epitomized in Pope John's greeting to the Rabbi of Rome, "I am your brother Joseph!" To the other religions of the world was extended admiration of their spiritual values. Each of these stances would lead that church to new and surprising positions in the years to come. It should be noted that Dr. Ruben Huenemann, the first President of United Theological Seminary, was an official observer to Vatican II in 1965.

Alongside these remarkable events of the times there were other ecumenical events that would influence the life of the seminary. On May 11, 1961 the Unitarian Universalist Association completed its merger. In the same year Lutheran bodies agreed to form the Lutheran Church in America. For the Seminary the decisive event was the Third General Synod of the United Church of Christ meeting on July 4, 1961, in Philadelphia. Here the

13. Ruben H. Huenemann, First President, 1960-70

14. Louis H. Gunnemann, Dean, 1960-74

15. Statue of Joshua, in memory of Karl J. Ernst

constitution of the new church was ratified and the continuing bodies of the Congregational Christian churches and the Evangelical and Reformed Church ceased to exist. The birth of the United Church of Christ, combining two church bodies of diverse ethnic, religious and theological traditions, provided the impetus for a new venture in theological education. At the same time the uncertainty of the church in relation to theological education would continue to create difficulties in establishing the school. The lack of denominational policy regarding theological education imposed the need for a certain amount of creative improvisations on the persons responsible for the maintenance and subsequent merger of the two schools.

With the adoption of the Basis of Union on May 4, 1960, events moved rapidly. The following month, on June 2, the Board of Trustees of Mission House Theological Seminary voted unanimous approval of the Basis of Union.[4] According to the provisions of the agreement nine persons were elected to the Board of the new seminary. On June 16, the Administrative Committee of the General Council of the Evangelical and Reformed Church approved the Basis of Union. The next week, on June 22, the General Conference of the Congregational Churches, at a special meeting in Denver, approved the document by a vote of 112 to 10, of the approximately 148 delegates present, and elected their representatives to the new board of trustees.[5]

The following day, June 23, 1960, the nine elected by the Mission House Board and the nine elected from the General Conference met to elect nine additional persons to the board, four laypersons and five clergy. The Rev. W. W. Hiller was elected temporary chair of the new Board and the Rev. Walter Odenbach, temporary secretary. Ruben H. Huenemann was

---

[4]Minutes of Special Meeting, Board of Trustees, Mission House Theological Seminary, Y.M.C.A., Milwaukee, June 2, 1960.

[5]Roland G. Kley, *United Theological Seminary: The First Ten Years*, New Brighton: United Theological Seminary, 1971, p. 20.

authorized to represent the new seminary in the Minneapolis area and to set up a temporary office for the school.[6]

Twenty-three of the twenty-seven elected board members were present for the first meeting, held at the St. Paul Hotel in St. Paul, Minnesota, on Sept. 6, 1960.[7] At this organizational meeting of the board Henry Reifschneider was elected Moderator pro tem and Walter E. Odenbach as secretary pro tem. It was decided that the Constitution and Charter of the school should be drawn up by the new President of the Seminary, consulting "with his spiritual and legal advisers" and in conformity with the Basis of Union. The selection of a site was given over to the Executive Committee of the Board, after hearing an appeal for consideration of a campus in Duluth owned by the University of Minnesota. The financial needs of the new school received much attention, noting both the resources and funds from the two previous schools, the possibilities of support from the church, and the importance of making the needs of the school known to a wider constituency.

The patterns for organization of the Board and the Seminary were a matter of deep concern and discussion. An Executive Committee of nine members was authorized, including a Chairman, Vice-Chairman, Secretary and Treasurer. The Executive Committee members were Edward Sayler, Mrs. Lawrence Schoen, Carl Hansen, Erwin Koch, Henry Reifschneider, Fred Schneider, Harry Baumer, and a C.C. layman to be chosen by the executive committee. Only then were the officers chosen: Edward Sayler as Chairman, Henry Reifschneider as Vice-Chairman, Mrs. Lawrence Schoen as Secretary, and Erwin Koch as Treasurer. Ruben H. Huenemann was officially selected as the first president of the new school though he had been serving as president pro tem for several months. As its final action the Board

---

[6]Minutes of the Meeting at Denver, Colorado of the Eighteen Board Members of the merged Mission House-Yankton Seminary, German Congregational Church, Denver, Colo. June 23, 1960.

[7]Minutes of the First Meeting, Board of Trustees, United Theological Seminary, St. Paul Hotel, St. Paul, MN, Sept. 6, 1960.

also selected the name for the new school: United Theological Seminary of the Twin Cities.

Approval of the Basis of Union, election of a Board of Trustees and the choice of a President did not assure the location and the establishment of the new seminary. On-site leadership was of critical importance at this time. Choice and purchase of an appropriate building site had to be undertaken immediately. An equally critical matter was the introduction of the seminary concept and vision to church, community and business leaders as well as educators. Not least among the immediate needs was the establishment of relationships that would assist in local and national promotion and fund-raising.

President Huenemann's exceptional leadership in the establishment of United Seminary was exhibited in the transition period from 1960 to 1962, and was continued in the decade of the Sixties. Huenemann came to the presidency from a pastorate in Faith Evangelical and Reformed Church in Milwaukee, Wisconsin. He had also been the chair of the Board of Trustees of Mission House Seminary after its separation from the college. Huenemann had deep roots in the Evangelical and Reformed Church, with several from his family having served in pastoral positions in that church. The oldest member of a large family of siblings he presented an imposing physical appearance and recognized leadership qualities. He brought a wide acquaintance within the denomination, twenty-five years experience in the pastoral ministry, and considerable familiarity and interest in religious and secular education. A lifelong association with Mission House included a childhood and youth spent within a mile of the campus during the years his father had studied for the ministry and later served the Emmanuel Church nearby. He had served as chaplain at the annual meeting of the Congregational Christian Churches in 1961, and had also been moderator of the 1953 General Synod of the Evangelical and Reformed Church at its meeting in Tiffin, Ohio.[8]

---

[8]After graduating from the Academy of Mission House Huenemann taught in several rural schools in South Dakota. He attended Luther College, Decorah, Iowa, for his B.A. and then received his B.D. from Mission House Theological Seminary. While a pastor in St. Louis, Missouri, and Lodi, California, he pursued graduate studies at Eden Seminary, Washington

When Huenemann accepted the presidency of Mission House he was a reluctant but committed candidate.[9] He felt that he did not have the academic qualifications for the position, with only an honorary doctorate. The situation on the Mission House campus was unclear because the relationship to the denomination was uncertain and the future in question. The place of theological education in the emerging United Church of Christ was a matter of debate, both structurally and financially. The resources for a new school in the upper Midwest were tenuous at best. Yet he accepted the position with the encouragement of James Wagner, President of the E&R Church, and the approval of Dean Sayler at Yankton.[10]

When Huenemann moved to Minneapolis in September of 1960 he was President of both Mission House Theological Seminary and United Theological Seminary of the Twin Cities. A more challenging job could not have been imagined. His days were filled with meetings with local church leaders and educational representatives seeking to interpret the new school and soliciting their support. He was responsible to two boards of trustees and their separate agendas. He was deeply involved in negotiations with the denominational leadership. He was speaking at church functions, visiting colleges to recruit students and interpret the new venture in theological education. Huenemann had to organize the publicity that was necessary to disseminate information about the new school. Also he had to develop a strategy to retain previous support and at the same time elicit new contributions. He was involved in the many minutiae of administration such as letterheads, brochures for distribution, receipt of gifts from individuals and congregations, and chartering the new school. Increasingly he was concerned with the location of the campus in the Twin Cities area and the selection of a

---

University and Pacific School of Religion. He received honorary doctoral degrees from Franklin and Marshall College and Heidelberg College.

[9]Letter from LHG to RHH, Sept 10, 1960. "I am delighted about many of the developments, and especially about your election to the office of President of United Theological Seminary. I need not congratulate you for you did not seek this office. But I do want to assure you once more of my great confidence in you, and also I want to pledge my heartiest cooperation to you in this work."

[10]Letter from RHH to James E. Wagner, Nov. 6, 1959, and letter from LHG to Edward Sayler, Nov. 17, 1959.

site. All of this he handled out of an office located in his apartment in Minneapolis, without a secretary. In the supportive role filled by many women of that time Clara Huenemann uncomplainingly maintained the household and answered the telephone.

Meanwhile the programs at Mission House and Yankton had to continue. Since Dean Gunnemann had been the acting president of Mission House for the school year 1959-60, upon the resignation of Arthur Krueger, he was familiar with the institutional details as well as the academic program. With Huenemann in Minneapolis much of the day to day work of administration had to be carried out by Gunnemann. Yet regular correspondence between the two kept a healthy working relationship as the hopes and dreams of the years became a reality. At Yankton Dean Sayler continued his leadership of that school though illness was to make that role increasingly difficult for him.

The faculty that had been gathered at Mission House in 1958 was coming together as a team. Each year an Integrative Seminar was held in the Fall to deal with a Key Book and to bring the faculty and students into dialogue about issues of critical import to the church and theological education. In the Fall of 1960 the topic was The Old Testament and Preaching, with a focus on Wilhelm Vischer's *The Witness of the Old Testament to Christ,* supplemented by Sigmund Mowinckel's *The Old Testament as Word of God*, and Brevard Child's *Myth and Reality in the Old Testament.* Presentations on the topic were made by three faculty members and sermons preached by two other faculty to illustrate the theme. In the Fall of 1961 the topic was Preaching to Contemporary Man, with a focus on Rudolph Bultmann's *The New Testament and Mythology,* supplemented by Gabriel Vahanian's *Death of God*, and John Macquaries's *The Scope of Demythologizing*. The format was similar to the preceding year and involved issues that made the Gospel relevant in the contemporary era.

Another factor bringing the faculty together was the on-going experience of the Tri-Faculty Conferences that met just before the opening of the school year. In 1960 the three faculties of Eden, Lancaster and Mission House met at Mission House and discussed the topic of Worship and Ethics. There were also reports on the recent AATS meeting and the progress of Mission House's relocation. Theological discussions as well as social events helped the faculties to understand both themselves and each other.

One initially unsettling factor was the resignation of Frederick Herzog to accept the position in Systematic Theology at Duke Divinity School in the Fall of 1960. Herzog had been a strong voice and theological critic in the development of the plan to enhance the school and seek its relocation. With Herzog gone only Gunnemann remained to express the original vision. The two of them had been especially close in both personal relationship and theological understanding. The search for a replacement was begun and Robert H. Bryant of Centre College, Kentucky was selected as the new teacher of systematic theology.[11] However he could not leave his position until the Fall of 1961. Therefore an interim was sought and located in the person of Milos Strupl, from the Reformed Church of Hungary whose special interest was in the Unitas Fratrum. Strupl entered easily into the faculty and became noted for his culinary skills as well as his teaching ability. The rest of the faculty sought ways to retain him as a colleague. He was suggested to Yankton as a possible addition to their faculty. There was hope he could be added to the Mission House faculty, but the budget would not permit it. At one point he was even proposed as the first new faculty member of United Theological Seminary. But all attempts to retain him came to naught and he went on to teach at Defiance College in Ohio.

Of course much of the energy and enthusiasm of the Mission House faculty was directed toward the building of the academic program of the new seminary. There were position papers to write and to evaluate. A continuing program for students who would move from Mission House to the new school had to be devised. Meetings with the faculty from Yankton had to be organized and attended. The days of preparation were full and exciting.

One major event during that period helped to mark the close of an era: the lectures of Karl Barth at the University of Chicago in April of 1962. The world famous theologian from Switzerland made his first trip to the

---

[11]Bryant had done his B.A. at William and Mary College and his B.D. and Ph.D. at Yale University.

United States, particularly encouraged by his son Markus who was teaching at Chicago. He presented a series of lectures on Evangelical Christianity. The faculty of Mission House Seminary attended those lectures on Thursday, April 25, 1962. Though listening to Barth's rough English in a heavy German accent was difficult they heard his call for a form of American theology that would comprehend the American scene with its accent on freedom. This call was accepted by the faculty and was incorporated into their concern for the new program of theological education at United Theological Seminary.

Another mark of the end of an era was the Centennial Commencement of Mission House Seminary and Lakeland College. From June 2 to 5 a series of events celebrated this historical moment in the life of the two schools. They began with a Historical Pageant to commemorate the history of the schools and the lives of the many folks who had been dedicated to the development of these institutions in the German Reformed tradition. The pageant was written by Eugene Jaberg of the seminary and the actors included faculty and students from the college and seminary as well as area residents. On Sunday there was a Communion Service in the morning and the Centennial Commencement in the afternoon at which Dean Elmer Homrighausen, of Princeton Theological Seminary, a Mission House graduate, was the speaker. On Monday and Tuesday the Centennial Convocation had as its lecturers Martin E. Marty, then associate editor of the *Christian Century* magazine and a Lutheran Pastor, on preaching in the contemporary scene and Bard D. Thompson, professor of Church History at Lancaster Seminary, on the Heidelberg Catechism. At a banquet on the evening of June 4 the honored guests and speakers were the three emeriti professors of Mission House, Karl J. Ernst, Josias Friedli and Ernst Fledderjohn, who together represented 75 years of teaching service. It was indeed a fitting conclusion to the long and distinguished history of Mission House Theological Seminary.

Yankton School of Theology was also confronted with the uncertainties of a great transition. With the formation of the United Church of Christ its relationship to the denomination needed to be clarified. Though it was a direct expression of the General Conference and was governed by the Board of Education it had already opened up to the "English" constituency by training ministers for the English speaking churches. Because it was in part dependent for support on the Congregational Christian Churches through the Board for Home Missions, the suggestion from the Board that it merge with Mission House was perceived as a mandate from the church rather than a decision taken by the faculty.[12]

Consequently this suggestion raised real questions for the faculty. They had carved out a significant mission of training ministers for the churches in the states of the Great Plains and westward. In the faculty minutes apparently a primary concern was not only the placement and ministry of the graduates but also the service that the students provided to the congregations in the region, with placement and supply a major topic of virtually every faculty meeting. When the final Obenhaus report was to be received the faculty discussed its possible import. Dean Sayler noted that Yankton was an ideal place for a school of theology for its "rural attitudes and scale of values." Eisenach suggested that closer relations to Chicago Theological Seminary might be an alternative. Ernest Sprenger noted that the Dakota Associations favored continuation of the location in Yankton.[13] When the report from the Obenhaus study was received the study was reported to favor a united seminary and that two locations were discussed: Yankton and Minneapolis. The faculty agreed that they would follow the recommendation of the church if it should propose a united seminary, but that it would also make "no recommendation for the location."[14] From Truman Douglass they had heard that there should be a reconsideration of the three major potential centers: Minneapolis, Denver and Seattle. At the following faculty meeting they had heard from Wesley Hotchkiss that there would be a new committee to report to the church on its policy regarding theological education and the suggested location for a United Seminary.[15]

---

[12]In the minutes of the Faculty of Yankton School of Theology there is virtually no indication of the conversations with Mission House and no record of their discussions about the issues.

[13]Minutes of the Faculty Meeting, Dean's Office, Friday, October 2, 1959.

[14]Minutes of the Faculty Meeting, Deans' Office, Wednesday, October 21, 1959.

[15]Minutes of Faculty Meeting, Dean's Office. Monday, November 15, 1959.

At this meeting the faculty indicated, "We shall be ready to unite with any proposed Congregational seminary for this region." From these discussions and actions it becomes apparent that Yankton was a reluctant partner to the merger. It knew that it had to do something in the light of the changing situation, both in theological education where its program no longer was adequate for the training of ministerial leadership, and in its relationship to the church that was changing because of the merger.

Once the Basis of Union had been agreed upon the faculty at Yankton took up the discussion of the curriculum for the new seminary. Their conclusion was that the new curriculum "should give expression to the particular concerns that have been the guiding motivation of our School of Theology."[16] However these particular concerns were not explained and it seems that they expected Dean Sayler to provide the voice for those concerns. Ironically that meeting to discuss the curriculum was held in the home of Dean Sayler who was already terminally ill. On the 13th of January 1961 Dean Edward Sayler died of cancer and his funeral was held at the First Congregational Church of Yankton. This was a grievous blow to Yankton School of Theology and to the prospects of the new seminary of which he had been elected Chairman of the Board of Trustees. A strong voice for the interests of Yankton and the values that it sought to incorporate into the new school had been stilled. The balance of power had shifted even more to Mission House and many from the Yankton side would feel that their voice had not been adequately heard.

In the meantime another shift had taken place in the Yankton faculty with the coming of Allan R. McAllaster in the Fall of 1960. John Cobb, the previous professor of Biblical Studies, had left his position that summer. As an outsider to the Yankton scene, coming from the English tradition, Cobb seems to have felt left out of the decisions about faculty supply preaching in

---

[16]Minutes of the Faculty Meeting of the School of Theology, Nov. 14, 1960.

16. Allan R. McAllaster, Dean of School of Theology, Yankton and Old Testament, 1960-84

17. Robert H. Bryant, Constructive Theology, 1961-91

18. W. Strobel, Christian Nurture, 1962-87

the local congregations.[17] McAllaster was also from the English tradition as he came from a large pastorate in Lawrence, Massachusetts, which he had served while finishing his doctorate at Boston University in Old Testament. McAllaster had entered the ministry later in life, having gone to college after his service in the Navy during World War II. A graduate of Asbury Theological Seminary, his religious roots were in the Free Methodist tradition though he had moved his ministerial standing to the Congregational Christian Church. Upon the death of Sayler, McAllaster was appointed acting dean of Yankton School of Theology and had to take up the leadership for Yankton though he had not come out of that tradition nor had he been with the school more than five months.

McAllaster was faced with a daunting task. He had to lead the faculty in its discussions of the issues regarding the formation of the new seminary; he had to negotiate the issues that faced Yankton College as it lost its School of Theology and formed a Department of Religion; and he had to interpret these concerns to the General Conference. To relieve him of his heavy teaching load Bozarth taught the introduction course to Old Testament and Sprenger taught the introduction to New Testament courses.[18]

The negotiations with Yankton College, under the leadership of President Rondileau, indicate some of the ambiguity with which the School of Theology entered into the merger with Mission House. The School of Theology had to set up a Department of Religion, which would remain at Yankton. It was that faculty that set up the requirements for graduation with a religion major or minor. It included a set of requirements that reflected strongly the pastoral orientation of the program with electives in preaching and worship, which were to help those "boys serving churches." The question of teachers for the religion program was also raised. As Howard Bozarth was approaching retirement he agreed to stay on at Yankton as one of the faculty in religion for a year, and then retired at Elon College in North Carolina. The other faculty member was sought from outside the current faculty. The

---

[17]Memo to Dean Sayler from James Harrel Cobb, attached to minutes of the Faculty Meeting, October 2, 1959.

[18]Minutes of the School of Theology Faculty Meeting, June 6, 1961.

search resulted in the election of Fred Kirschenmann, a Yankton graduate who was finishing his doctorate at the University of Chicago, to assume the position in the Fall of 1962.[19]

In addition to the need to establish a Department of Religion there was the question of the continuance of the B.Th. degree at Yankton. A memo from McAllaster to President Rondileau outlined the agreement that Yankton would continue to offer the B.Th. degree, though the fifth year of theology would be taken elsewhere and the credits transferred to Yankton College that would award the degree.[20] In accepting the agreement Rondileau indicated that a committee consisting of the Dean of the College and the two religion professors would be the admissions committee for the continuing B.Th. program.[21] It is significant that the new United Theological Seminary was not designated as the site of the fifth year of theological studies! What reservations were felt in that regard were not noted in any official document. The source of the impetus to carry on the B.Th. program at Yankton is not clear, especially when the theological school was supposedly to be merged with Mission House Seminary and the seven year plan that had been originally proposed would find its fulfillment in the new program of the new school. There is no evidence that any students were ever admitted to the continuing B.Th. program, and those students who had been in the B.Th. program transferred either to United Seminary or to another school.

At the last meeting of the School of Theology Faculty on May 17, 1962, several actions were taken.[22] Academic prizes were awarded for the 1961-62 school year. Five graduates were recommended for the B.Th. degree. Loans to several students were granted. And the Dr. Edward Sayler

---

[19]Minutes of the Board of Education of the School of Theology of Yankton College, Yankton, SD, held at Yankton, SD, on January 10, 1962.

[20]Memo from Allan R. McAllaster to President Rondileau, May 19, 1962.

[21]Memo from Dr. Rondileau to Dr. McAllaster, May 22, 1962.

[22]Minutes of the School of Theology Faculty Meeting, May 17,1962 (and concluded on May 18th).

Memorial Fund was established to provide a scholarship for students who had financial needs and demonstrated sociological sensitivity. With these actions the School of Theology ceased to exist.

The German churches which had been served by the former School of Theology accepted the challenge to raise $100,000 for the new seminary. The assets of the School of Theology were designated for United or to the college's department of religion. Those who had favored the merger with Mission House, including conference ministers and Board members, made diligent use of President Huenemann to maintain personal, direct contact. He was invited to speak and be resource leader at conference and association meetings. As late as June 1963, at a General Conference meeting held in Scotts Bluff, NE he was confronted by two laymen who tried to oppose the fund raising campaign. However the Conference voted overwhelmingly to continue its support.[23]

---

[23]Interview with RHH by ALM, at UTS, August 19, 1991.

CHAPTER 5

CONSOLIDATING A FACULTY

With the modifications in both faculties, the differing views and experiences of theological education, and the separate locations of those persons who would form the new faculty the task of consolidation was not easy. Initially there was only a President for United Theological Seminary. No other academic officers were elected or appointed. The Basis of Union had stipulated that the faculties of the two schools would become the faculty of the new school. Louis Gunnemann of Mission House, due to his tenure and experience, as well as his vision of the new school, took the lead in the initiative that would result in the building of a significant program of theological education. It was not until the second meeting of the Board of Trustees, on May 22-23, 1961 that he was elected Dean of United Theological Seminary. At the same time Allan McAllaster was elected Registrar of the new school. The question of Dean of Students was left in abeyance.[1]

The first introduction of the proposed Seminary to the Twin Cities community occurred on January 25, 1961, at a luncheon meeting held at the YMCA in St. Paul, MN. The meeting had been arranged by the President to introduce the concept of United Seminary to the Twin Cities area. Local clergy, selected laypeople, and educators had been invited to the luncheon,

---

[1]Minutes of the Annual Meeting, Board of Trustees, United Theological Seminary of the Twin Cities, Lyman Lodge, Excelsior, Minnesota, May 22-23, 1961.

and over 200 people responded. Dr. H. Richard Niebuhr, the noted ethicist and Professor at Yale, had accepted the invitation to be the speaker. On the afternoon before the set date he was forced to decline due to the death of his mother. Frantic telephone calls to several known theologians resulted in the acceptance by Dr. Charles Taylor, executive secretary of the American Association of Theological Schools, of the invitation. He interrupted his schedule to fly to the Twin Cities where he provided an appropriate address. He spoke on the need for theological education not only in the church but also in the world. Such education was necessary because there was a need for more ministers and that it was crucial to provide more than the tricks of the trade. Taylor had been a strong supporter of both Mission House and the proposed new seminary. At this meeting Dr. Alvin Rogness of Luther Theological Seminary extended the welcome of the other theological schools in the Twin Cities.[2] For most of the faculty members present it was the first occasion for personal contact between Mission House and Yankton. Though there was no formal meeting of the faculties, at least names received faces and acquaintances could be initiated.

The first formal meeting of the faculty of United Theological Seminary was held on April 14-15, 1961 at Plymouth Congregational Church in Minneapolis.[3] Present for the meeting were President Huenemann, Professors Howard Bozarth, Robert Bryant, George Eisenach, Louis Gunnemann, Paul Hammer, Theophilus Hilgeman, Eugene Jaberg, Allan McAllaster, Arthur Merrill, Ernest Sprenger and Milos Strupl. Roland Kley was absent due to illness. Allan McAllaster chaired the meetings and Arthur Merrill was elected secretary of the faculty.

Huenemann set the tone for the meeting with his initial comments on the context in which the discussion of the curriculum and its principles should take place. He particularly stressed that the new school needed to listen to voices that were looking beyond merely intellectual concerns for the preparation of "better pastors." These voices were identified as the Church,

[2]Kley, *The First Ten Years*, p. 26.

[3]Minutes of United Theological Seminary Faculty Meeting, Minneapolis, MN, April 14-15, 1961.

the Ecumenical Movement, the secular community and the United Church of Christ.

The major discussion focused on a paper entitled "Theological Education at United Theological Seminary," prepared by a committee of faculty at Mission House and distributed before the meeting to both faculties.[4] Here one can discern some shifts in the understanding of theological education that marked the new school in its beginnings. The first major shift was the understanding that the basis of the task was the Word of God, known through the scriptures and revealed in Jesus Christ. Though the formulation was rather typical and traditional there were accents that made it different in tone. On the one hand the *event character* of that Word was emphasized. Whereas the Neo-orthodoxy of the time was also concerned with that dimension of the Word it was seen as having doctrinal significance. But for this faculty the event character of the Word was an encounter that saw the Word as not something beyond or above the human realm but coming out of that encounter in the human situation. Though the language largely reflected what would later be called the "Biblical Theology Movement" those who participated in the discussion had their own particular understanding of that language. This can be seen in the backgrounds of the two biblical scholars, Hammer and Merrill.

Hammer had studied for his doctoral degree at the University of Heidelberg, in Germany under the tutelage of Gerhard von Rad and Gunther Bornkamm. It had been Bornkamm who in his 1948 article on "The Stilling of the Storm in Matthew" had initiated the approach to Scripture that would later be called redaction criticism.[5] A student of Rudolph Bultmann, he was concerned with the relationship of church and tradition in the Scriptures. It was in the intersection of church and tradition that the event character of the Word could be discerned and made available for the ongoing self- understanding of the community of faith.

---

[4]The final form of the statement can be found in the first *Announcements*, 1962-63, of United Theological Seminary of the Twin Cities.

[5]Eldon J. Epp and George W. MacRae, eds. *The New Testament and its Interpreters* (Atlanta, GA: Scholars Press, 1989).

Merrill on the other hand had studied at the University of Chicago under the guidance of J. Coert Rylaarsdam and Robert M. Grant. The "Chicago School" of that time was not only one where process theology was prominent, but also where the socio-historical legacy of Shailer Mathews and Shirley Jackson Case remained strong. This socio-historical approach had two important dimensions. One assumption was that to understand one first had to know what methods one was employing to study the phenomena under consideration. Whereas Liberal and Neo-orthodox theologians were concerned with doctrine the Chicago School was concerned with method. The other aspect was a concern for context. In this respect the Chicago School became known as environmentalists, for it was the context that provided the key to understanding a thinker or movement. As Mathews said, the "efficiency (of leaders) is always dependent upon coherence." And that coherence was to be found in method and context.[6] Thus Scripture came out of a context that must be delineated so that one can understand its message for its time and place.

In the discussion of the faculty on the position paper the issue of the understanding of the Word of God was thereby joined though there were a variety of understandings in the faculty and no final agreement was reached. It was noted that the matter would need further discussion and clarification. Yet it was a significant move for it set the Scriptures as the basis for understanding the character of theological education. In the previous curriculum at Mission House the organizing principle was the personal relationship to Jesus Christ, as Word of God, and known through the tradition, reflected in the Key Books and the Heidelberg Catechism. The ecumenical vision had shifted from what Gunnemann would call an "ecclesial piety" to a focus on the Biblical tradition.

This movement was no doubt enhanced by the presence of Robert Bryant who had done his theological study at Yale Divinity School and whose doctoral dissertation had focused on the authority of the Bible.[7] Having

---

[6]Jerald C. Brauer, "A History of the Divinity School: Creatively Out of Step," *Criterion* 29:3 (Autumn 1990) 12-17.

[7] *The Authority of the Bible*, Minneapolis, MN: Augsburg Press, 1968.

studied under H. Richard Niebuhr, among others, he contributed to the understanding of the Word of God in the community by insisting that the formulations not reflect the current danger of "Christomonism" with its concomitant danger of individualizing the Gospel. The afternoon of the first day Bryant presented a paper entitled "The Word of God and the Scriptures." The Word of God as revelation was seen there as including God's initial action and human response in obedience. Thereby the Word is seen as dynamic, as becoming, rather than a static symbol.

Notes from that discussion point to a desire to see the relation of the person to the Word as a continuing involvement in community, with that involvement always viewed in relation to the world. The Church's responsibility, as the interpreting community, was for that world.

Though the discussion of the nature of theological education at United Theological Seminary would continue and take a variety of turns the faculty was able to reach a sufficient consensus to accept the Mission House document and publish it in its first catalogue.

A related matter that took considerable time at that first faculty meeting was the place of the Biblical languages, Hebrew and Greek, in the curriculum. The tradition of Mission House had been to require both of the biblical languages for graduation with the B.D. degree. All the courses in exegetical theology presupposed this competency. It was not a denominational requirement but the studied response of the faculty in its understanding of theological education. On the other hand Yankton had not required the languages for the B.Th. There was therefore a spirited discussion of the matter and the faculty in the Biblical area were asked to prepare a recommendation. They were not able to reach an agreement. Hammer and Merrill held out for the importance of the requirement. McAllaster, though also agreeing on the importance of the languages, felt he had to support the Yankton position that the languages were not necessary. In the end the faculty agreed that in principle the requirement was valid, though its validity would need to be tested in the working out of the curriculum. However, "due to historical circumstances" the curriculum would have to provide for a B.D. program without the languages. Here was an issue that would again arise to confront the faculty in its discussions.

Perhaps the most significant outcome of these initial discussions was the decision that Theology (the Word of God) would be the integrating principle of the new curriculum. As a theological seminary the offering of the curriculum was not just a series of courses to be completed but a coherent whole discernible in its orientation and focus. That focus and orientation should lie beyond any one discipline or area of study. The perception was that one did not study theology and then apply it practically but that the ministry of the Church in the world was itself a theological task. Nevertheless the structure of the curriculum continued the traditional quadrivium of Biblical Theology, Historical Theology, Systematic Theology and Practical Theology, and the movement of studies was seen to emerge from the foundation of Biblical Theology. The curriculum would therefore include basic courses in the respective areas that would provide the ground from which theological competence would develop. Comprehensive examinations at the end of the second year would gauge the degree of theological competency that the student had attained. Electives would be offered in two or more fields and integrate theological understanding in terms of the functions of the ministry of the Word. Specialized electives in the various fields would also be offered. A thesis would be the final integrating experience of each student.

Having set the basic principles and guiding structures for the curriculum two committees were formed to begin implementation. The Committee on Educational Program, consisting of the faculty from Mission House, were to flesh out the divisions of theological study and the specific courses, including the integration of a program of Field Work. The Committee on Educational Requirements, consisting of the faculty from Yankton, were to spell out the degree programs, admissions and graduation requirements and related areas. With those tasks set the first faculty meeting of United Theological Seminary concluded. There was a great sense of accomplishment as well as awareness that much work lay ahead.

The second meeting of the UTS faculty was to take place in Webster Groves, MO at the time of the Tri-Faculty Conference held at Eden

Theological Seminary.[8] There were four sessions of that faculty meeting that stretched over four days, August 28-31, 1961. The major task was to receive the reports from the various committees so that an initial catalog could be published to present the program of studies at UTS. As usual there was attention not only to principles but also to the precision of language and editorial aspects of the documents. One report that was not easily accepted was that of the Committee on Grading. The matter was tabled and not resolved at that meeting. The issue of the biblical languages was raised again, though this time by the biblical faculty. They stated that they would not run a parallel sequence of interpretation courses for those who did not take the biblical languages as they did not want to create a two-tiered student body. The attempt would be made to incorporate both groups of students into a single set of courses.

A significant action of the meeting was the decision to call the published program of studies the *Announcements* rather than the more typical designation of catalog. This decision reflected the perspective of the Dean and the faculty that they were presenting an integrated view of theological education in the light of which prospective students were invited to participate in this program of studies. The seminary was not offering a catalog of courses from which the students could choose according to their predilections. The concern for the integration of theological studies was there from the beginning and marked the character of the program at United.

Another issue that began to emerge at this meeting was the composition of the faculty at United. Eisenach of Yankton was not able to attend due to his health. Since he was approaching retirement the viability of his participation in the new faculty was a question that would take some time to resolve. Strobel, who was appointed by Yankton but was still in graduate school, also was unable to attend due to his schedule. Sprenger, of Yankton, announced that he would be taking a leave of absence to study in the area of Historical Theology. He would not be available for faculty service at the

---

[8]Minutes of the United Theological Seminary Faculty Meeting, Webster Groves, MO, August 28-31, 1961.

beginning of the opening term. In view of these various factors, and the nature of the curriculum that had been developed, the faculty recommended to the Board of Trustees that, "there be a beginning of investigation to find a man in Systematic Theology with a special competence in ethics." The vision of the educational program was not to be limited by the resources of the presently available faculty.

The third and final meeting of the faculty before the opening of the school was held in the YMCA in Minneapolis on Dec. 2, 1961.[9] Present for this meeting were Huenemann, Gunnemann, Bryant, Hammer, Hilgeman, Jaberg, Kley, McAllaster, Merrill and Sprenger. It would be the last time that Sprenger met with the UTS faculty. Bozarth had already decided to stay at Yankton as part of the new department of religion. And Eisenach had written to Huenemann that he would not be able to accept the appointment to the faculty of United due to his illness. That left McAllaster in the very difficult position of being the only person who had continuity with the program at Yankton.

There were three major items on the agenda for that meeting. Probably the most important for the on-going history of the school was the appointment of a new person in the field of Theology and Ethics. Two candidates were interviewed and James B. Nelson was elected. He was pastor of the Congregational Church in Vermillion, South Dakota, who had done his doctoral work at Yale University under H. Richard Niebuhr and James Gustafson in ethics. The faculty present voted unanimously to recommend the call of James Nelson to the new chair of Ethics in the field of Systematic Theology. He was asked to respond to the call by December 15, 1961, so that he could be included in the new Announcements. However he felt that his work at the church in Vermillion had just begun and that in all fairness he should not accept the call to the faculty until the Fall of 1963. Both the Board and the Faculty considered him such an outstanding candidate that the request was honored.

At this meeting it was also voted that the Faculty call the attention of the Board Committee on Faculty to the necessity of another person in the

[9]Minutes of United Theological Seminary Faculty Meeting, Minneapolis, MN, Dec. 2, 1961.

field of Historical Theology. The nature of the curriculum and the awareness that Hilgeman would be retiring from the faculty in 1965 were the reasons for this request. It further reflected the hope of the Mission House faculty that the services of Milos Strupl might be retained.

The third major issue facing the faculty was the question of whether it should offer a M.A. in Christian Education. The matter was discussed at some length but the decision was made not to announce such a program at that time. Christian education was undergoing serious reconsideration and it was not certain that United could propose a program that was in keeping with the theological program that had been established. The nature and necessity of such a program were not clear to the faculty.

With this last meeting the character of the new faculty and program at United was set - not in stone nor as an unchangeable reality but as an experiment in theological education that would be expressive of the ecumenical commitment. Both faculty and curriculum would change as the circumstances called for new responses in new contexts. But the program had been launched and the commitment and enthusiasm of the faculty were high.

CHAPTER 6

THE BATTLE OF SEMINARY HILL

The building of the new campus would prove to be a more complicated and convoluted process than was originally anticipated. The very location of the seminary had been a matter of debate, at times acrimonious. The Obenhaus study had looked at the Twin Cities, Seattle and Denver as possible locations. Depending on the data that was emphasized one could argue for any of those sites. It appears to have been the Mission House Board that pushed most strongly for the Twin Cities, seeing the need for a strong metropolitan area located in the midst of a fairly numerous constituency. Yankton would have preferred not to move at all so that it could retain its rural atmosphere and values. In the Board for Home Missions of the Congregational Christian Churches the arguments tended to focus on Seattle as a field of endeavor that would open up new possibilities.

Other sites also called for consideration. A letter from Detroit, Michigan, sought attention as a possibility. And a campus for sale in Duluth, Minnesota, the old campus of University of Minnesota - Duluth, was suggested as a northern locale for the new school.[1] It was the Committee of Four that recommended the decision to locate in the Twin Cities and that was supported by the respective bodies that were represented by that committee.

---

[1]Minutes of the Board of Trustees, Sept. 6, 1960.

One of the major tasks that faced Huenemann in his new job as President was the identification and securing of a site within the Twin Cities area. Much of his time seems to have been devoted to this task, as reflected in his correspondence with Dean Gunnemann. Many possibilities were pursued. It had been hoped by some of the staff of the Board for Homeland Ministries that the seminary would be located in proximity to the University of Minnesota that is the major educational resource of the area. At that time the University was in the process of a campus expansion on the West Bank of the Mississippi River. It was a depressed area in need of urban redevelopment and Huenemann explored the site possibilities with city and university planners. However a site on the West Bank adjacent to the new development of the University of Minnesota had to be abandoned. Not only would the cost be prohibitive, over a million dollars for a minimal plot of land, but also the plans for redevelopment were far from complete and would not be in place in time for the school to open in the Fall of 1962.[2] Another option that was pursued was the development of the campus in conjunction with the relocation of Bethel College and Theological Seminary. Discussions between Huenemann and President Lundquist of Bethel led to the conclusion that their move would take some time beyond the schedule to which United was committed.[3] Sites in Golden Valley, to the west, and Bloomington, to the south were also investigated but they did not meet the criteria which had been set for the new campus.

Helping Huenemann in site selection was an advisory committee of three laymen, all very knowledgeable realtors in the Twin Cities and members of churches in the E&R and CC traditions. They were Rohland Thommsen, Robert Reid and Richard Thomson. All gave generously of their time in the pursuit of the location for the seminary.

---

[2]Letter from RHH to LHG.

[3]Letter from RHH to LHG, Sept. 30. 1960.

19. Constituting Board of Trustees, 1960

20. Groundbreaking Ceremony, October 1961.
Left to right: Allan R. McAllaster, Dean of Yankton School of Theology; Ralph Hoffman, Chair of the Board of Trustees; Samuel Schmeichen, Chair of Building Committee; Ruben H. Huenemann

21. Construction of the Main Building, 1962

At the Executive Committee of the Board of Trustees on January 2, 1961, they recommended the purchase of an approximately 63 acre site in New Brighton on the northern edge of the Twin Cities. Shaped like a large "L" the northern part was covered with oak trees and the southern part, which had the highest elevation, was bare.

At the time New Brighton was developing from an independent small town into a burgeoning suburban area. Real estate developments were taking over former farm land. In the area of the seminary property were three barns, only one of which was still part of a farm operation and that for pigs. In the early years the pigs were known to get loose and come visiting on the campus. The area was still accessible to wild-life, and deer, fox and pheasant were seen crossing the campus.

The property was owned by a Dr. Widen who was willing to sell the land to the school for $190,000 with a down payment and a three year contract for deed. It met the criterion of accessibility, located on the major belt highway that was then designated State Highway 100, roughly equidistant from the two cities and fifteen minutes from the University of Minnesota. It was on the western edge of Ramsey County in the midst of a residential area where sewer, water and gas lines were available. To the south was the Minneapolis City reservoir that meant that area would not be developed. To all concerned it appeared to be an ideal site. Following the luncheon at which Dr. Charles Taylor spoke on January 25, 1961, the faculty members visited the site and were very pleased. As Dean Gunnemann was to say to Huenemann, "Our response to the new site was especially enthusiastic. All of the faculty were like young boys after they looked over the property. They are still excited about it. We do hope that the purchase contract will go through and there will be no delays in the acquisition."

Those hopes were soon to be dashed. The seminary had to apply to the Village Council for a special use permit because the property had been zoned for residential use. The Planning Commission of New Brighton had no objection to the special use permit. However the residents of the Lake Forest development immediately east of the seminary and living along Forest Dale Road entered into the fray and objected to any change in projected use.

Their primary argument was that the use for religious purposes would take valuable land off the tax rolls. Behind this official stance were other mixed and varied motives. Some thought that the presence of a large group of young men would be a hazard to their properties and their daughters! Others wished to have the property retained as open ground for their own use. Some felt they had been promised by the original developer that the land would become part of the Lake Forest development and would bring in more single residence housing. Huenemann noted to Gunnemann that most of the vocal opposition were Roman Catholics who wanted to see the land developed residentially so that there would be more support for the local parochial school. On the other hand the local Catholic priest, Father Paul Koscielski, supported the Seminary. He said, "We have our schools and they have the right to build theirs."

So it was that the request sparked a long and protracted series of negotiations, marked by a series of council meetings, vote reversals, neighborhood meetings, public hearings, petitions and letters. By March 20 Huenemann was becoming quite concerned about the process and said, "I find that the cultural and sociological climate is such that the board of the seminary should give serious consideration to the possibility of locating the seminary elsewhere. We owe an obligation to faculty families and generations of students to provide a setting in which they can do their work without blind, nonsensical harassment."

After a public hearing on April 25 the council postponed action until the following week. A further postponement meant the issue would not be decided until May 9. At that meeting two petitions were submitted, one bearing 355 signatures in favor of the seminary and the second with 239 signatures in opposition. It appeared that the issue was settled when the vote of the council was 3-2 against the seminary. The majority felt they were supporting their political constituency among the Lake Forest residents, though they did not actively oppose the seminary themselves. This action led to a letter from the New Brighton businessmen urging reconsideration of the action, as well as a letter from Fred Fisher, attorney for the seminary, pointing out that the basis of the action had no standing in law. The removing of land from the tax rolls was not a legal basis for denying the permit according to Minnesota law. So on the 16th of May the council voted to reconsider its action. A special meeting May 23 led to a further delay. Though the council chambers were packed, including many trustees who were present in the area due to the annual trustees meeting, the council refused to act.

The "Battle of Seminary Hill," as it was called by a St. Paul newspaper came to a climax and resolution on June 23, 1961, at a New Brighton Council Meeting when the vote of the council was 3-2 in favor of granting the special use permit, subject to agreement on development plans. There were last minute attempts to impose limitations on the permit. Some felt seminary families should pay tuition for their children in the public schools. Others thought that fees should be paid for fire and police protection. Others wanted a buffer zone between the seminary and the community! And some thought that the seminary should provide a recreational area on its campus for the community. However these various proposals did not claim the support of the council and they passed into history.[4]

Throughout this conflict the expert legal counsel of Fred Fisher played an important role. His contributions to the Seminary extended far beyond this initial controversy and helped the school resolve many legal questions. Out of this conflict also came invaluable publicity for, through the headlines in the newspapers, the Seminary became widely known in the Twin Cities. In addition it created a loyalty among those who supported the Seminary through this difficult winter.

While the negotiations with the New Brighton City Council were underway Huenemann interviewed a half dozen of the leading architectural firms in the Twin Cities. Local members of the Board joined in some of the interviews and performance checks on the most promising firms were made. At the same meeting of the Executive Committee at which the site had been approved the committee also met Kenneth Whitehead, Vice-President of Cerny Associates, who was engaged as the architect for the new campus. He expressed his desire to consult with the faculties at Mission House and Yankton to help him comprehend the full program of the seminary. A

[4]A summary of the actions and reactions can be found in Kley, *The First Ten Years*, pp. 29-30.

Planning Committee was appointed to work with the architect. This committee consisted of Samuel Schmiechen, co-pastor at St. Paul's Evangelical and Reformed Church, Alvin Wolff, president of Purity-Ohleen Dairy, and Kent Youngdahl, administrative officer of the Hennepin County Highway Commission.[5] Marian Toren, a laywoman from St. Paul, was later added to this committee.

Whitehead had been the project architect for several large buildings in the Twin Cities including the recently completed terminal building at the Minneapolis-St. Paul International Airport. He visited the respective faculty groups and listened attentively to the concerns of those who would be using the buildings. As an advocate of the principle that form follows function his suggestions were highly utilitarian and functional. In his proposed master plan were provisions for two major buildings consisting of a classroom building and the library, two apartment buildings, for married and unmarried students, a student commons, and ten faculty residences. At a later stage he suggested that the chapel, an administration building, and a retreat center be built. The initial project, comprising the classroom and main buildings and the faculty homes, carried an estimated cost of $1,720,000, including site work, construction and equipment and furniture. This initial stage was intended to serve a student body of approximately 150 students.

The master plan for the campus was accepted by the Board of Trustees at its meeting on May 22-23, 1961 and authorization was given to borrow up to $750,000 for the initial construction. A model of the master plan was made by Cerny and Associates and was displayed at the General Synod Meeting of the United Church of Christ in Philadelphia that July, where it attracted much attention. It offered tangible expression of the hopes and dreams for an ecumenical seminary.

The faculty at Mission House had attempted to state in its first response to the architect its understanding of the design of the buildings. "The spirit to be expressed symbolically in the design and layout of the buildings should include reference to the following: the unity of the community of faith and learning as it is expressed through its commo

[5] Letter from RHH to Mrs. Lawrence Schoen, Nov. 7, 1960.

worship, study, discussion, fellowship and service; the ecumenical nature of theology reflected in the universal tradition and the universal outlook of the Church; the seminary as the intellectual center of the Church's life as it is expressed in the service which the seminary renders to the Church, and to the world in behalf of the Church, in the name of Christ, confronting human wisdom and endeavor with God's wisdom and will; and the timeliness and timelessness of the Gospel."[6]

This vision of the seminary was to raise some critical questions when in October the initial exterior sketches of the buildings were presented by the architect. It was the sketch of the library building that raised objections from the faculty at Mission House. As the dominant building on the campus, two stories high and 100 feet on each side, it was located on the highest point of the campus. The initial concept had large bays on the first floor and a series of narrow windows on each side on the upper floor, much like the public library in Minneapolis. The faculty's objection to the design was that it appeared to them to produce a rather squat building, looking more like a fortress defending itself from the world. This seemed to be a direct contradiction of the faculty's view that the seminary should be open to the world and inviting rather than in a defensive posture. So they suggested that the bays of the first floor be extended to the second. This would open up the building as well as provide for vertical lines that would be symbolic of the seminary's dependence upon God in its upward sweep.[7]

The initial reaction of the planning committee and Huenemann was to question the suggestion of the faculty. They felt that the original design said that this was a library, and expressed openness with strength.[8] The faculty and Gunnemann were not satisfied with this response and pressed the issue. Huenemann was willing to have the exchange of ideas, though he said he could not record any positive impression of the faculty's suggestion. He

---

[6]"Suggestions for the Architect for the United Theological Seminary," attached to a letter from LHG to RHH, January 11, 1961.

[7]Memo from Mission House Faculty to Kenneth Whitehead, October 16,1961. Sent by LHG to RHH for forwarding to the architect.

[8]Letter of RHH to LHG, October 19, 1961.

was concerned that the faculty and planning committee not become deadlocked over this issue and that a satisfactory compromise be reached.[9] By the 10th of November the staff at Cerny's had come up with an alternative proposal that incorporated many of the suggestions of the faculty. As Huenemann would say, "I believe it should meet their unqualified approval. It is certainly more dramatic; I'm not sure that it is either more practical or better architecture."[10] These last words were to prove prophetic for the building that was built when "electricity was penny cheap" would turn out to be costly when fuel bills would climb in the nineteen-seventies and eighties!

Before construction began the scale of the first phase of the plan was reduced by the elimination of the proposed buildings for a student commons, and student housing. Even so the resources of the new school were stretched to the limit. Further fund-raising was inhibited by two campaigns that had been initiated earlier. The United Seminary Appeal of the Evangelical and Reformed Church and the Christian Higher Education Fund of the Congregational Christian Churches were not scheduled to be concluded until the end of 1961. So the appeal for capital funds could not be launched as a general appeal to all the area churches, but needed to be addressed specifically to the two respective constituencies. The alumni of Mission House and the churches they served were asked to raise the moneys to underwrite the faculty homes. These homes were needed for several reasons. As Huenemann was to say, the merged faculty needed to work together in closest harmony, with opportunities for frequent consultation. The houses were also an economic necessity for the school because there could be no funds in the operating budget for faculty housing allowances.[11] It was easier to raise funds for the construction of homes because of the parsonage tradition and the housing pattern at Mission House. The total faculty housing fund was more than $300,000 by the time the books were closed. The alumni of Yankton and the churches of the General Conference were

---

[9]Letter from RHH to LHG, November 6, 1961.

[10]Letter from RHH to LHG, November 10, 1961.

[11]Memo from RHH to Board of Trustees, September 22, 1961.

asked to raise $100,000, to underwrite the building of the classrooms, and they met that commitment.

Ground was broken for the new seminary in New Brighton on October 27, 1961, with Ralph Hoffmann, Conference Minister of the South Dakota Conference and the new chair of the Board of Trustees, turning the first shovel of earth. Civic leaders in attendance included the Governor of Minnesota, Elmer L. Anderson, Congressman Joseph Karth, Mayor Arthur Naftalin of Minneapolis and Mayor Bernard Skrebes of New Brighton. Mayor George Vavoulis of St. Paul sent greetings. Following the service a dinner program was held at the New Brighton village hall, the scene of the earlier debates over the granting of the permit to use the property. At the dinner program the Right Rev. Philip McNairy, then Suffragan Bishop of the Protestant Episcopal Diocese of Minnesota was the principal speaker. This seminary was going to attend to the other denominations and to the attendant society.[12]

Site preparation would take the rest of the construction season in the Fall. It was Spring when the actual construction of the buildings began under the aegis of the Wichter Construction Company. Despite an extremely rainy Spring the building program had advanced sufficiently for the laying of the cornerstone on May 20, 1962. Faculty and Board members expressed the hope that the school would be ready for the opening of its doors in the Fall. That morning the faculties from Mission House and Yankton had preached in a number of churches in the Twin Cities area and the choir of Mission House Seminary had sung in several churches. In the afternoon the crowd assembled on the new site surrounded by mud and without any direct surfaced roads. Only the floor of the classroom building had been poured and the supporting pillars for the walls were in place. The library and administration building was visible as a hole in the ground with only the beginnings of the basement walls. To the east the faculty homes were under construction but facing the problem that the weight of the water in the clay was collapsing several of the foundation walls!

---

[12]Kley, *The First Ten Years*, p. 32.

Nonetheless it was a day of celebration. The visions and dreams of faculty, seminary leaders, board members, church leaders and others were coming to fruition. The cornerstone was laid in the entry to the classroom building and contained items selected by Roland Kley, Librarian of the Seminary. Among the memorabilia were not only historic documents related to the two previous schools but also documents recording the new developments. A copy of the certificate of licensure and ordination of the Rev. Christian Schoepfle, who was the first student enrolled at Mission House in 1862 was included and marked not only the centennial of that tradition but the purpose of United to prepare men and women for the Christian ministry.

The Rev. Carl Hansen, minister of the Minnesota Conference of the United Church of Christ, was the speaker for the day. In his address he noted "Our seminaries are the training centers where our men (sic) must learn to communicate with effectiveness and clarity; where they shall learn how to love even when they are despised for Christ's sake, and where they can learn the fine art of being both in the world and yet not of it. To United Theological Seminary of the Twin Cities we of the church look for that preparation of those called by God into his special service such as shall be the source of the revitalizing and renewing of the Church of Jesus Christ in our day."[13]

It is to that vision and commitment as it was worked out in the days that followed that we shall attend in the following chapters. The foundations had been laid. Now it would be seen if the hopes and dreams could be fulfilled.

---

[13]Kley, *The First Ten Years*, pp. 33-37.

PART THREE

A NEW VISION OF THEOLOGICAL EDUCATION

CHAPTER 7

MYTHS OF THE PIONEER DAYS

It was the turbulent 60's when the United Theological Seminary of the Twin Cities opened its doors for classes on September 27, 1962. On that day an army of sheriffs and police blocked the entrance of James Meredith into the University of Mississippi. As a result of the decision of Brown v. the Board of Education public education in the South was opened up to Negroes. However the society that had formed the barriers of segregation was determined not to surrender easily or peacefully. On that day Congress had authorized the use of force, if necessary, to prevent Cuba from becoming a threat to the security of the Western Hemisphere. Thus both the issues of race and peace were engaged as the school began the struggle to find its identity and mission in the midst of those disruptive times. Yet in the excitement and exhilaration of building a new school the participants tended at first to see those issues as remote, though they could not be ignored.

The school year began, as it has for the past thirty years, with a student-faculty retreat. It was held on September 24-25 at Lyman Lodge, the YWCA camp in Excelsior, MN. The retreat provided an occasion for the orientation of the students to the new school and its vision of ecumenical theological education for ministry. As Gunnemann was to write to the Retreat Committee: "It will be important to create something of the 'spirit' of the Seminary at this Retreat and to interpret the purposes and character of the school."[1] The theme chosen for the Retreat was "The Witnessing and Learning Community," and that theme was developed in terms of both the church and the seminary. On the night of the 25th the Huenemanns held a reception at their home, 2781 Forest Dale Road, New Brighton, for "all students and their wives or fiances."

The following day the students registered for classes. That evening the first opening Communion Service was held with Professors Jaberg and Strobel assisting President Huenemann in the service of word and sacrament. The communion service was the first held in the new chapel, the all purpose room at the west end of the classroom building. For that first communion a table needed to be brought into the room and a lectern from one of the classrooms. The seating was individual white plastic stacking chairs. It could not have been plainer in an early New England church or Quaker meeting house. Yet the fervor of the assembled people was evident in the strong singing of the hymns and the thanksgiving to God for having the opportunity to participate in this great experiment.

When the Registrar, Allan R. McAllaster, gave his report on enrollment that first term the student body consisted of forty-six students, 43 of them B.D. candidates and three of them seeking certificates of graduation. There were no auditors or part-time students. They represented 14 colleges, with 22 from Lakeland College and 8 from Yankton College. They came from 15 states, with 12 from Minnesota and 12 from Wisconsin.[2] In that student body there was only one woman, though she would transfer to another school to get a master's degree in religious education. A second woman, Harriet Ann Johnson, would enroll in the second term, January 1963, and take a course of studies prescribed by the Minneapolis Presbytery of the United Presbyterian Church, USA. On February 2, 1964, Johnson was the first woman ordained to the ministry by the Minneapolis Presbytery. The service was held at Shiloh Bethany Church near the campus. She had been a

---

[1]Memo from LHG to Arthur Merrill and Eugene Jaberg, July 13, 1962.

[2]Registrar's Report, October 12, 1962.

22. Student Body and Faculty, October 1963

23. Student Apartments, 1965

24. Graduation on the Mall, 1969

missionary in Japan for ten years and would return there to continue her ministry. That may have been the reason why the presbytery was willing to ordain her.

Myths are the stories by which a community defines itself and finds the meanings of its life. As later faculty would claim, a number of myths were generated in the early days that continued to inform the way in which life was lived in the emerging seminary. Among those myths were the stories of early life on the campus.

When classes opened in September of 1962 the construction of the campus was still in progress. Only the classroom wing could be used for the functions of the school. In it all the daily activities of the seminary were carried out. Of the six classrooms only four were used for classes. The last two rooms on the east end housed the temporary library. Faculty and students assisted in unloading and placing the books. Planks across the sand and mud led from the truck to the entrance. In classroom E stacks of temporary shelving for the most necessary books were set up. The rest of the 11,000 volumes remained in boxes stacked in order and labeled according to their contents. Classroom F became the workroom, office and reading room of the library. Here reserve books were available and the librarian and his staff of one assistant attempted to carry on the functions of the library including the acquisition and processing of books.

Between the classrooms were two very small rooms converted into offices for the Dean and Registrar. They shared the only secretary, Alice Strobel, who had a desk in the same small room with the Dean. Next to the Registrar's office was the only rest room which had to serve the entire seminary community. In the times between classes the only available space for faculty and students was the hallway where coffee and doughnuts were made available for a morning break. Here one could watch the finishing touches being made on the classroom building as well as the on-going construction on the main library building. That building would become available for faculty, administrative offices and the library in April of 1963

Access to the Seminary was difficult at best for the main access road of Fifth Street was not completed nor paved. From the east one entered the campus through the roads that came through the faculty housing, and even those roads were not paved until November of that first Fall. Some portions of Driftwood Road, which fronted the seminary on the east, required surfacing three times because of the frequent heavy rains. From the West one approached through Columbia Heights, past the public high school, and entered the campus from East Upland Crest. As Gunnemann would say in his announcements for the opening of the school year, "Since construction will continue awhile after the opening of school, students will find that some things will not be in order. Patience and forbearance are not only laudable virtues, but will be most useful in this situation!"[3]

The students surely needed patience and forbearance. Single students were housed in apartments leased by the Seminary in the community. Married students needed to find housing in the area and were resourceful in the variety of types of housing they located, including motel apartments. The Seminary provided suggestions but the students had to make arrangements for themselves. Student wives had to find employment in the area without having lived in the community more than a few days or weeks. For those seeking employment as teachers Superintendent Ralph Reeder of the Mounds View School District was most helpful. He was a member of the United Church of Christ in New Brighton. The hardships and difficulties the students faced forged a community of tightly knit persons who shared many of the same experiences.

Food service at the seminary could not be provided until the library basement was completed. Lunch time meant either bringing one's own brown bag or leaving campus for a meal. When space was available Alvin R. Wolff provided kitchen equipment and booths for the dining area to make food service possible.

Moving the faculty families into the homes still under construction required many improvisations and adjustments. The Huenemanns had moved to the edge of the campus where the Seminary had bought an existing house adjoining the property of the school. Here the President not only lived but also worked, since the basement family area was converted into an office for him and a secretary. For many months the double garage served as a

[3]*Announcements for the Opening of the Autumn Quarter, 1962-63*, August 14, 1962.

storage shed for furnishings and books belonging to various faculty members. The faculty homes under construction were expected to be occupied in August. The persistent rains of the Spring and Summer had delayed completion of the homes. When Gunnemann visited the campus in July he reported that the houses in the south circle were just receiving their roofing. To Merrill he wrote, "As far as weather here is concerned, you are the lucky man; your house is dry...The Gunnemann house is just a hole filled with water; I've always talked about living in a tent, but I think Noah's ark would be more appropriate!"[4]

As it turned out Merrill and Hilgeman were the first to move into the faculty homes in September. Grading was still progressing in the area and the homes were not yet finished. Initially there was no heat or water in the houses, only electricity. The first Saturday night the Merrills, with two small children, and the Hilgemans had to walk down Driftwood Road to the Huenemann home to get their showers! As the weeks progressed the other homes reached the point where their residents could settle in. In the meantime most of the faculty lived in apartments in adjoining communities. Some had to bring their children to the campus each morning to meet the public school bus, and pick them up at the end of the day. As each family moved in the others helped in moving their household goods into the respective residences.

Because of the incomplete state of the faculty homes the McAllaster family did not move from Yankton to the campus until October. The Gunnemann family moved in with the Merrills, using the basement for their family area and a back corner for their son Jon, who was an entering student at United. Meals were taken in common. The Gunnemanns moved into their new home the first of November, the day after Katherine was born to the Merrills. Emma and Ron Barz, who were on the staff of the Seminary, lived initially in the basement of the home of Bob and Alice Strobel until a house for them was finished. Ron was the maintenance man and Emma would later manage the kitchen of the seminary.

---

[4]Letter from LHG to Arthur L. Merrill, July 24, 1962.

While the faculty homes were still under construction for several months a number of amusing and not so amusing incidents occurred. Neighbors would often enter the homes to see how construction was progressing, even when the residents were already ensconced. The building committee made many an unannounced visit to check on the work of the construction company. Finally the faculty resisted these visits and asked for notification before the committee marched through the homes. And as is true of any new construction there were defects in what was done and changes in the midst of the progress being made. The homes proved to be very comfortable and efficient living spaces. The building committee and architect were concerned that they be similar to eliminate rivalry. However they were sufficiently distinct from each other, and at the same time linked to the overall campus design. No home could look directly into another nearby, and privacy was preserved in the midst of community.

Paving of the campus roads and sodding of the lawns were not accomplished until November. In the meantime there was mud everywhere, around and in the classroom buildings and the faculty homes. Planks provided temporary walkways. When the Gunnemanns moved into the Merrill home the van driver attempting to get close to the house to deliver the household goods sank the van into the mud. Later it was pulled out by one of the Caterpillar tractors of the construction company. There is also the apocryphal story that one afternoon on returning home from the classrooms Merrill had his rubbers pulled off by the mud of the roadway. There he remained stranded until rescued by Bryant who went for a pair of galoshes which permitted the resumption of the journey home, the rubbers forever lost in the mud.

Out of these events came the values which informed the school in its early days. Community was forged in the midst of difficult circumstances. Cooperation and the willingness to pitch in to accomplish the task at hand was the mark of many situations. The desire to forge a new school overrode the tendencies to look out for oneself or complain about the hardships.

25. James B. Nelson, Christian Ethics, 1963-

26. Thomas C. Campbell, Church and Community, 1963-65, 1974-79

27. Donald R. White, Historical Theology, 1965-

28. Emile J. Naef, Christian Faith and Personality, 1966

29. Chris M. Meadows, Christian Faith and Personality, 1967-70

30. H. Wilson Yates, Church and Community, 1967-

CHAPTER 8

A COLLEGIAL FACULTY

The sharing of common hardships in the early days no doubt helped to draw the faculty together. The forging of the faculty into a community of teachers and scholars, however, was an ongoing process. One factor during the first year was the almost weekly faculty meetings to discuss the programs and policies of the school. That first academic year recorded forty-four faculty meetings, the first one held at the President's home. The President presided at the faculty meetings and each meeting was opened with prayer. At the initial meeting the Student Handbook, outlining academic policies, was discussed and the issues of grading received paramount attention. At these meetings there was established a basic norm of faculty process. Decisions were to be reached by consensus rather than by majority vote, though votes were taken once the agreement had been achieved. This style of decision making was encouraged by Gunnemann who was seeking to weld the faculty into a common force for the benefit of the school. At the same time it tended to sublimate conflicts that were real and could have strained the body politic.

Alongside this consensus model of decision making was the involvement of the faculty in most of the decisions that affected the institution. The faculty was not only concerned with the academic program but also with those other institutional matters that impinged upon the academic program. Therefore one finds in the minutes of the faculty many issues that are not properly the concern of the faculty, such as the food service. The story is told of an early faculty meeting at which the question was raised as to the location of the pencil sharpener. It was discussed that the pencil sharpener had been located at one place at Mission House and at another place at Yankton. For United the pencil sharpener had therefore to be in a new and neutral place! This was not an efficient use of faculty time and effort but it surely involved them at all levels of seminary life. It bound them to the purposes and functions of the institution as much as to their specific professions.

This egalitarian view of the faculty was manifested also in the policies and procedures of the faculty. However it was not until the end of the first academic year that a committee on Faculty Procedures was formed[1] and specific procedures were developed.[2] For a faculty of only nine members a rather elaborate structure was proposed. Fourteen committees were named under three major rubrics: functional committees, advisory committees and policy committees, that ranged from concern for the handbook for students to the self-study of the seminary. This organization proved to be too complex and lasted for only two years. By the end of the school year 1964- 65 a reorganization of the committees attempted to reduce the number of meetings. Committee membership was not decided on the basis of rank or tenure but on the interests of the faculty members and their skills, and were appointed by the President and Dean.

One policy that particularly marked the self-understanding of the faculty was the development of the Faculty Field Fund. In part due to "horror stories" from other faculties there was the concern that the faculty not be so involved off campus that the work of the school suffer. A self-limitation of no more than four engagements per month were to be taken by an individual faculty member. And more significantly the honoraria from those engagements were to be placed into a common treasury, the Faculty Field Fund. It was felt that this would help to enforce the policy of off campus engagements as they would not accrue to anyone's personal benefit. This fund was in existence for over a decade and was used by the faculty to

---

[1]Faculty Meeting Minutes, June 4, 1963.

[2]Faculty Meeting Minutes, July 23, 1963.

finance a range of concerns. In the early years it contributed to the development of the grounds by paying for plantings not within the budget. It also helped faculty attend special meetings abroad as well as in this country, and paid for racial justice programs and student participation in community events.

Another manifestation of the egalitarian nature of the faculty is that rank and seniority were never a major factor in committee appointments nor in academic processions. In the early years the President was the moderator of the Faculty and presided at meetings. When he was not available the Dean acted in his place. As the sixties and their emphasis on participatory government grew in force the faculty finally petitioned the President to have the faculty elect its own moderator. When the petition to the President was presented it was not favorably received for it appeared as a challenge to his leadership and his participation in faculty decisions. But he soon recovered the crumpled petition and agreed to it in principle if not whole heartedly for it removed him from a significant involvement with the faculty. When the moderator was elected by the faculty it was not an office that symbolized power. The effective principle of choice became the fact that the moderator was chosen from those who had just returned from sabbatical leave, perhaps as a penalty for having been relieved of the on-going work of the seminary. And no moderator served more than one year at a time. In later years the moderator would also have the dubious distinction of being the marshal for all academic processions. In those processions the order of march was determined by alphabetic listing rather than seniority or rank, a way of life that continues until this day.

However the issues of rank and title continued to be a concern for the school. When the faculty was formed all those who had received a doctoral degree were automatically designated professor in their field of expertise. Those who had not yet received their doctorates were either assistant or associate professors, partly factored by their length of service. That first faculty all received the same rate of pay, $7000.00 per year plus fringe benefits. Only the President and Dean received more for their administrative responsibilities, and that additional pay was only a token of their value to the school. As the various members of the faculty completed their doctoral work[3] it created a faculty where virtually all members were or would soon become full professors. So a committee of Paul Hammer and Roland Kley was formed on April 20, 1965, to examine the question of ranking. Their report proposed that Bryant, Gunnemann, Hammer and McAllaster be full professors, Kley, Merrill and Nelson associate professors, and Jaberg, Strobel and White assistant professors. This meant that several of the faculty were demoted in rank. Because rank was not tied to salary there were no cuts in pay and all were still receiving the same salary. At the same time when these rankings and titles were reported to the Board of Trustees more definitive policies on tenure and promotion were also proposed and adopted by the Board.[4]

On December 9, 1962 the President and the first faculty members were installed. At a service of worship at St. Paul's United Church of Christ in St. Paul the Rev. Dr. Ralph Hoffman, chair of the Board of Trustees presided at the ceremony and inaugurated the first president and nine faculty members. Dr. James I. McCord, President of Princeton Theological Seminary, delivered the inaugural address. McCord said the seminary is a "microcosm of the church" and must be free not from the church but for the church so that the church may be free. "It should be a community which hears the word of God and which is more disciplined by the word of God than any other Christian community."[5]

As is true of many faculties, however, the teaching staff of United did not remain stable for very long. Already James B. Nelson had been called to the faculty and began his long tenure in the Fall of 1963. During the first academic year Dr. Shirley Green of the Department of Town and Country Church of the UCC suggested a joint appointment by the national church and the seminary. Such a person could help the churches in the Great Plains as well as bring an emphasis on the rural church to the Seminary and so continue the concerns that had been expressed by Yankton. These negotiations resulted in the appointment of Thomas C. Campbell as associate

---

[3]Merrill received his doctorate in 1962, Strobel in 1965, Jaberg in 1967.

[4]Minutes of the Board of Trustees, June 14-15, 1965.

[5]Kley, *The First Ten Years*, p. 40.

professor of church and community. He began his initial brief but significant association with United in the Fall of 1963.[6] With these two appointments the balancing of the faculty with persons from the Congregational Christian side of the UCC was also accomplished.

With the impending retirement of Theophilus Hilgeman in 1965 as well as the need to enhance the offerings in the field of Historical Theology a search for a person in that field was also inaugurated in the first academic year. Three candidates were interviewed and on February 12, 1963 Gerhard Spiegler, a doctoral candidate at the University of Chicago, was recommended to the Board of Trustees for appointment. He asked that his appointment be delayed until the Fall of 1964 while he finished his dissertation. However in the Spring of 1964 Spiegler expressed his regrets and indicated that due to personal factors he had taken a position at Haverford College in Pennsylvania.

Consequently the search for a person in Historical Theology had to be reopened. During the school year 1964-65 three more candidates were interviewed and recommended to the Board of Trustees. Donald R. White accepted the invitation and was appointed to the position, beginning his teaching at United in the Fall of 1965 as the replacement for Hilgeman.[7] This search indicated the problems that a new and not yet established school had in obtaining top ranking candidates for its position. It took a person of vision and courage to associate with a not yet recognized institution. As a consequence those who joined the faculty became committed to its vision of an ecumenical theological school for the church.

On the same day that the Board of Trustees named White to the faculty in Historical Theology it also received the resignation of Thomas

---

[6]Campbell, a native of Minnesota, had received his B.A. from the University of Minnesota, his masters degree from Kent State University in Ohio, his B.D. from Yale Divinity School and was completing his doctoral work at the University of Chicago Divinity School. He had served as pastor of the First Congregational Church in Newton Falls, Ohio, for four years.

[7]White was a native of Youngstown, Ohio, receiving his B.A. degree from Berea College, Kentucky, his B.D. from Chicago Theological Seminary and his M.A. and Ph.D. from the University of Chicago Divinity School. Prior to his arrival at United he had taught as an interim for one year at Carleton College, Northfield, Minnesota. He was a member of the United Presbyterian Church, USA.

Campbell who had accepted a call to Yale Divinity School. This was a serious blow to the school, for Campbell, as we shall see had been influential in the reformulation of the curriculum into a new and dynamic structure. His dual position called for much effort and the task of balancing the demands of both faculty work and denominational responsibility became impossible. For Campbell only leaving seemed to resolve the dilemma. Even at the point his leaving there were those on the faculty who were considering ways in which they could bring him back to a full time position.

A third action on that fateful meeting of the Board of Trustees was the resignation of Ernest Sprenger from the faculty. For three years he had been pursuing graduate work to qualify him for a faculty position but the ill health of his wife led him to abandon that goal. He left graduate work to become pastor of the UCC church in Ritzville, Washington, a position that he would serve until his retirement from the active ministry.[8]

The replacement of Campbell on the faculty was no easy task for he had set a standard for the position in Church and Community that was not easily met. Two candidates were interviewed in the Fall of 1965 and one, Alan B. Anderson, was recommended to the Board of Trustees. However by November Anderson declined the invitation with regrets. This turn of events however opened up the opportunity to invite Prof. Victor Obenhaus, from Chicago Theological Seminary, as Visiting Professor of Church and Community. Obenhaus commuted to the Twin Cities that Spring to teach at United. For the following year Gordon Nelson was appointed as Instructor in Church and Community while the search for a permanent appointment continued. Because his appointment was the first on the faculty as a term appointment the school did not know how to negotiate the situation with grace and dispatch and his departure caused him hard feelings.

With the start of the new curriculum and a long standing commitment by the faculty to have a person in the field of Christianity and Psychology the position was initially filled with an interim appointment, Clyde J. Steckel, campus minister at the University of Minnesota. The Faculty moved quickly to invite Emil J. Naef for an interview on April 12, 1966. This new position

[8]Minutes of the Meeting of the Board of Trustees, June 14-15, 1965.

was an attempt to balance the social concerns with the personal aspects of the faith. In Naef the faculty discerned a person who could bring psychology and theology into a fruitful and significant dialogue. Unanimously they recommended him to the Board of Trustees. That Fall he moved his family to the campus and began his teaching at United. Little did the faculty and administration realize that behind the promising prospects of this newest member of the faculty lay a history of deep depressions. It was with great sadness and sense of loss that the community learned of his death by a self-inflicted gunshot wound beside a lake in Minneapolis on the morning of November 19, 1966. In a memorial tribute President Huenemann said, "Today United Seminary owes a debt of gratitude to a man who sought with all his being to teach devotion to ultimate human meaning, never to hide behind familiar religious phrases, never to be content with pat answers, never to accept false premises, but rather always to search out the hidden realities, to acknowledge an ultimate responsibility, to open the springs of divine insight....What hunger remained unsatisfied, or what burden proved too heavy–this we shall never know. We can only surmise that he would have felt the challenge of all such questions, and sought to measure the quality of his search by the scale of eternal and ultimate meanings."[9]

With Naef's death two vacant positions vacant needed to be filled that were critical to the new understanding of the curriculum. Several candidates were interviewed for the position in Church and Community, including Gordon Nelson who was teaching on a term appointment. In the end a young scholar by the name of H. Wilson Yates who was finishing his doctoral degree at Harvard University was elected by the faculty and recommended to the Board of Trustees.[10] Though several candidates were considered for the position in Christian Faith and Personality only one candidate was invited for an interview, Christopher Meadows, a doctoral candidate at Princeton

---

[9]Kley, *The First Ten Years*, p. 78.

[10]Yates, a native of Missouri, received his B.A. from Southeast Missouri State College and his B.D. from Vanderbilt Divinity School. Yates was an ordained member of the United Methodist Church.

Theological Seminary.[11] With his strong credentials in counseling and theology he was an attractive candidate. During his brief tenure Meadows was instrumental in the formation of the North Central Career Development Center.

In the Sixties there was great turmoil in the ministry and many were questioning if the pastoral ministry was any longer a viable form in the culture. Many pastors were leaving their churches and moving either into special ministries or out of the ministry altogether. The formation of the Career Center offered a neutral space, sponsored by the denominations but not within the formal structures of the church, where ministers could look at their careers and make the necessary decisions on the basis of testing and counseling. The creation of the Center was first suggested by Bishop Philip McNairy of the local Episcopal diocese, and resulted in a growing cooperation between his denomination and the seminary.[12]

Both Yates and Meadows began their teaching at United in the Fall of 1967. Since both were in the process of finishing their doctoral dissertations their lives were full with their teaching responsibilities and their writing. As the deadline for their dissertations approached Marian Hoeft, the secretary to the President, offered her services as typist for the final drafts to be submitted for oral defence. Many were the nights when the midnight oil burned as the deadline neared. But the whole community was able to celebrate the successful conclusion of the marathon task.

When the Yates arrived on campus they lived initially in the home of the Jabergs who were absent on sabbatical leave. During the year a new home had to be built on the campus for them. This was the last faculty home built, and rounded out the number to twelve faculty homes, plus the President's home.

The faculty at last was at full strength. The projected positions had been filled with attractive and competent teachers and scholars. A sabbatical

---

[11]Meadows, also a southern product, took his B.A. at Baylor University, and his B.D. at Southern Baptist Theological Seminary. He had earned a Th.M. at Princeton Theological Seminary. His standing as a minister was as an American Baptist.

[12]Interview with RHH, August 20, 1991.

program, that had been inaugurated in the academic year 1965-66, was in progress and being used to maintain the skills and interests of the faculty.

However a faculty is never in stasis. In the academic year 1967-68 Paul Hammer, professor of New Testament Theology, resigned to take a teaching position at Colgate Rochester Divinity School. This was a blow to the school for Hammer had been a very popular lecturer in the churches of the area and a vibrant interpreter of the school and its program. He had been a dynamic force not only in the establishment of the original curriculum for United but also in the revision of the curriculum in 1965. Hammer had also been a key player in the negotiations to link the theological schools of the area to the University of Minnesota in a graduate theological program.[13] When that linkage failed, due to issues of Church and State, Hammer reportedly became discouraged and began to look elsewhere for a challenge.

With Hammer's departure the search for another teacher in the field of New Testament raised one of the first real controversies within the faculty. Two candidates were brought to the campus for interviews in the Spring of 1968. Both men were strong candidates for the position and each brought their own distinctive contributions to the understanding of the New Testament. One had a focus on the Gospels and the theological dimensions of the text. The other had an emphasis on the Pauline materials and the concern to relate the Scriptures to the ethical issues of the day. When the faculty first met to discuss the two candidates they were unable to reach a consensus and agreed that the matter be held over. The Administrative Committee was asked to investigate whether there were other candidates available.

Compounding the emotions of the discussions was the fact that on April 4, 1968, the day the faculty reconvened, Martin Luther King Jr. was shot and killed in Memphis, TN. The faculty in the biblical field, Merrill and McAllaster, were convinced that a biblical theologian was needed for the

---

[13]Robert Duffett, in his doctoral dissertation, *The History and Development of the Doctor of Ministry Degree at the Minnesota Consortium of Theological Schools: 1957-1985*, p. 299 mistakenly identifies Hammer as Professor of Philosophy. He apparently confuses Paul Hammer and Paul Holmer, professor at Yale Divinity School, who had taught at the University of Minnesota.

position. In the end, by secret ballot, Henry A. Gustafson was selected as the recommendation to the Board of Trustees.[14] In Gustafson United gained a teacher who would become well-beloved by students and faculty alike.

With the expansion of the faculty and the changes over time the faculty came to represent the ecumenical vision that had guided the development of the school. Though the early faculty represented primarily the two traditions of the UCC, the Evangelical and Reformed Church and the Congregational Churches, even that faculty had come from a wider variety of various backgrounds, including the traditions of Presbyterian, American Baptist, and Free Methodist. The new persons added to the faculty were from the Methodist, American Baptist, Presbyterian and Covenant churches. Though the search was always for the best teachers and scholars the goal to have a variety of church traditions was expressed and implemented. The ecumenical mix by the end of the sixties was varied, but primarily represented the so-called mainline denominations.

---

[14]Gustafson, a native of Minnesota, had received his B.A. at North Park College and his B.D. at North Park Seminary. His Ph.D. was from the University of Chicago. He was an ordained minister in the Evangelical Covenant Church where his views of Scripture were often under scrutiny in that conservative context.

CHAPTER 9

THE NEW CURRICULUM

A faculty, as crucial as it is to the life of a school, is not effective unless there is a vehicle to express its vision and direct its efforts. This requires a curriculum that can embody the vision and guide the hoped-for outcomes. When the seminary opened its doors it had a curriculum that was rather traditional. It was divided into the usual four fields of biblical studies, historical studies, theological studies and practical studies. However the so-called practical fields were perceived by the beginning faculty as theological fields and they sought to integrate them through biblical and theological studies into a more holistic vision of both theological education and the mission of the church. From the beginning the faculty recognized that there needed to be a dialogue with the fields of psychology and sociology and projections were made to meet that need. Behind the curriculum was what one might call a modified neo-orthodox position that could embrace the variety of positions within the faculty.

One innovative contribution of the first curriculum was its perception that field education was a significant part of the curricular design and needed to be attended to as seriously as any other discipline. Field education was not seen primarily as a service to the churches nor as a remunerative position for the students but an integral part of the theological curriculum. The danger would always persist, however, that this dimension of the program would be seen as technical and practical training and make the school look like a trade school.

Initially two units of field education were required for graduation. "Although it contributes to the correlation of 'doing' and 'knowing' in student experience, it is designed primarily to aid the student's growth as a person and in his understanding of the ministry and mission of the Church."[1] The first unit was a placement in a church context to observe and understand the various functions of ministry. The emphasis was on observation rather than practice. The second unit was the opportunity to be involved in the practice of ministry, based on the theological training to date, and in a context of sustained ministry. These units of field education were not in the curriculum under Practical Theology nor under Integrative Courses for they were an integral part of the program.

A clinical year could be taken as an internship but was not required. There was to be no payment for the first unit of field work as it was an assignment of the Seminary. There was remuneration for the second unit but all moneys received were placed in a pool and distributed equally to all participants. Student pastorates were discouraged because it was felt that they tended to perpetuate patterns that were unreflective and uninformed by theological understandings.

Another aspect of the early curricular design was its concern that the theological disciplines be integrated in the practice of ministry. Here was a theme that would continue in various ways in successive revisions. Therefore a series of "integrative courses" was designed for the Senior year of studies. These courses were focused on specific Church functions: preaching and worship, Christian nurture, Church polity and organization, Christian social responsibility and pastoral care. In them the student was to correlate the knowledge and skills derived from the basic disciplines with the practice of ministry. All these courses were to be taught interdepartmentally. As often is the case the ideal was better than the implementation but the goal had been set and the concern was to continue.

A curriculum is never a static entity and there would be both minor and major changes. For United Theological Seminary the major change came in 1965 with the introduction of "The New Curriculum" as it would be

[1]*Announcements: 1962-63*, p. 13.

called for many years. This new curriculum was the consequence of a number of factors. Among them the most significant were the coming of new faculty members who had not been present for the initial planning and the radical changes that were taking place in American society. But the character of the student body was also changing. When the Seminary had opened a majority of the students came from the two "feeder" schools of Lakeland and Yankton Colleges. Increasingly the students enrolled from a variety of institutions of higher education, many of them state sponsored schools where the concerns of religion had been insignificant or lacking altogether. For the entering student the usual background in the liberal arts or the life of the church could no longer be assumed.[2]

In the light of these factors, and others, the faculty established a self-study committee. Current influential books, like Harvey Cox's *The Secular City*, were read and discussed. Position papers were written by various faculty members and discussed. Informal sessions on the nature of theological education and its pedagogy were held. Out of this mix of perspectives came the realization that the curriculum needed a radical reformulation to carry out its mission of theological education with an ecumenical perspective, and focusing on the formation of the person.

Crucial to the process was the dynamic and charismatic leadership of Tom Campbell during his two-year stint as professor of church and society. It was he who gave the new curriculum its theological underpinning and coherence. Steeped in the theology of Paul Tillich he proposed the rubric of dialogue between church and world. Tillich's method of correlation understood that to be human raised ultimate questions and the Christian faith was the source of the answers to those ultimate questions. One therefore needed to begin where the students were, or in the colloquial idiom of that day, "where it is at!" Rather than beginning with the tradition and applying it to the issues of the day, one was required to begin with the human situation to raise the crucial questions and issues of the day.

---

[2]Keith R. Bridston and Dwight W. Culver, *Pre-Seminary Education: Report of the Lilly Endowment Study*, Minneapolis: Augsburg Publishing House, 1965.

As Nathan Pusey of Harvard and Charles Taylor of the AATS were later to say, "At United Theological Seminary of the Twin Cities the curriculum begins, not with ideas, but with the realities of human existence in the light of the message of the Christian church. The *ground* of that curriculum is personal faith in God made known in Christ, its *context* is the life of the church in mission, and its *method* is that of dialogue."[3] Consequently the first year of study was tailored to the student's relation to the world and culture in which one lived. Here three courses were developed that focused on "The Christian Faith and the Social Order," "The Christian Faith and Human Personality" and "The Christian Faith and Economic and Political Life." These courses, as their titles indicate, were dialogues between the faith and culture. It was assumed that the students brought an understanding of the culture in which they lived. But if they were not aware of the current issues the courses of the first year included field trips in which the student was confronted with major issues of present human concern. These included trips to the inner city ghetto, public housing, rural communities, political institutions, and industrial systems.

To enhance the dialogue the student needed to have a theological basis for that conversation. To that end each student also participated in an "Integrative Seminar" each week in which all the teachers of the first year students joined to discuss and learn a basic theological stance. The theological works used in these integrative seminars were Reinhold Niebuhr's *The Nature and Destiny of Man* and Paul Tillich's *Systematic Theology*. The intent was not to make the students into little Niebuhrs or Tillichs but to see how a theological system worked and to provide categories for the dialogue between church and culture. In these seminars, as well as elsewhere in the new curriculum, we see the continuance of two basic elements of the original curriculum, the theological character of seminary education and the concern for integration.

On the basis of this work in dialogical theology the student was to investigate in greater depth the resources of the Christian tradition, the more

[3]Nathan Pusey and Charles Taylor, *Ministry for Tomorrow: Report of the Special Committee on Theological Education*, New York: Seabury Press, 1967, p. 98.

typical courses of a theological curriculum. The second year of the curriculum therefore focused on the classical studies of the Christian tradition. But even here the accent on dialogue was not lost. Twice during the Middler Year, as it was then called, the student was required to participate in a week-long immersion experience focused on a particular issue that confronted the Christian faith. These immersion experiences could include dialogue with scientists, campaigning with a political candidate, registering Negro voters in rural Mississippi, or a trip to Chicago's Ecumenical Institute. At the end of the second year a set of comprehensive examinations evaluated the student and measured the growth in understanding that had resulted.

In the third, or Senior Year, greater choice was allowed but the emphasis was on the functions of ministry. For as Louis Gunnemann said, "What is required in this kind of professional training is not education for work in a particular institution but development of the capacity to use a variety of institutional forms creatively."[4] This was not only true of the third year but of the whole program as it attempted to build in a variety of experiences through field education, integrative seminars, the immersion experiences and the comprehensive examinations. Field education was taken concurrently with courses throughout the seminary experience and the field seminars were integrated with the other courses. Field education embraced parish, special and secular ministries to awaken the students to the variety of forms that the church might take in the world.

Two basic transformations resulted from this new curriculum. One was the reformulation of courses, to provide an integrated and theological perspective. An example of this reformulation was the reorganization of the biblical courses. Traditionally biblical studies had been predicated on the study of the biblical languages, followed by exegetical courses, introducing historical and literary concerns, and climaxing in biblical theological study. In the new curriculum that order of biblical studies was reversed. If the focus was the dialogue of faith and culture, then one needed to start with theology

---

[4]Louis Gunnemann, "From Purpose to Curriculum," *Theological Education,* Vol. 2 (Spring 1966) 177-183.

for that dialogue. Consequently the initial course in the biblical field was a course in biblical theology, using the works of Gerhard von Rad and Rudolph Bultmann. This was heavy material for beginning students. Yet it provided opportunities for the students to write papers that brought the biblical perspective into interaction with a present concern, whether it be poverty or Vietnam, contemporary drama or art, racism or alienation. On the basis of the theological study one could then move back into the study of specific biblical material and finally to the languages as a tool for study. This approach finally made it possible for the faculty to deal with the question of the biblical languages that had become such a hurdle for many of the entering students. The motivation for the study of the biblical languages comes not from a requirement or hurdle to overcome but is the consequence of an involvement in the material that leads to a desire to enter with greater depth into the biblical sources.

The second major reformulation of the new curriculum was a new pedagogical approach. Not only were the students to begin with issues that were close to the heart of their own inner integrity, and from those explore the theological resources that may offer answers. But the students were also to take responsibility for their own learning with an emphasis on independent study from an inductive approach. To enhance this perspective each course was designed to meet on a single day of the week, using a variety of pedagogical approaches throughout the class day. With this structure the student did not have to shift gears from class to class within the course of a day. Rather the one day scheduling permitted a variety of methods, not only lectures but also group discussions, reading time, and field trips. Wednesdays were kept free from classes as a time of study and field education involvements.

The new curriculum was acclaimed from different viewpoints. Bridston and Culver, in their study of pre-seminary education, noted that the curriculum took seriously the fact that entering students did not have the traditional backgrounds in the culture of the church.[5] Henry B. Adams, director of Church Ministries studies of the National Council of Churches,

---

[5]Bridston and Culver, *ibid.* p. 138.

praised its concern for a learner-centered approach to education and invited Dean Gunnemann to share the understanding of the seminary's curriculum at the January 1967 meeting of the National Council's Department of Ministry in Atlantic City.[6] Pusey and Taylor observed that "The Seminary helps its students 'to think theologically,' to come to grips with ultimate realities...and communicate with their fellows amid the complexities of contemporary technological culture."[7] Faculties from Canada and the United States both corresponded with the school and came to visit and discuss the issues of theological education that the new curriculum raised.

---

[6]Kley, *The First Ten Years*, p. 65.

[7]Pusey and Taylor, *Ministry for Tomorrow*, p. 98-99.

31. UTS Choral Society, 1965-66

32. Demonstration against Viet Nam War, Larry Mens, Student

33. Dennis Banks and Clyde Bellecourt, AIM Leaders, with Gene Jaberg at Fall Retreat, 1971

34. UTS Players doing "In White America."
Left to right, Cyril Paul, Lee Neuhaus and Randall Reddin

CHAPTER 10

ACHIEVING ACCREDITATION

There can be little question that the new curriculum and its innovative approach to theological education contributed to the ultimate achievement of accreditation by the Seminary. However the path to accreditation was not an easy one. Neither Mission House Theological Seminary nor the School of Theology of Yankton College had ever been accredited by the American Association of Theological Schools. Mission House had been an associate member and Dean Gunnemann had served on the executive committee of the AATS. The integral relationship between the church and the seminary for both schools had meant that accreditation had never been a significant factor in their history. With the formation of United as a new venture in ecumenical education accreditation became a significant goal. Without accreditation the school could not attract students from those denominations that required graduation from an accredited school of their ministerial candidates.

The first hurdle to be overcome was the requirement for continuity in the educational program itself. Until the seminary had graduated at least one class that had gone through its whole life at United the school could not make application for accreditation. In this respect it was considered to be a new institution, even though it carried forward the traditions of Mission House and Yankton.

To exist it needed students. And it rapidly became apparent that the new school could not long depend on the two former feeder colleges to provide a steady stream of candidates. The initial thrust in recruitment was a high-profile but low pressure event called the "Conference for College Students."[1] Under the leadership of Thomas Campbell the college conference was designed as an opportunity to invite college students to the campus. The focus was not on the discussion of issues of ministry directly, but to look at some of the critical problems facing the church and society. Campus pastors and students were invited to join in the reflection on a pressing concern from a theological perspective and by observing the seminary in that reflective task the visitors would see the relevance of theological education.

The first college conference was held for three days in January 1964. Outside leadership was provided by William Stringfellow, the noted Episcopal lawyer and layman, and William Benedict, director of the Chicago City Missionary Society, to look at the theme "The Challenge: Change or Conservation" as it focused on the city. Not only were the visiting students involved in the presentations and discussions but under the leadership of Campbell a bus tour of the city was taken to look at the various aspects of the community from a sociological and theological perspective. Attendance at a movie was followed by an analysis of the content of the movie and of the audience.

This pattern continued for six years and focused on the major issues of the time: the new morality, peace and war, the population explosion, China, governance on campus and in the nation. The campus community was enhanced by the presence of noted theologians, such as Robert Fitch, John Bennett, Ralph J. Potter Jr, Henry Pitney Van Dusen and Franklin Littel, as well as representatives of business, government, the press and law. Senator Eugene McCarthy was one of the speakers in 1965 and Ambassador Braj Kumar Nehru, India's ambassador to the U.S. spoke in 1967.

Another important way in which the seminary made contact with both the church and society was through drama. In the Fall of 1964 the Simpson Players performed at United. They produced P.W. Turner's *Christ in the*

---

[1]The College Conference was initially supported by a grant from the Hill Family Foundation through its executive director Al Heckman.

Concrete City. The performance was reviewed in the student paper *Kairos* by Jon Gunnemann, and also led to the development of a drama company on campus. In the Summer of 1965, following an "Ecumenical Clinic on Drama in the Church", which featured Malcom Boyd as the keynote speaker, the Interchurch Theater Company began a series of productions which included drama focusing on racial issues. The intent was to confront church people with the issues of the time in the form and language of the day. Under the direction of Prof. Gene Jaberg this vehicle brought together students, church members and members of the black community. Each summer a series of plays were produced and presented in the courtyard of the library building. Playing to full houses the plays were an important part of the growth of the school. In the end the project became involved with the Theater of Involvement, under the direction of the Rev. William Livingstone of the United Ministries in Higher Education at the University of Minnesota. The last season, 1973, was held at the Wayzata Community Church (UCC), in a suburb on the western edge of the Twin Cities.

Students and faculty also joined together in the UTS Choral Society. Under the direction of students and also professional musicians, the choral society sang for special occasions on campus and also took Spring tours, during the vacation period, into areas and churches served by the Seminary.

The various forms of the arts were important to the life of the school. Often there were exhibits of artists' works in the hallway of the classroom building. A piece of art that has become particularly identified with the seminary is the sculpture "Joshua" by Herman Schwagereit of Essen, Germany. The piece was first seen by alumni at the General Synod of the United Church of Christ and purchased as a memorial to Dr. Karl Ernst, Professor of Exegetical Theology at Mission House. The piece was dedicated on April 19, 1966 and continues to grace the courtyard of the main building.

In spite of the College Conference and other recruitment efforts the student body grew slowly. The initial year there had been 50 students, two of whom were women. In 1964 there were 61 students, 70 in 1965 and 68 in 1966, of whom three were women. The lack of student housing in the early years was no doubt a hindrance.

On June 10, 1964 ground was broken for student housing, twenty-four units of single bedroom apartments that could be used for single students or for married students without children. One apartment was reserved for Ron and Emma Barz who continued to serve as maintenance man and cook for the seminary. The major funds for this project came from the Churchmen's Fellowship of the United Church of Christ, and the name of the building reflected this generous gift.

Recruitment is always crucial for an educational institution and United has always struggled with that issue. On the one hand there was the strong belief that the quality of the program and the innovation of the curriculum would attract students to this new venture. Many have noted that the brochures and *Announcements* of the Seminary were most attractive and a positive factor in recruitment. On the other hand there was recognition that United was in competition with other schools for a limited number of candidates. The Seminary did not want to enter into a bidding war for students. Not only were there limited funds for such an attempt but it was inconsistent with the values and self-understandings of the school.

In 1967 a grant of $7,000 was received from the George D. Dayton Foundation of Minneapolis to underwrite a program of student recruitment. The money was to be used for a seminary student who would spend an intern year interpreting the seminary program to college students. The position of student interpreter reflects the ambiguity that the school felt about recruitment, for the task was seen as primarily that of interpreter rather than recruiter. Michael Groh, a graduate of 1969, was the first student interpreter and initiated a long line of students in that position. After graduation Groh became one of the founders of Y.E.S., Youth Emergency Service, in Minneapolis, a telephone hot-line for troubled youth.

By the end of the Sixties the enrollment had grown from the original 50 students in 1962-63 to 118 students in 1969-70 in the basic professional program. In addition an average of 27 students registered annually for the post-B.D. and graduate programs. A total of 108 students had graduated from the seminary by 1970. The diversity of the student body was becoming apparent. Students had come from 103 colleges and universities in 28 states and several foreign countries. Nineteen denominations were represented by those students, including not only the traditional denominations but also Assemblies of God, Evangelical Free, Mennonite, Moravian and Roman Catholics.[2]

Of course all theological schools in the United States experienced growth of their student bodies in the Sixties, and United participated in that growth. Some of that growth was due to the increasing protest against the Viet Nam war. Concern about the war and the current political system led many to consider ways to find alternatives. Theological schools provided a way to evade the draft. But not all who came sought to evade the draft and many of those who chose this alternative were seriously seeking the meaning of their lives and of the world in which they lived.

This ambiguity is reflected in the experience of John Hawley who was a first year student in 1968-69. Though enrolled in seminary he sought conscientious objector status from his draft board on moral and personal grounds rather than religious training and belief, and refused classification as a seminary student. His draft board refused his request and a state appeal was also denied. More than 100 persons gathered at the Federal Office Building to support Hawley when he was arrested. Protest songs were sung, speeches were made, including one by Mulford Q. Sibley, the University of Minnesota professor who had not only been Hawley's adviser as an undergraduate, but was also a strong activist in the anti-war movement.[3] This was the first peaceful demonstration of the newly-formed Seminarians for Peace, which included students from United, Luther and St. Paul Seminaries.[4]

Another major existential factor in the continuing life of the seminary was its financial basis. Both Mission House and Yankton had received their primary support from the churches to which they were integrally related. With the merger of the United Church of Christ the new denomination took

---

[2]Kley, *The First Ten Years*, p. 115.

[3]Sibley would later, after retirement from the University, become adjunct professor at United in 1983-84.

[4]Kley, *The First Ten Years*, p. 95.

over the obligation of support for the seminaries that had been given by the Evangelical and Reformed Church for its three seminaries, including Mission House. This support was promised for ten years, out of the regular budget of the Church. The amount of subsidy however was reduced and never adjusted for inflation. Yankton School of Theology had been supported by both the German Conference of Congregational Churches and the Board of Home Missions of the Congregational Christian Churches. With the merger of the schools the German Conference pledged $100,000 for the new buildings, recognition of which was the identification of the classroom building with that gift.

These factors led to a precarious position, financially, for the new seminary. Huenemann, in addition to his administrative duties, had to be the chief fund raiser for the institution. With great diligence and effort he was in the field, speaking to local congregations, interpreting the school to the various judicatories, contacting individuals who might provide support, and defending the school in the councils of the denominations. His was the unenviable task of finding the financial resources to make the vision a reality and the dream find concrete expression.

At the end of the first year of school Huenemann would report to the Board of Trustees that the net income for operating expenses had been $153,301.25 and that the expenses had been $164,472.22. This resulted in a deficit of $11,170.52![5] It was obvious to all that a new form of funding needed to be sought. At the General Synod of the UCC on July 4, 1963, he requested a meeting of the Conference Ministers of 17 midwestern conferences who were brought together and apprised of the financial problems not only of United but of the theological schools in the region. At this meeting, chaired by Robert Inglis, Colorado Conference Minister, it was decided that there needed to be a regional support effort for the three seminaries in the area, Chicago Theological Seminary, Eden Theological Seminary and United.

Working with the conferences the three seminaries would approach the local congregations for support of theological education and to ensure

[5]Minutes of the Annual Meeting of the Board of Trustees, June 17-18, 1963.

leadership in the future for those churches. This joint effort became known as the Seminary Regional Support Program. The administration of the program was underwritten by the schools, and committees in the conferences were responsible to help in the interpretation of the task. The goal of the program was to encourage each congregation to give 2% of its annual budget to theological education. This appeal, which later came to be known as CUE (Chicago, United, Eden), would become a significant factor in the budgets of the three schools. In 1965 the joint effort had raised $63,000 of a goal of $87,000 for United's portion.[6]

The urgent need for United was not only the annual operating budget but also capital funds. To the Executive Committee of the Board of Trustees, on November 1, 1966, the President proposed a Capital Funds Campaign of $1,750,000. This ambitious proposal included the liquidation of the present mortgages (500,000), a new administration and continuing education building (300,000), additional student apartments with a gymnasium (250,000), a retreat house and roadway in the north woods (250,000), scholarship endowment (250,000) and a continuing education endowment (250,000). This proposal was presented as the second phase of campus development that had been part of the original master plan for the seminary.[7]

The plan was adopted by the Board of Trustees at their annual meeting May 28-29, 1967 with the modification that it include the cost of a new faculty house for Wilson Yates, and the goal was set at 2 million dollars. Ketchum Inc., a national fund-raising firm, was hired to formulate the campaign. They advised delay and more ground work in the larger Twin Cities community. When the Board met again in 1968 it was announced that the contract with Ketchum Inc. had been terminated. However funds needed to be raised immediately, and the President was "cautiously optimistic" about the outcome. At this point the first development officer was hired at United, Richard Paul Turner, a lay Christian Brother, whose contacts with the

---

[6]Report of President Huenemann to the Board of Trustees, June 14-15, 1965.

[7]Minutes of the Executive Committee of the Board of Trustees, November 1, 1966.

community held forth the promise of a successful campaign. At the meeting of the Executive Committee on the 13th of October 1969, Turner would report that only $426,422.65 had been raised, no buildings had or would be built, and the Board had to borrow $25,000 to undergird the operational expenses.[8] Like many such campaigns this one ended quietly and short of its goals.

A third critical factor in the effort to achieve accreditation was the state of the library. When the school opened in September of 1962 there were only 11,000 volumes in the collection. As both merging schools had been part of college libraries there had been no effort to develop independent collections. When Mission House Seminary separated from Lakeland College the faculty made a concerted effort to build up the seminary library and that provided what library there was available for the new school.

The collection, though solid, needed to be expanded as the Seminary looked forward to accreditation. At the Annual Meeting of the Board on June 15, 1964 the Librarian, Roland G. Kley, proposed that the budget be almost doubled to $34,750 to enhance the acquisition of materials for the library, but the Board did not accept the proposal. When the AATS visiting team, invited by the Seminary, came in November 1964 for a pre-accreditation visit they noted that "the library is the outstanding area of need."[9] Not only was the periodical collection spotty and the back-issues limited, but the book collection was weak in several areas.

This report gave the administration of the school the means to push for the improvement of the library. At the next Board of Trustees meeting the proposed budget for the library was increased to assist in the purchase of materials and the increase of the staff. Further a library committee was formed with faculty representation. The whole faculty was urged to participate in the identification of resources that would build up the

---

[8]A mail vote was taken by the Board of Trustees in August 1966 to authorize this borrowing.

[9]Kley, *The First Ten Years*, p. 54.

collection. In the school years 1965-66 and 1966-67 the library was able to add over 4000 volumes a year, doubling the collection.

When accreditation did come on December 27, 1966 the efforts concerning the library fell short. One of the two notations received was in relation to the library that was judged inadequate in holdings and building. However this notation provided the stimulus to continue to enhance the library. Clair Wilcoxen was hired as assistant librarian beginning in the year 1966-67 and two clerical staff were added. In June 1967, Raymond P. Morris, Librarian at Yale Divinity School, was invited to consult with the librarians of the theological schools in the Twin Cities. Out of that consultation came the proposal to the Hill Foundation that the libraries jointly develop their serials collections and publish a joint catalog of their serials holdings. And in May 1968 the decision was made to reclassify the holdings to the Library of Congress system to make the collection compatible with the other libraries of the area. Formerly the Union Theological Seminary Library system of classification had been used.

All these efforts increased the holdings of the library. However the question of the building remained. Though stacks were added to hold the collection, the space for the library was limited. The need for more space was to be included in the capital campaign for new buildings. On the basis of that campaign proposal the AATS removed the notation about the space for the library building. But as has been noted the campaign did not succeed and the problem of space remained to haunt the library for years to come.

Nonetheless the quest for accreditation continued. On May 1, 1966 the seminary submitted its self-study to the American Association of Theological Schools as the first formal step in the process. The heart of that self-study was the new curriculum with its church-world polarity for developing skills in theological reflection. The teaching and instruction of the faculty were not directed to indoctrination but to engagement in theological reflection. To this end the faculty were focused in the encouragement and nurture of the students in preparation for ministry.

The self-study was cognizant of the fact that there were areas that needed attention. The clarification of the role of the Seminary in the United Church of Christ was a major concern. The need for closer cooperation with the other schools in the Twin Cities area, not only in library but also in instruction, was noted. Problems of recruitment and on-going supervision and counseling of students were in need of attention. And the need for continued re- appraisal of the new curriculum and of the seminary as a whole was suggested.[10]

In November of 1966 a team of examiners came to the campus for interviews and a close look at the operation of the Seminary. The team consisted of Dean Gordon E. Jackson of Pittsburgh Theological Seminary and Dean Lowell D. Lund of the Lutheran School of Theology at Chicago. Their positive report led to the December 27, 1966 announcement that United Theological Seminary was fully accredited by the American Association of Theological Schools. It would mark a significant milestone in the brief history of the school that had opened its doors only four years previously. Beside the notation on the library there was a further notation that the resources of the school were not adequate for work beyond the basic B.D. Degree. At the same time that United received its accreditation Bethel Theological Seminary, its neighbor in adjoining Arden Hills, also received its accreditation.[11]

The joy over the achievement of accreditation could not overcome the concerns regarding the relationship to the other theological seminaries in the area and to the denomination. The task of theological education in always done in the context of multiple relationships. It is to the consortium and the denomination that the story will now turn.

---

[10]*Self Study of United Theological Seminary of the Twin Cities.*

[11]Kley, *The First Ten Years,* pp. 80-81.

CHAPTER 11

THE GROWTH OF CONSOLIDATION

With its vision of ecumenical theological education and its concern that the Seminary work cooperatively with its theological neighbors it is not surprising that United took the lead in the process that led to the development of the Minnesota Consortium of Theological Schools.[1] That leadership was embodied in the person of Louis Gunnemann. It was his memo of January 23, 1964 to the key administrators of the four Protestant schools that led to the crucial meeting of February 7, 1964. He was seeking to find ways in which the schools could cooperatively work to offer a program of continuing education to pastors in the area and to establish a joint graduate study program. That meeting was held at United and present for the meeting were Presidents Lundquist (Bethel), Rogness (Luther), Zeidler (Northwestern) and Huenemann (United). The Deans of the four schools were also present: Johnson, Hansen, Roth and Gunnemann (Bethel, Luther, Northwestern, and United respectively), along with Kent Knutsen, Director of Graduate Studies for Luther.

This historic meeting led to three major conclusions that would shape the character of the Consortium in the years ahead. First it noted the need to design a continuing education program that would transcend

[1]The early history of the Consortium is well documented in the doctoral dissertation of Robert G. Duffett, *The History and Development of the Doctor of Ministry Degree at the Minnesota Consortium of Theological Schools: 1957-1985*. Unpublished Ph.D. Dissertation, The University of Iowa, 1986. I am indebted to this work in telling the story of the Consortium.

denominational lines. Second it saw the possibilities for seminary faculty and programs to be involved in an interdisciplinary curriculum with university faculty people. Third, it proposed the assessment of the demand in the region for graduate theological education and the need to offer this jointly.[2] This meeting also reached the conclusion that the presidents and deans would continue to meet to discuss the various concerns of common interest. It became known as the Presidents and Deans Committee.

Significant though this meeting was, two other factors contributed to the development of the Consortium. Seven years earlier Gunnemann, in the process of seeking the relocation and merger of Mission House, had called together a meeting of the presidents of the Protestant seminaries in the Twin Cities. This meeting was to assess their response to the idea of and need for an ecumenical theological school in the area. The participants were Zeidler of Northwestern Lutheran, Lundquist of Bethel, Rogness of Luther, and Christenson of Augsburg.[3]

This earlier meeting was to influence the outcome of the relocation and merger of Mission House and Yankton for the assembled Presidents were positive in response to the possibility of that happening in the Twin Cities. For the future Consortium this meeting would also be critical for it represented the first time the presidents of the four schools had met at the same time and place! Gunnemann would later write, "The response was unexpectedly warm and receptive and is summed up in Dr. Rogness' statement that the strong Lutheran, Roman Catholic and Baptist constituencies in Minnesota had made for an inhibiting parochialism. He ended by saying: 'We need an ecumenical seminary and we will welcome you.'"[4]

---

[2]Minutes of the Inter-Seminary Consultation, February 7, 1964.

[3]Augsburg Theological Seminary would merge with Luther Theological Seminary in 1963 when its denomination merged with other Lutheran groups to form the American Lutheran Church.

[4]L.H. Gunnemann, unpublished manuscript, p. 20, n. 13. Huenemann, in an interview 20 June 1991, also noted the cordial attitude may have stemmed in part from the common background Rogness shared with Huenemann at Luther College, Decorah, Iowa.

The February, 1964, meeting was not the first cooperative effort of the theological schools in the Twin Cities. Already in the academic year 1963-64 the librarians had begun to meet to find ways to cooperate in the marshalling of library resources in the area. The first librarians to meet were David Gustin of Bethel, Norman Wente of Luther, Curtis Paul of Northwestern, Father Clyde Eddy of St. Paul Seminary, and Roland Kley of United. It was the librarians who led the way in showing that the schools could cooperate and that they could work together. This group would become known as the Minnesota Theological Library Association and has met regularly ever since, resulting in the most fruitful and tangible program of resource sharing that the Consortium has so far produced.

It was not until 1967 that the two Roman Catholic seminaries were invited to join the cooperative effort. St. Paul Seminary, the diocesan seminary, was invited on April 7 of that year to be a participant or observer in the cooperative work of the seminaries. Following its acceptance the Presidents and Deans extended an official invitation to St. John's Seminary and School of Theology. It too accepted the invitation. The reason for the delay in invitations and the ordering of the sequence is not given in the records.

Another factor leading to the development of the Consortium was the presence of the Interseminary Student Movement that had come out of the ecumenical movement of the Fifties. In 1962-63 there was a regional meeting of the ISM at Luther Seminary and students from the local seminaries attended. The theme of that meeting was "The Word of God in the Inner City."[5] At that time the students came to meet one another and develop their own concern for interseminary cooperation. This movement, however, would never be a very strong or active force on the local scene. In the Sixties it could at times agree on anti-war demonstrations but the theological character and differences of the separate schools were not conducive to any large scale cooperation.

---

[5]Kley, *The First Ten Years*, p. 43.

One of the first educational projects to emerge in the growth of the Consortium was the formation of an Interseminary Course. It was initially offered in March of 1965 when students from United, Bethel and Luther could register for credit in the course "The New Morality." The course was limited to five or six upper-class students from the three schools and was team taught by James Nelson of United, Clarence Bass of Bethel and James Burtness of Luther. Students from Northwestern Lutheran and St. Paul Seminary were permitted to audit the course.

Interseminary courses have continued through the years and have offered the opportunity for students to learn together and for faculty to work together. The topic of the courses changed from year to year, depending on the needs of the schools and the interest of the faculties who taught together. Many different combinations of schools and faculty resulted in some rich offerings. In addition a joint course between the seminaries and the University of Minnesota was developed which focused on Rural Communities and Economics. This course continued for a number of years thanks to the financial underwriting of the Wilder Foundation.

Other educational cooperative efforts were explored, including the possibility of students taking classes at other seminaries and the exchange of faculty between the various schools. This enriched the possibilities for the students beyond what was available or traditional in their respective institutions. For example, in the Fall of 1968 Father Killian McDonnell of St. John's University taught a course on "Ecclesiology of Vatican II" at United while Professor Nelson offered a seminar on "Church-State Relations" at St. John's.

Another type of cooperation among the schools has been the sponsorship of various events in the community with groups not connected directly with the seminaries. One of the first such cooperative events was the co-sponsorship of the Faith and Life Dialogue in November of 1966. This effort of saturation evangelism took the form of The Town Meeting in the Twin Cities. Focusing on "The Care of the City" the theme was explored through civic, educational, religious and mass media channels. The purpose was to have citizens in the region relate their personal, moral and religious concerns through a variety of programs and resources.

A specific contribution of United to this effort was the production of the play "In White America" by the Interchurch Theater Company, directed by Professor Jaberg. He also participated in the production of a television documentary on the use of leisure.[6]

The one area in which the schools have not yet found a way to cooperate is the adoption of a common calendar. Though it would enhance the cooperative work of the schools such an arrangement has never achieved agreement. The internal politics of each school and the relationships with church constituencies beyond the campus borders have proved to be insurmountable in attaining this goal.

A major cooperative program of significance for the consortium was the establishment of a joint Th.M. Program. Gordon Johnson, Dean of Bethel Seminary, convened a meeting in February of 1965 at the request of the Presidents and Deans Committee with faculty members from the four Protestant schools in attendance. This committee agreed that the idea of a joint or cooperative effort was important and sought further investigation of the possibilities.[7]

By the end of 1965, however the Presidents and Deans appointed another committee to review what had been already done and to present another proposal for a possible joint program. This committee came to the conclusion that post-B.D. studies should be of two kinds, a non-academic program that would provide refresher courses in a continuing education format, and an academic program that would lead to an advanced theological degree. As the schools were already doing the first kind of programs a joint effort in this area was not deemed necessary. If a joint academic program were to be mounted the choice of the committee was for the establishment of an institution for advanced studies that would draw upon the resources of the faculties and facilities of the four schools. They also suggested that a joint program could be mounted in which the schools would have their own programs, but where there would be close cooperation in admissions

---

[6]Kley, *The First Ten Years*, p. 79.

[7]Minutes of the Presidents and Deans Committee, February 4, 1965.

standards, reciprocity in courses, use of the libraries, and joint announcements of all offerings and programs.

The Presidents and Deans Committee received this report and after serious discussion adopted the alternative program in which each school would have its own program, focused on the areas of study that they could provide for the joint offering. A Joint Graduate Program Committee was elected in which the representatives were, Dorris Flessner from Northwestern, Clifford Larson from Bethel, Kent Knutson from Luther and Louis Gunnemann from United. The committee drew up the standards for the joint Th.M. degree and became the administrative body for the program.

The proposal of the joint Th.M. Program was greeted with enthusiasm and quickly adopted by the faculties of Northwestern, Luther and United. United offered the program its emphasis on Christianity and Culture, with the concern to interpret the faith in the light of the contemporary institutions of society. The faculty at Bethel was in favor of the joint Th.M. Program but was faced with a public relations problem and institutional identity questions if they participated in a joint program. They therefore sought the opinion of their Board of Regents who approved the action to proceed with the planning for the degree but at the same time requested a study of the implications of the joint program for their constituency, which had a strong separatist tendency.

By November of 1968 the Bethel faculty, proceeding on the basis of the Board's action, after analyzing their strengths and weaknesses decided to offer a Th.M. Degree in Old and New Testament studies. They felt the pressures of their constituency and proposed that the program begin in the Fall of 1969. In the meantime the administration mounted a strong public relations campaign to support this action. At the July 1969 the delegates to the General Conference of Baptist Churches approved the program. A strong dissident group castigated the school for associating with those liberal schools, especially United.

It was almost two and a half years from the first planning committee to the implementation of the joint program. Many of the issues raised at this time would come back to affect later developments. The Catholic schools were not disinterested observers to the process but felt that this program did not fit into the understanding of their vision and mission. Most priests went on to Catholic institutions for further graduate work. Also they did not have a post B.D. Program to which this program could relate. The proposed graduate program did not appear to enhance the priestly functions, especially spiritual formation. At that time spiritual formation was still primarily a Roman Catholic concern.

In the meantime the desire of United Theological Seminary to relate to the University of Minnesota had not been lost. It was a natural relationship to be pursued in the light of the dialogical nature of the curriculum and the school's wish to be associated with other schools of higher education. Also the conversations with the other theological faculties since 1964 had included this component among the issues that were discussed. Therefore it was no surprise when Paul Hammer, Professor of New Testament at United, put forth the proposal to link the Consortium schools with the University.

Hammer proposed establishing an ecumenical center for joint graduate theological study adjacent to the University of Minnesota. This center would not only enrich the academic programs of the seminary students and graduate programs of the Consortium but would also be a place where University students could enroll and participate in the programs of the Consortium schools. The hope was that by being a Consortium endeavor, ecumenical in nature, it could overcome the University's resistance to participating in religious studies. The center would be governed by an independent Board of Trustees, consisting of 24 members nominated by the six schools, four from each school, which would incorporate to hold property, determine policy and hire staff. Hammer worked closely with Bryce Crawford, Jr., Dean of Graduate Studies at the University, in developing this proposal of which Crawford was a strong supporter. Hammer also received encouragement and support from other members of the University administration, including Elmer Learn, Assistant to President Malcolm Moos.

At the same time United had embarked on a long-range planning process using the consulting firm of George Nelson, Inc. Hammer was also involved in that process and was able to use the resources of the consultants in the development of his proposal. George Nelson, Inc. offered to be the consultants to secure the land, develop a plan of financing and determine the size of the building. This was an ambitious undertaking and reflected the enlarged vision of the Seminary.

When the proposal was presented to the Presidents and Deans Committee on March 8, 1968 each school was asked to provide $500 from each school to underwrite the exploration of the project. At the same time the Joint Graduate Program Committee proposed that the Consortium pursue some kind of graduate union and that a plan to that end be drawn up. Within a week the Presidents and Deans Committee met again. At this point they raised the question whether a graduate program of the theological schools should be academic or professional in nature. To examine this question they chose Kent Knutsen of Luther to make a study, which was underwritten by assessing each school $500.00. The minutes of that meeting clearly reveal that there were two perspectives in the schools. On the one hand there were those who felt that the future of the consortium was in the area of academic graduate study. On the other there were those who tended to favor professional graduate study. The two reports received on March 8 reflected those two positions.

While the Knutsen study was in progress the Danforth Foundation indicated an interest in the ecumenical theological center, particularly as it was focused in the relationship to the University of Minnesota. Therefore, Ruben Huenemann, on behalf of the six schools, submitted a proposal to the Danforth Foundation to fund a study investigating the feasibility of such a center.[8] The proposal for the project was not funded. Hammer left United at the end of the school year 1967-68 and no strong voice picked up his leadership on the ecumenical center. The University for reasons both internal and external did not choose to initiate any actions that would further the development. As a consequence the initiative was lost and the center died a quiet death, more of neglect than intentional termination.

However, the Knutsen study kept alive the hopes of those that envisioned an ecumenical graduate theological center. It was known that the

[8]RHH to Luther H. Harshbarger, Danforth Foundation, October 1, 1968.

faculty at Luther Seminary favored an academic doctorate. Knutsen had a good grasp of the central issues and was granted the freedom to pursue the issues involved. The objectives of the study were described by the Presidents and Deans as follows:

> To discover what if anything can be done by our seminaries together to effect for our several churches and their ministries academically respectable programs of advanced theological training and what degree programs might reasonably be incorporated in such a program.[9]

As is evident the commission was worded with sufficient ambiguity that the outcome could not be preconceived. And Knutsen was encouraged to visit other such centers where joint programs were being carried out.

It was hoped that his report would be completed in a brief period. However it would be June of 1969 before the report was finished. It was delayed not only by difficulties in visiting the other centers but also by the fact that Knutsen was elected President of Wartburg Theological Seminary in Dubuque, Iowa.

In that report, which was received by all faculty and board members of the six seminaries, Knutsen proposed several actions to achieve the stated goal of his commission.[10] First, he proposed the seminaries should establish an agency that would be a "quasi- educational institution" to make possible the offering of degrees by the various schools. It would be like a brokerage agency with a director and budget but have no property or faculty of its own. Second, that agency would be the vehicle for a professional doctorate and a master's degree in the art of ministry. Such a professional doctorate would be similar to one offered by San Francisco Theological Seminary. Third, this new organization would attempt to evaluate the need for and the possibilities of offering an academic doctorate.

---

[9]Minutes of the Presidents and Deans Committee, May 2, 1968.

[10]Kent S. Knutson, "A Proposal for Cooperating in Graduate Education among Minnesota Theological Seminaries: A Preliminary Report," July, 1969.

The immediate consequence of this report was the formation of the Minnesota Consortium of Theological Faculties.[11] Until this time the schools had been working informally and under the guidance of the Committee of Presidents and Deans. What had been achieved was the result of informal power and strong leadership, especially the guidance and vision of Louis Gunnemann. With the Knutson report a means for accomplishing the goal of cooperative graduate theological education was available that would not tie the schools into a structural relationship but would permit the faculties to cooperate. The plan was especially important from the point of view of Bethel, which would have had trouble linking itself institutionally to the more liberal schools. Therefore on February 27, 1970 the Presidents and Deans authorized a committee to develop a plan for the organization of the consortium. By the end of that calendar year the six schools had ratified the "Articles of Agreement" with minor amendments and on December 11, 1970 the presidents and deans moved "...that we declare ourselves a Consortium on the basis of the agreement."[12] A means for offering the professional doctorate had been established. It would take some time before the degree was actually offered, but the Consortium had become a reality that would provide the means for cooperation among the schools in a more systematic and planned way.

From the point of view of those who had high hopes and great dreams for the Consortium it is a shame that the vehicle has never fully carried out those hopes and dreams. For some of the schools denominational heritages may well have restricted their possibilities. For United it has been a lack of funding and possibly a fear that some degree of freedom would be lost. Institutional constraints and external limitations have forced the consortium to act cautiously and seek the lowest common denominator. The Twin Cities area has a rich theological resource in the six seminaries, one of five such concentrations in the nation. However the schools have remained tentative and tended to look inward when the possibilities of cooperation and joint

---

[11]Duffett, *History*, p. 313 incorrectly identifies the organization as a Consortium of Schools.

[12]Minutes of the Presidents and Deans Committee, Dec. 11, 1970.

effort were proposed. Even United's role in often carrying the flag in the attempt to bring together the schools has been more limited than it might wish to acknowledge.

CHAPTER 12

THE UNITED CHURCH OF CHRIST AND ITS SEMINARIES

Theological schools, and particularly denominational seminaries, are by their very nature ambiguous creatures, related to both the church and the academy. In the European tradition theological schools are usually departments of the universities, and often formed the basis on which the universities were founded. That tradition has its continuation in the American scene with the founding of such great schools as Harvard, Yale, Chicago, etc. The rise of denominational seminaries, however, is a peculiar feature of the American experience. They are the consequence of the forces that converged in the nineteenth century and which also resulted in the Sunday School and the Christian Endeavor movement.[1] Education had become the American way of transcending economic class or social status, as well as providing access into the denominational structures.

When one looks at the closely-related seminaries of the United Church of Christ one quickly discerns that they were all founded in the nineteenth century, from Andover in 1807 to Yankton in 1885. Since then the only new formations were the mergers of Andover Newton in 1931 and of United in 1960. Each school was founded to provide ministerial leadership for the churches to which it was related, usually by congregations and leading ministers who saw the need for an intellectually trained leadership. Yet

[1]Speech by Robert W. Lynn, President's Dinner at UTS, Oct. 1990.

there was a significant difference in the two major streams that formed the United Church of Christ.

The seminaries in the Congregational Christian tradition were founded as autonomous and independent schools. The only clear exception to that was the School of Theology at Yankton, which was governed by the Board of Education of the German Congregational Churches. The primary relationship of these schools to each other was through membership in the Division of Higher Education of the Board for Home Missions. Not until January 29, 1956 when the Congregational Christian Council of Theological Schools was formed was there an organization devoted solely to the interpretation and support of theological education. This Council had as its aims the symbolization of the denomination's concern for the education for ministry, the improvement of theological education in the schools, the interpretation of theological education to the churches, a channel for cooperation with denominational and other organizations, and making known the resources available in the seminaries to the denomination.[2] In June of 1957, with the impending merger of the church, the Evangelical and Reformed Seminaries were also represented on the Council. Originally eleven seminaries formed the Council, with Howard University joining later.[3] From 1956 to 1960 the Council met annually in January at Buck Hill Falls, PA in conjunction with the General Council of the CC Churches to which it was primarily related.

In 1958 the Council called for a Commission on Theological Education within the new United Church of Christ, which would be directly related to the General Synod. However the constitution placed the theological seminaries under the Council for Higher Education that also had responsibilities for the colleges related to the church. At the General Synod of 1961 in Philadelphia the Council was dissolved and awaited the formation

---

[2]*A Short History of the Congregational Christian Council of Theological Schools*, mimeographed paper, no date or author. Perhaps it was written by President Frederick W. Whittaker of Bangor who was the secretary of the Council throughout its history.

[3]The eleven schools were Andover Newton, Bangor, Chicago, Hartford, Harvard, Oberlin, Pacific School of Religion, Union (NY), Vanderbilt, Yale and Yankton.

of the Council for Higher Education under the Board for Homeland Ministries.

The Evangelical and Reformed Church seminaries had developed a quite different relationship to the church even though they too had been founded by congregations and ministers. Here an organic relationship to the Church was the norm, for the whole Church was perceived as engaging in the task of theological education. The seminaries were the centers where that task was focused. As a consequence the faculties and chief administrators of the schools were called to serve the whole Church and approved by the General Synod. The presidents of the seminaries were given voice and vote at the meetings of General Synod by virtue of their office. The primary funding for the seminaries came from the national budget of the denomination, and from special appeals, such as the United Seminary Appeal that had a two year goal of $2,000,000. Within this organic relationship there was a high degree of academic freedom and institutional security for each of the three seminaries.

Similar to the CC seminaries the E&R seminaries were related to each other through a Commission on Higher Education that also had responsibilities for the denominationally related colleges. It was not until 1959 that the E&R formed a separate Committee on Theological Education. The other interrelationship between the seminaries was the annual Tri-Faculty Conference. When the United Church was formed the Tri-Faculty Conference dissolved after its meeting in the summer of 1962. Attempts to form Inter Theological Faculty Conferences following that format failed, due to lack of interest among the faculties, the difficulty of identifying a time when they could meet and the cost of sustaining the larger meeting.

The first two General Synods of the UCC had little to say about theological education. What little they did say had to do with student loan requirements and the concern for aid for students under care of the associations. It was not until the third General Synod in Philadelphia that specific action was taken and here it was reactive to the development of United Theological Seminary. For those who opposed the formation of the school a method of sidetracking the issue was to call for a study of theological education in the UCC. The motion called for a survey which "would take into account existing seminaries, their present resources and future potential, geographical location, per student costs in various areas, and all other possible factors, keeping foremost the future of the entire United Church." This survey was to determine the future giving of the denomination and the working out of a strategy for location of the seminaries.[4] Fortunately for United it did not pass. The other significant expression of concern was that the report of the Division of Higher Education "expressed its desire that the United Church continue its support of these institutions [colleges and seminaries], as necessary, at least during the next decade."[5]

An "Advisory Committee on the Seminaries and the Church" was appointed to carry out the intent of the 1961 motion of General Synod. Three consultants were appointed to this committee, Herman Morse, Charles Taylor and Douglas Horton. In 1963, at the Fourth General Synod in Denver, they reported on the development of the Seminary Regional Support Program (CUE) and recommended national support of the seminaries. They also employed the Rev. Ross W. Sanderson to make a survey of the seminaries as the basis for making further recommendations. His report was made to the Executive Council of the Church on August 15, 1964. In it he appears to suggest that the seminaries should relate to interdenominational agencies, rather than the prevailing wisdom that encouraged relationships with universities. For him "ecumenical" was a term without fiscal meaning. He concluded his report with the optimistic note "The UCC can make two wonderful discoveries: 1) These children of ours...are potentially one of the most unitive factors in our existence as a church..., and 2) the revival of some form of vigorous association among these schools might prove a prime event in the history of the United Church."[6] Among his observations was the gratuitous question: "How can

---

[4]Vote 61-GS-54.

[5]P. 51.

[6]Report of Ross W. Sanderson to the Advisory Committee on Theological Education of the Executive Council of the General Synod of the United Church of Christ. August 15, 1964.

we help United to grow up a Joseph among brethren, capable of being a great leader of his people without becoming obnoxiously a favorite son?"[7]

Concretely, on the basis of the Sanderson Report the Advisory Committee recommended to the Executive Council the formation of a Council for Theological Education and a budget item of $950,000 for the work of that proposed council. The Executive Council did not approve the formation of the proposed council "at this stage in the life of the church" and asked the Council for Higher Education "to develop a sound and feasible plan for participation of the Church in the financial support of the seminaries related to the Council."[8] At the fifth General Synod (1965 in Chicago) the Synod upheld the position of the Executive Council but continued to affirm its continuing concern for theological education. It did, in typical fashion, ask for the Council of Higher Education to continue to study this problem and report to the 1967 General Synod.[9] As to the request for more funds for the seminaries the Synod, in accepting the report of the Council for Higher Education, "directs the Budget Committee to assign high priority to the meeting of the demonstrated needs of the seminaries when it determines the allocation of any available funds in excess of $11,500,00 in each of the years 1966 and 1967."[10] This action indicates little support for the expectation was that there would be a budget shortfall.

The Division of Higher Education responded to this action of the General Synod by authorizing yet another study of theological education in the United Church of Christ. This time Professor Paul M. Harrison, of the University of Pennsylvania, was engaged to conduct the study.[11] Significantly, but immaterial to the questions being asked in the church about theological education, Harrison concluded his report by proposing a program

---

[7]*Ibid.*

[8]Vote 65 3EC 6.

[9]Minutes of the Fifth General Synod, p. 113.

[10]65-GS-276.

[11]Paul M. Harrison, *Theological Education and the United Church of Christ*, mimeographed, 1967.

of continuing education for ministers in their own locales, as an extension program of the seminaries, using groups of ministers and working with other institutions, so that the ministers might become specialists where their interests and community problems coincided. These group ministers would serve as adjunct professors and have student interns on a one or two year basis. This program, he argued, would tie together the work of the seminary, ministry, the churches and regional and national offices of individual denominations. His proposal looked very much like the program used in the Federated Theological Faculty of the University of Chicago under the leadership of Dean Jerald C. Brauer ten years before!

The Sixth General Synod in 1967, at Cincinnati, received the Harrison Report and responded with a proposal that a "high-level" Commission on Theological Education be "re-constituted" to evaluate the report, set long-range goals, propose procedures, suggest possible time schedule and make suggestions for the support of the seminaries in the interim. This motion was referred to the Business Committee[12]. This resolution then appears in the minutes again, only to be referred back to the Report Committee on the Executive Council, which had also supported the formation of a Commission on Theological Education.[13]5 In the meantime the Ohio Conference and eleven other conferences and associations had sent overtures to the General Synod expressing their concern that support of the institutions of higher education in the United Church was eroding and might be discontinued in 1971. The report of the Board of Home Missions sought to reassure those who had submitted the overtures and supported the formation of a separate committee for theological education.

The final action of that General Synod was to direct the Executive Council to appoint and convene a temporary Commission on Theological Education. This Commission would consist of twelve members, none of whom would be a member of a UCC related seminary or staff or a member of the board or staff of an instrumentality of the UCC.[14] Before the Seventh

[12]67-GS-19.

[13]67-GS-31.

[14]67-GS-158.

General Synod would meet the Commission was appointed and met five times.

When the Seventh General Synod met in 1969, in Boston, the report of the temporary Commission on Theological Education was presented. Its primary proposal was that there should be a Committee on Theological Education, consisting of 15 members, appointed by the Executive Council and nominated two by the Council for Church and Ministry, two by the Division of Higher Education, two by the Seminary Section of the Council for Higher Education, and nine members at large. The previous limitation of no seminary staff person and no staff person of an instrumentality of the church was also maintained. A significant move was that the responsibility for maintaining the national support level promised to certain seminaries was to be lodged in the Executive Council rather than the Board of Homeland Missions as of January 1, 1970. Further the budget of the Committee on Theological Education was also to be a line item in the budget of the Executive Council.[15]

It appeared to the seminaries that a major battle had been won. At last they appeared to have a specific and visible structure that would bring theological education into the mainstream of the denomination. The identification of the national support for seminaries was now a possibility in the budget of the Executive Council.

When the Committee on Theological Education reported to the Eighth General Synod, in Grand Rapids, two significant actions were taken. One was the recognition that not only were there thirteen seminaries "historically related" to the United Church of Christ, but also that of these there were seven schools that had a "particular relationship" with the denomination in terms of close historical ties, critical financial needs, and a major number of students for ministry from the denomination. The other action by the committee was the acceptance of a formula for support of the seminaries. It recognized that the goals of the previous synod had not been met and that the schools were hurting. So the committee proposed that there be a continuation of the support promised the previous E&R Schools but

[15] 69-GS-117.

also funding of special projects, especially in the communities of racial and/or economic transition. However in the budget suggested by the committee itself the figures for the three schools were less for 1971 than for 1970, and the ordering of the names of the schools shifts from giving priority to the three former E&R schools to a greater equalization among the seven closely related seminaries.

When the Committee on Theological Education reported to the Ninth General Synod in 1973, in St Louis, the language of its report represents a classic example of purported compromise which results in the direct opposite of what it intends. In Section 1 it states that "it recognizes a national responsibility for the support of theological education" and will provide funds from basic support in Our Church World Mission. In Section 3 it states it "recognizes a regional responsibility for the support of theological education" and recommends that funds for the support of the six, later seven, seminaries be the responsibility of the Conferences and local congregations. The consequences of such language might not have been great if the Committee on Theological Education had been able to continue and interpret its meaning.

However, at the same 9th General Synod, the Office for Church Life and Leadership (OCLL) was created and this body was designated as the inheritor of the functions of the Council for Church and Ministry, the Council for Lay Life and Work, the Committee for Theological Education, the Commission on Worship and the Theological Commission. In a single body, encompassing a range of responsibilities, the UCC had consolidated the task of development of lay and professional leadership in the church. It was therefore OCLL that was to interpret the meaning of the text left by the Committee for Theological Education. The decision of OCLL was that the support of the seminaries would not be primarily, if at all, a national responsibility! Furthermore it claimed that it had received no funds specifically earmarked for theological education, and that there should be no official or even ex officio representation from the seminaries on OCLL. It did finally designate $100,000 for special projects in Theological Education in the fiscal year 1975. So any national responsibility for the support of the institutions was undercut. In a strange twist of reasoning OCLL thought that the seminaries could offer increasingly special services at the same time the support of the institutional base was decreasing.

Since 1975 the United Church of Christ, at the national level, has had a tendency to make high sounding resolutions and statements about theological education and its significance for the church, but to do nothing substantive with regard to institutional support. What has finally happened is that the temporary pattern developed by CUE and first suggested by the administration of United has now become the normative pattern across the nation for UCC seminaries. In 1977 the 11th General Synod noted the four regional support programs, one for Lancaster from four Pennsylvania conferences, one for Bangor and Andover-Newton from six New England conferences, CUE-Midamerica from 16 conferences and Pacific School of Religion supported by the Western conferences. At the same time it continued to recommend that local congregations give two percent of their budgets for the basic support of seminaries.

Today the situation is not greatly different. Since 1985 an organization of Presidents of the closely-related seminaries has been linked to the Executive Council of the UCC. The seminaries are in a position not unlike that of 1983 when President Avery Post of the UCC said, "We have some owning and gathering to do at this point."[16] The lack of denominational support has forced the administrators of the seminaries into direct action. The seminaries have become dependent upon regional resources, community support and the good-will of individual congregations. When Huenemann resigned in 1970 it was in large part due to the exhaustion that was the consequence of this difficult financial situation, as well as the invitation to accept the position of Conference Minister for the Central Pacific Conference with headquarters in Portland, Oregon.

[16]Minutes of the Thirteenth General Synod of the United Church of Christ, 1981, p. 121

PART FOUR

TRIALS AND TRIUMPHS

CHAPTER 13

TRIALS AND TRIUMPHS

As the decade of the founding of the Seminary ended it was clear that the times were changing. They had already changed from the radicalization that had occurred in the 60's, stemming from the movements for racial equality and the student protests for peace and free speech. In May of 1970 at Kent State University in Ohio four students at a peace rally were shot by the National Guard. The peace movement was to change forever and the deep questioning of the government was to become a way of life in America. This was a profound change from the relatively optimistic days of May 1960 when the Basis of Union was signed for the formation of the Seminary. If "the book" of the Sixties was Harvey Cox's *The Secular City* the book of the Seventies was Charles Reich's *The Greening of America*. His thesis was that if the "Grandfather" of American society was the individualistic entrepreneur and the "Father" was the technological and corporate state, then the children were the present generation characterized by Consciousness Three. These were the bell-bottomed, beaded, latter-day flower children who sought a more innocent, peaceful and loving kingdom. In theological education there were also great changes marked by the deaths in 1971 of Reinhold Niebuhr, William F. Albright, Gerhard von Rad and Roland DeVaux.

It should not have been surprising that in 1970 Ruben H. Huenemann, the first President, announced his resignation from the Seminary. He had taken up the challenge of the formation of an ecumenical seminary and had committed his efforts to that end. He had worked long hours in committee meetings and board efforts to carry forth the vision of a Seminary in the upper Mid-west. Weekends he had forayed forth to speak in congregations large and small to instill the understanding of theological education in the Church and to raise funds to bring it to fruition.

Huenemann was to say to the Board of Trustees "It has been a strenuous and in many ways a rewarding decade. The newly developed school has experienced the favor of God. He provided tasks to keep us busy, He provided critics to keep us humble, He provided changes to keep us alert, He provided successes to keep us satisfied, He provided friends to keep us encouraged, and He provided financial supporters to keep us solvent...This seminary can be expected to move positively in the directions indicated because a decade of cautious experimentation has already occurred. The results need not be lost, for they will surely commend themselves to concerned church leaders in the future."[1]

With characteristic insight Huenemann realized that he had accomplished the task that had been set before him. The time had come to move on and let others lead it into the new decade. It was with great regret that his resignation was accepted. At the farewell dinner, held at the Calhoun Beach Manor in Minneapolis, a student, William Hunt wrote a poem in honor of the occasion which ended:

Changes mean
We never know what we have done.
Only what we have tried.
The universe of what we intended
Moves around our heads
Like the giant star-clouds
Of Magellan. The things we love
And make sacrifices for are
Stars inside the clouds,
Moving; dying; changing;
Exploding into new forms;
Holding still;
Long filaments of light
Over New Brighton
Late on the darkest nights.

---

[1]President Huenemann's final report to the Board of Trustees, September 17, 1970.

Huenemann accepted the call to become minister of the Oregon Conference of the United Church of Christ, which he served until his official retirement. Even in that retirement he continued to serve the church as interim minister in congregations across the nation and continues to live in Portland, OR. In his place an interim president was appointed, Dr. Richard Kozelka, former dean of the School of Business Administration of the University of Minnesota. An active layman in the United Church of Christ, he had played a vital role in the steps that led to the forming of the Seminary. He had also served as the first chairman of the Advisory Council of the Seminary. In his quiet and unassuming manner he held the school together in this first major transitional period. He provided for a time of catching one's breath and for looking forward to a new era.

Yet the life of the school went on. Lance Barker was appointed Assistant Professor of Ministry Studies, bringing additional help to the Ministry Studies Program as an integral part of the curriculum. Barker had come to the Faculty as an assistant to Prof. Victor Obenhaus while Nelson had been on sabbatical leave. His experience in the Detroit Industrial Mission, as part of his research for his doctoral dissertation, gave him a good basis for understanding the role of the church in the urban community.[2]

Another important appointment in 1970 was the result of the resignation of Chris Meadows, who had accepted a position at Vanderbilt Divinity School. The search for a professor of Psychology and the Christian Faith led to the call of Clyde J. Steckel.[3] Steckel was the Campus Minister for the United Ministries in Higher Education at the University of Minnesota. In that position since 1963 he had been involved in the life of Seminary in several ways. He had been on the Advisory Council of United

[2]Barker, a native of Nebraska had received his B.A. from the University of Wyoming and his B.D. from San Francisco Theological Seminary. His graduate work was at the Divinity School of the University of Chicago from which he received his M.A. and Ph.D. He was an ordained minister in the United Presbyterian Church, U.S.A.

[3]Steckel, a native of Anderson, IN, had studied for his B.A. at Butler University and his B.D. at Chicago Theological Seminary. His M.A. and Ph.D. were from the Divinity School of the University of Chicago. His service to the church was expressed through his experience as a parish minister, hospital chaplain and campus minister and assistant professor at Illinois College. He was an ordained minister in the United Church of Christ.

and had provided important leadership of that council. Also when the new curriculum had been instituted he had been the interim faculty member for the Psychology and the Christian Faith course. His administrative and counseling roles at United would prove to be highly important for the development of the school.

There were changes in the nomenclature of faculty positions, reflecting the changes that had taken place in the curriculum and personal changes in teaching emphasis. The By-laws of the Seminary were changed to have the Academic Dean become the Dean of the Seminary, and surely Gunnemann was The Dean, as all referred to him. A Director of Graduate Studies was also added to the administrative structure of the school, and Arthur Merrill was appointed the first Director, overseeing the Th.M. and M.A. Programs. Though the school had never practiced overt discrimination, for the first time a policy of non-discrimination on the basis of race, gender, national origin or religious affiliation was formulated and adopted. In the curriculum the substitution of an evaluation process alongside grades was instituted. This reflected the changes in the student perception that grades were competitive and did not truly evaluate their progress in the educational program.

Perhaps one of the most significant changes in the interim period was the start of the theological journal, *Theological Markings.* This was the brain-child of Dean Gunnemann and reflected his great concern to provide a forum wherein both the seminary and the church would engage in discussion of the theological issues of the day. Mission House Seminary had had its *Bulletin* and the three seminaries of the Evangelical and Reformed Church had had their *Theology and Life.* Since the formation of the United Church of Christ and United Seminary there had not been a forum to mark the discussion of the major issues confronting those institutions.

It was appropriate for *Theological Markings* to mark the beginning of the second decade of the Seminary. The first issue that appeared in the Spring of 1971 contained the lectures which celebrated the tenth anniversary of United. In the Fall of 1970 former faculty were invited to return and present those lectures. Thomas C. Campbell of Yale Divinity School,

35. Henry A. Gustafson, New Testament Theology, 1968-89

36. Lance R. Barker, Ministry Studies, 1970-

37. Clyde J. Steckel, Theology and Psychology, 1970-

Frederick Herzog of Duke University and Paul Hammer of Colgate Rochester Divinity School were the featured lecturers. In style the new journal was characteristic of the publications of the new school, with a generous use of wide margins, a clear and neat type style, and a carefully crafted cover. The character of the school in that anniversary year was also marked by the granting of two honorary doctorates. Here both the external concerns and internal nature of the Seminary were evident. On June 7, 1970, an honorary degree was conferred on Andrew J. Young, then executive vice-president of the Southern Christian Leadership Conference. Then Young was known as "one of Martin Luther King, Jr.'s young lieutenants" and was a minister of the United Church of Christ. He would later become prominent as Ambassador to the United Nations and mayor of Atlanta. The end of the anniversary year was marked by the granting of an honorary doctorate to Theophilus F. G. Hilgeman, the first faculty member to retire at United.

In the meantime the Board of Trustees had appointed a Search Committee to find a new President. The committee was chaired by Ralph Hoffmann of the Board of Trustees and included two students, Richard Gerber and Richard Seaman, and two faculty, James Nelson and Louis Gunnemann. From 35 potential candidates the committee received data on 20 persons and interviewed five finalists. On June 10, 1971, the second interview was held with Dayton D. Hultgren and the committee recommended him to the Board of Trustees as their candidate for the presidency of the Seminary.[4]

Hultgren was in some respects an unlikely candidate. The committee had hoped to attract a theological educator of some stature, but those candidates were not available. A Presbyterian minister, Hultgren had received his degree in educational psychology from the University of Minnesota, his thesis focusing on the continuing education needs of clergy. He had worked at the University of Minnesota and at the time of his election

[4]Hultgren, a native of North Dakota, had his education at Mayville State College, B.A. and the University of Dubuque, School of Theology, B.D. His M.A. and Ph.D. were from the University of Minnesota. He had been employed in the Counseling Center of the University of Minnesota and the Individual Learning Center of Macalester College. He had been a parish minister in Akley, IA and was ordained in the United Presbyterian Church, U.S.A.

had been the Director of the Individual Learning Center at Macalester College in St. Paul. He had not been familiar with United nor had he been related to it in his work. As often happens with a search committee a special chemistry between Hultgren and the committee developed. He was invited back for a second interview on June 10 and the conversation ranged long and wide. Hultgren expected to depart and be notified later but Hoffman told him the interview with the other candidate had been canceled.[5] By the end of the afternoon he was their candidate and United had its second President. On June 23 the Faculty was notified of the selection, expressions of gratitude were noted to the faculty members of the committee and the faculty asked for a retreat in the Fall with the new President to get acquainted.[6] The inauguration of the new President was held Sunday, October 31, 1971, at Hennepin Avenue Methodist Church in Minneapolis. The Rev. Kenneth B. Smith represented the United Church of Christ at the ceremony and brought greetings.

Though Hultgren's own formal relationship to theological education had been limited to his training at Dubuque Theological Seminary he brought skills in organization and management that became recognized throughout the Association of Theological Schools. As he took up the leadership of the Seminary he was faced with two major problems. One was the organization of the school that was facing a rapid increase in enrollment and in which the consensus style of governance was experiencing strain. The faculty was expressing concern for its involvement in the many issues of administration. The other concern was the financial condition of the school. With the growth of the school the financial resources were not only strained to their limit but the budget had gone into deficit financing, with internal borrowing at its limits. When Hultgren had asked for a budget before his second interview the committee had not been able to locate a formal budget

---

[5]Interview with Dayton D. Hultgren, May 9, 1991.

[6]Minutes of the Faculty Meeting, June 23, 1971.

38. Dayton D. Hultgren
President, 1971-82

39. Thomas C. Campbell
Academic Vice President, 1974-79

40. Gregory H. Ritter
Vice President for Development, 1975-85

for him to peruse. For Hultgren there were four criteria for the viability of the institution: organization, management, long range planning and operating funds. It was the issue of organization which Hultgren attacked first. By the end of his first year he presented to the Board of Trustees a proposal for the reorganization of the seminary. In this proposal the administration of the seminary was made more distinct from the academic program and processes. The rationalization and bureaucratization of the institution were begun as a necessary step in the right direction. Under the President was to be a Vice President for Academic Administration, a Vice President for Development and a Vice President for Financial Affairs. Under the vice presidents were directors with support staff to undergird the process. Though this step was a necessary and important direction for the developing institution it created some problems for the Seminary. This rationalization and bureaucratization of the school laid an organization alongside the original structure in which the decision making process was the primary prerogative of the Faculty. The Faculty was used to working in a collegial and consensual mode. Bureaucracies work by much different principles and norms. To this day these two patterns remain in tension, sometimes creative and sometimes destructive. The metaphor that Hultgren used to try to bridge these two patterns was that of "avuncular" leadership. For him the "uncle" was the one who could support and encourage the "adolescent" institution.

Louis Gunnemann was appointed acting Vice President for Academic Affairs at the Board of Trustees Meeting when the reorganization plan was adopted. However he indicated his unwillingness to be a candidate or serve as the Academic Vice President. In part this was due to his expectation to retire in 1974 and he felt that he should not be the first incumbent for such a short period. As a consequence a Search Committee was formed to locate a new Vice President for Academic Administration. Fortunately the search could be conducted not under pressure but with careful attention to the needs of the school in this new and changing period of its life.

On February 9, 1974, the Board of Trustees accepted the recommendation of the search committee and appointed Thomas C. Campbell as the new Academic Vice President and Professor of Theology and Culture. It was a warm homecoming to the person who had been so influential in the life of the school when the "new curriculum" had been adopted in 1965. Here was the leader of theological acumen and stature that the Seminary needed to carry forth its educational task and ecumenical vision. A sociologist by training he could understand and work with Hultgren and each was able to complement the other. Together they made an excellent team of executive leadership.

After teaching at Yale Divinity School Campbell's theological leadership had been recognized when he was called to the presidency of his alma mater, Chicago Theological Seminary. When he had left United in 1965 several on the faculty had speculated that someday Campbell might return in a leadership role. By a series of coincidences, or Providence, Campbell accepted this new position.

Hultgren tells the story from his own perspective. The search was not going as hoped. Several candidates had been pursued but the two top candidates had withdrawn from the process. The question had been raised if Campbell might be a real possibility but those who thought they knew felt that this was not likely. Hultgren had to go to a CUE meeting in Chicago. Over the weekend he had a dream and in that dream Campbell was not only a candidate but had accepted. He thought he was losing his mind and told no one of the dream. After the CUE meeting Hultgren approached Campbell and asked if he could have a brief conversation with him. In Campbell's office he said, "Tom, is there any chance you would consider exploring the idea of becoming vice president of United?" Campbell broke into tears. Hultgren quickly asked if he had offended him. He said, "No, but your timing couldn't be more timely. I can't even discuss it this minute. Could you give me a couple of days?" So Hultgren called Campbell back toward the end of the week and he said that now he would like to talk to Hultgren. They met at the airport in Chicago. The story emerged that the morning of Hultgren's initial question Campbell had met with the Chair of the Board of Trustees of Chicago Theological Seminary and told him that he didn't like what he was doing. He was a teacher and had great difficulty being a president. Campbell and Hultgren talked through the evening and again the next morning. That's when Hultgren understood the timing and the reason

Campbell responded so emotionally when the issue was mentioned. As a consequence Campbell accepted the call and the formal process followed.[7] United was to be enriched beyond its expectations by Campbell's presence.

To fill the position of Vice President for Development the Seminary looked to the Development Office of St. Louis University that had produced many top flight leaders in the field. From that office it chose Richard Lohr as the first Vice President of Development at United. There had been previous development persons working for the Seminary but they had not been effective. At the time Hultgren arrived the incumbent was Richard Turner, a lay Christian Brother, whom Huenemann had hired. Turner was no longer effective and finally Hultgren terminated his employment. With Lohr in place the development office was finally organized and the process of undergirding the financial resources of the school was underway. A Vice President for Financial Affairs would not be appointed during Hultgren's tenure.

No doubt the most important contribution of Hultgren to the Seminary was the reorganization of the Board of Trustees. In its early years the Board was dominated by clergy with a sprinkling of significant lay leaders. Among those lay leaders one needs to mention the important contributions of Alvin R. Wolff, Ludwig Loos and Florence Partridge among others. In the beginning the character of the Board was important for it helped to maintain those historic ties with the various constituencies in the churches. However as the Seventies evolved the Board was needed to become more active in the educational process and contribute to the raising of funds for the seminary.

In the reorganization of the Seminary the first thing Hultgren did was to have the board meet three or four times a year, rather than annually. In that process the Board was composed of four significant committees overseeing the various activities of the school. When Ralph Hoffmann finished his service on the Board in 1970 he was succeeded by Carl Hansen, Conference Minister of the Minnesota Conference of the United Church of Christ, as Chair of the Board of Trustees. Hansen had been on the original

[7] Interview with Dayton D. Hultgren in the office of ALM, 9 May 1991.

Board and returned for a final term of service. Hansen was soon to retire and in his place Forrest L. Richeson, pastor of First Christian Church in Minneapolis, became Chair of the Board.

An important person to the Seminary during Hultgren's tenure was William Driscoll, a business person of the Twin Cities area. In more ways than most realize he was instrumental in helping the Seminary achieve fiscal stability and in having the Trustees become more involved in the life of the school. A quiet and unassuming person he had been on the fringes of the seminary for several years. After Hultgren arrived he made an effort to become acquainted with Driscoll. Their first meeting was over bean soup in the dining area of the Seminary. Then Hultgren outlined what he knew of the fiscal and academic situation of the Seminary and what concerned him about the situation. Driscoll responded that if that was what the Seminary was about he would like to be a part of it. He had previously been asked to serve on the Board but had not wanted to be part of a "knife and fork club" which was how he regarded annual board meetings.

During his first year on the Board Driscoll was elected Treasurer. At his second or third meeting after he gave his treasurer's report, Bill put the paper aside, stood there a while and said, "When I came in here I didn't know I was going to say this. I am embarrassed as a trustee, because none of us, including me, thinks enough of the institution to put our own money in." Upon saying this he challenged the others. "If between now and the end of the year, June 30, all of the rest of you trustees will together give $5000 to the operating budget, I will match it and give $5000. If all of you can raise and commit $10,000, I'll give $10,000. In fact, if all of you together can give $25,000, I'll match it with $25,000 and I'll be the happiest $25,000 giver this place has seen." Then he sat down. The silence was profound. Finally the Chair acknowledged the challenge but there was no discussion. They didn't raise the $25,000 but the final total was about $16,000. For the first time the Trustees had been challenged to give, and that set a precedent that carried through the years and made the gifts of the Trustees important to the Seminary. That was the character of Bill Driscoll, quiet, unassuming but with a deep conviction and a growing commitment to the Seminary. In 1975 he was elected Chair of the Board and served well in that capacity.

While the reorganization of the Seminary progressed the financial condition of the school worsened. Each year brought larger and larger deficits. For a school with an endowment not larger than $500,000 this was a serious challenge. One direction in which the Development Office moved was to attempt to raise money from key individuals, firms and corporations, foundations and through deferred giving. The latter takes many years of cultivation and with no one working regularly in the field the prospects are difficult to project. With the former groups the major issue tended to be that giving to a specifically religious body was not part of their ethos or norms. Even when the school in question was an ecumenical seminary, serving at least nineteen different denominations, firms and foundations were reluctant to support a theological school. At one Board of Trustees meeting Lohr reported that 30 foundations had been approached for gifts but with no success.[8] Yet the annual budgets of the Seminary continued to include line items for income from firms and foundations.

One major factor in the financial distress of the school was the loss of support from the national bodies of the United Church of Christ. By the time Hultgren arrived the financial commitment of the Church to the seminary had reached its conclusion. The reorganization of the national instrumentalities and the formation of the Office of Church Life and Leadership changed the patterns of giving. By 1975 OCLL was giving only program grants and not institutional support. Yet already in 1972 Hultgren presented a paper outlining the issues that pertained to the support of the seminaries by the United Church of Christ.[9] The Church was reducing institutional support but asking for increased services. His plea was for a joint planning for the future of that relationship, a plea that was not heard, or if heard, not acted upon. He concluded by stating that, "The need is for churchmen of will, vision and commitment beyond self-interest who will give leadership at this time in a manner which exemplifies responsible Christian stewardship and statesmanship." Hultgren had sought and received dual

[8]Minutes of the Board of Trustees Meeting, Oct. 20, 1973.

[9]Dayton D. Hultgren, *Observations on the Present Status of the United Church of Christ and its Seminaries*, May 30, 1972. Mimeographed paper.

standing in both the Presbyterian Church and the United Church of Christ. He sought vigorously to be a voice for theological education in the councils of the Church. He exercised important leadership through a difficult time in the relationship of the seminaries to the denomination. One important initiative was the formalization of the CUE (Chicago, United, Eden) regional support program and the hiring of a director who would make the needs of the seminaries visible.

In the short run alternatives to reverse the cash flow problems had to be sought. The first action taken in that respect was the move to sell the wooded area on the north side of the campus. There were thirty acres of oak woods that had been saved with the hopes that a retreat center could be built in that area. However with the change of times the mood of the church was not to retreat but to be engaged in the great social issues of the times. It was felt one should be out on the streets demonstrating and protesting the forms of racism, sexism and poverty that were engulfing the society. The woods had also become a liability to the Seminary. As an open and unprotected area they had become the haunt of youths in the neighborhood and the FBI suspected that drugs were being bought and sold in the shade of the old oak trees. Periodic fires brought out the local fire department and incurred charges against the seminary for such protection. So it was with little regret on the part of the school that a developer was sought and by 1974 the woods had been sold for $213,750, more than the original cost of the land for the total campus. Today gracious homes are to be found on what was once the hilly and wooded property of the school.

With the proceeds of the sale the intra-fund indebtedness was reduced, a bank loan was retired and a major campaign fund drive was established. The latter entered into the lore of the school with its campaign slogan, Eight by Eighty! The goal was to raise eight million dollars by 1980. Lohr, the Development officer, created a slide presentation that told "THE UTS STORY" and indicated the needs of the school and the hopes for its future. As was the case with other previous major fund drives this one also failed to reach its goal. Its ambitions were beyond the reach of the institution.

A later generation of students found the slide presentation and used it as a basis for a skit on the school. One of their revisions of the story was that its goal was to build a swimming pool for the students, whose dimensions would be eight by eighty!

However the financial stability of the school could not wait for the completion of a capital funds campaign. As an interim measure the Board of Trustees authorized the formation of a Board of Consultants.[10] Its task was to raise $600,000 as an emergency fund that would undergird the budget until 1980 when the campaign was scheduled to end. The leadership of the Board of Consultants was accepted by Harry Piper, President of Piper, Jaffrey and Hopwood in Minneapolis. Piper was a committed lay person and member of the Wayzata Community Church (UCC) and a graduate of United with a Master of Arts in Religious Studies. He had entered the program to further his interest in the Christian faith and the ethical issues of the day. His ecumenical interests were also expressed as chair of the Board of Directors of the Ecumenical Institute at St. John's University, Collegeville, MN, of which Gunnemann was also a member.

Apart from his leadership in the business community of the Twin Cities Piper was famous for a bizarre incident in his personal life. His wife Virginia was one day abducted from their home in Deephaven and held for ransom by two men who demanded a million dollars to release her. On his own personal signature he was able to obtain the money from the bank and he personally delivered the money to the assigned location. Virginia was later found handcuffed to a tree in northern Minnesota, shaken but unharmed by the experience. Though one man was arrested and tried for the kidnapping the money was never found. Both Piper and his wife later died of cancer and the bulk of his estate went to found the Virginia Piper Cancer Institute at Abbott Northwestern Hospital in Minneapolis. The emergency fund, however, was a success and the money raised by Piper carried the institution through some lean times.

---

[10]Minutes of the Board of Trustees Meeting, February 8, 1975.

41. Gayle Graham Yates,
Director of M.A.R.S. Program, 1974-76

42. Patricia Wilson Kastner,
Historical Theology, 1975-82

43. Mary Farrell Bednarowski,
American Studies, 1976-

44. Karen Smith Sellers,
Ministry Studies, 1977-88

CHAPTER 14

WOMEN AT UNITED SEMINARY

When United Seminary began its life in the Twin Cities the role of women in the school was rather typical for its time. Women were primarily understood as spouses of students and faculty. The initial organization for student wives was called "Seminettes" and was a carry over from Mission House days. The pattern was for the President's wife to offer evenings in her home on a regular basis to help the women understand their roles in the parsonage. This included even learning how to pour tea and the proper attire for various church occasions. However, from the beginning there were women in the student body, though few and usually not degree candidates.

Within a year the women's organization had changed its name to UTS Women and was under the guidance of Johanna Gunnemann and other faculty wives. The program was enlarged to include cultural events and participation in the larger community. In addition the Faculty was asked to offer evening courses for student wives that would help them understand the changes through which their husbands were going. Also the Faculty Wives met for social events and to assist in the hospitality of the Seminary. This typical pattern reflected the chauvinism and sexism of its times, coming out of the post World War II ethos of American life.

Even the academic life of the school was oriented to the male student, coming out of college and entering into pastoral ministry. Strobel had argued for offering a M.A. degree in Christian Education but the proposal had not been accepted by the faculty nor the administration. In other seminaries such a program offered women the opportunity to get into theological education and the ministry of the church. Eventually the Seminary was to offer a certification program in Christian Education, a program that offered one course a term for three years. This attracted some women from the area into the program of the school. The career of one woman offers insight into the emerging place of women in the development of United. Donna Wolff entered first into the certification program, then when the M.A.R.S. Degree was offered she entered and completed that program. Following that achievement, she finally entered the M.Div. Program and completed that degree.

It was not until the Fall of 1969 that the first woman was admitted to the B.D. (now M.Div.) program as a regular full time candidate for the degree. Marilyn K. Creel was to become representative of the women who came to seminary in the Seventies. She was a second career woman, having graduated from Syracuse University and then working first in the presidential campaign of Hubert Humphrey and then in the Oral History Project of the University of South Dakota at Brookings. Hers was a lonely path as the only woman in the professional degree program. She was not allowed to live on campus at first, that privilege being reserved for male single students or married students without children. Besides the administration would not let a single woman live in the apartments alone! She had to find housing off-campus until her senior year when finally she was permitted an apartment on campus. Her experience in the church and the society did not count in the seminary's understanding of what would be appropriate field ministry settings. The matter of field ministry was further complicated by her own desire to go into theological education as a career rather than the pastoral ministry.

Creel was soon joined by other women in the professional degree program and the issues of the Seventies became the issues of the Seminary. In response to an IRS inquiry the Seminary finally formulated a policy of non-discrimination, stating: "Discrimination with regard to race or sex has never been and is not now practiced."[1] However the statement of non-

[1]Faculty Minutes, February 10, 1971.

discrimination did not necessarily mean that the institution was not discriminating. Shortly after the adoption of that policy the Moderator of the Faculty, James Nelson, had to remind his colleagues that comments from several women had been received which indicated that there were times when male chauvinism appears in class and discussions.[2]

Yet the faculty was both astounded and confounded when within the month the three women in the B.D. Program confronted them with three demands which specifically affected women students.[3] First they asked for an evaluation of the priorities of the school in respect to housing, field work and faculty load. Also they asked for clarity and specificity in policy and procedures. And finally they asked for a clear delineation of specific alternatives to policies and procedures. The Faculty was stunned and had difficulty comprehending the issues. In typical fashion they asked the Self-Study Committee to conduct a study of the institution concerning discrimination, relative to both formal and informal institutional patterns. They also asked the Dean of the Seminary to analyze the material submitted by that committee and delegate the issues to the appropriate offices and committees. The dispatch with which the matter was handled no doubt was due to the fact that Martha Ann Baumer, one of the petitioners, was a cousin of the Dean and not known for her radical stance. She had wanted to enter seminary while it was still at Mission House but had been discouraged due to the prevailing attitudes in the church at that time. After further graduate work and a successful career as a high school English teacher she had finally entered United to pursue what had been a life long dream. Within a month the Dean reported to the faculty that issues regarding housing and field education had been analyzed and that actions were being taken to respond to the petition.

For the early women at United the path was not easy and the hurdles were often difficult. One way in which they were able to cope was the support they received from other women and from faculty wives. One

---

[2]Faculty Minutes, April 14, 1971.

[3]Faculty Minutes, May 12, 1971. The three women were Martha Ann Baumer, Marilyn K. Creel and Mary Anne Murray.

support group was formed and lasted several years with the assistance of Jean Merrill and Eleanor Steckel, faculty wives. To this group also came a few women who were enrolled at Luther Northwestern Seminary and found little support at their own seminary.

The Self-Study Committee presented a seven page, single spaced report on its discrimination study in April 1972.[4] It reported its findings of both male sexism and racial discrimination and made recommendations to the Faculty to address the issues. The issues were deep and painful, however, and there were two minority reports addressed to the Faculty at the same time. One came from a group of women whose basic concern was that the definitions of community extant in the seminary were in conflict with the practice of discrimination that was reflected in such matters as how faculty and male students addressed women, and the lack of role models for women on the faculty. The issue was one of alienation of the women from the community. A second addendum to the "official" report was a petition from the women students that a woman theologian be appointed to the faculty to replace Robert Bryant while he went on sabbatical leave in 1973-74.

When the Faculty met on May 10, 1972, the report of the Self Study Committee was received, with the provision that the issues be discussed, and the recommendations adopted and disseminated. The statement of the concerned women was appended to the official report, and the petition was referred to the Faculty Administration Committee with the request that they accept it and act affirmatively upon it. The specific reference to Robert Bryant and his sabbatical leave was deleted by the Faculty in its recommendation.

On June 4, 1972, the first woman M.Div. student was graduated from United Theological Seminary. To mark that auspicious moment the Faculty prepared a resolution that was read in honor of Marilyn K. Creel as that graduate. At the same Commencement two women received the M.A.R.S. Degree, Sue Ecker and Donna Wolff. Another first was the breaking of the tradition that the Faculty Wives serve the Graduates Reception. In this year,

---

[4]Report on the Discrimination Study, Self Study Committee, April 1972. Committee members were Clyde J. Steckel, Chair, James Nelson, Wilson Yates, Bill Kasemann, Richard Gerber.

and for many years following, the Faculty took responsibility for the preparation, serving and clean-up of that event, following the final Communion Service of the academic year.

It is symbolic of the times that it was also that summer, July 1972, when the first issue of *MS* magazine was published and gave expression to the growing feminist movement in the United States. The feminist movement had received its initial impetus and expression in the works of Betty Freidan (*The Feminine Mystique*) and Simone Beauvoir (*The Second Sex*). However the participation of women in the racial revolution of the Sixties had made them aware of ways in which their own situation paralleled that of the black experience. Though the United movement reflected that growing awareness of women as the Seventies began it never reached a truly revolutionary level.

In the academic program one of the first responses to the women's concerns for courses related to women's experiences and teachers who were women was the offering of a course in the Spring Term, 1973 on "Women and the Church" by Gayle Graham Yates who was pursuing a doctoral degree at the University of Minnesota in American Studies.[5] Yates was also selected as the Commencement Speaker for the ceremonies in June of 1973.

The issue of appointing a regular faculty member who was a woman continued to be raised. It became possible to make such an interim appointment in the Fall of 1973 with the coming of Patricia Wilson as the replacement for Robert Bryant who was on sabbatical leave. A native of Texas, Wilson had been raised a Roman Catholic and had entered the Sisters of St. Mary of Namur following graduation from high school. She left the order in a desire to find another way in which to fulfill her professional and personal goals. She completed her B.A. and M.A. at the University of Dallas and then received a scholarship and teaching assistantship at the University of Iowa to pursue a doctoral program. While in Iowa she was attracted to the First Congregational Church in Iowa City and became a member of that congregation. Later she sought and received ordination in the United

---

[5]Her dissertation was published as *What Do Women Want?*, Cambridge, MA: Harvard University Press, 1975.

Church of Christ and served as a parish minister in the Welsh Congregational Church. She received her doctoral degree in 1973 for her dissertation on "Jonathan Edward's Theology of Grace."

The response of the faculty, students and administration to Pat Wilson was extremely positive. Her full-time presence on the faculty was an experience that the community needed and found to be very important in terms of the dynamics of the increasing enrollment of women. By March of the year 1973-74 Nelson had written a memo to the Faculty Administration Committee raising the possibility of retaining Wilson. By April the Faculty had voted to recommend to the Board of Trustees that she be appointed to the Faculty by the Fall of 1975. The only catch was that there were no funds for the position. Fortunately Wilson gave the school time by marrying Ronald Kastner and moving to Iceland. Ron Kastner had a grant to research Icelandic Byzantine literature in preparation for his doctoral dissertation.

Gunnemann, who was still Dean, pointed out the urgency of the Faculty's request to the Board of Trustees. Requests for money were made to several sources including the Minnesota Conference (UCC) Task Force on Women in the Church. It was hoped that some money might be forthcoming as five of the nine members were associated with United, including the Chair, Karen Smith Sellers.

However it was St. Paul's United Church of Christ in Wheatland, Iowa, that came to the rescue. Their pastor, Harold Koenig, a graduate of Mission House and a friend of Wilson Kastner, helped the consistory come to the decision to pledge $2,400 per year toward the new faculty position. As Campbell, who in the meantime had replaced Gunnemann in the renamed position of Academic Vice President, said, "We cannot continue to advocate recruitment of women to study at the Seminary without ourselves doing all in our power to symbolize the full place of women in the teaching faculty."

With the pledge of the Wheatland church and the opening of the half-time position as Director of the D.Min. Program for the Consortium it became possible to make the appointment of Patricia Wilson Kastner to the Faculty as Assistant Professor of Historical and Constructive Theology. As the first woman faculty member on regular appointment she was to become a symbol for the school and for the women students who were to come in increasing numbers. By 1973-74 30% of the student body were women, a figure higher than that of any other A.T.S. school then, and the figure would rapidly grow to 50% by 1976.

With the arrival of ever more women students several issues began to emerge which would not be easily solved nor find unanimous agreement. Feminism itself would take a variety of expressions and move in different directions as the years passed. One major issue was the place of women in the Church. As an ecumenical seminary United was caught in the midst of a variety of understandings within the various denominations. Its own denomination had a long tradition of ordaining women, though the numbers in the past had been few and far between. Thus the Seminary had no problem with admitting and training women for the ministry of the church.

The issue of the placement of women in field settings and upon graduation remained an issue. As ministry studies in field settings was an integral part of the curricular structure the policy of non-discrimination for placement was adopted without question.[6] When churches indicated that they would not accept women in field placements they were notified that the Seminary could not use them as a location for field ministry. This stance was taken with the realization that some settings previously used were no longer available and that financial support might be withdrawn from the school.

The placement of graduates was a much more intractable issue though most of the major denominations were moving toward the ordination of women. When the issue arose before the General Convention of the Episcopal Church in 1973 the Faculty sent a petition and resolution to Presiding Bishop Hines supporting the ordination of women in the Episcopal Church.[7] No response was heard from the Bishop and the General Convention voted against the ordination of women. However the Seminary did attract Episcopal women who studied for the ministry in the hopes that the situation would change by the time of their graduation. Even a few Roman Catholic women came to study for the M.Div. in the expectation that

[6]The policy was adopted formally on Nov. 13, 1974 and reaffirmed at a Faculty Meeting on Jan. 12, 1976.

[7]Faculty Minutes, Sept. 26, 1973.

someday that church would change its stance. The policy of the Seminary was that it would not supply any names for placement of graduates to those churches that made sexist requests.[8]

Sexism within the Seminary, however, was not easily resolved. In the minutes of the Faculty the issue was raised repeatedly.[9] The primary focus of that discussion was the question of sexist language. Language is the form in which the human gives expression to the understanding of reality and shapes the perceptions of that reality. The Faculty had little difficulty in stating its position on the use of language concerning the human. Such usage would need to be inclusive and sensitive to the issues that had been raised by the feminist movement. When it came to the language about God the issue became much more complex. In the end the Faculty encouraged inclusive language in this realm of discourse but did not mandate it. This issue continues to be debated and becomes evident when new members to the community come from contexts in which there is little sensitivity to the problems of inclusive language. Though adjunct faculty and visiting preachers are apprised of the issue the mere fact of their being notified does not always bring compliance with the seminary's norms.

Initially the increase of women students also had its impact on the question of housing. Single women were finally permitted to live in the student residence building. And as more women commuted to United a commuter apartment was eventually set aside for their use.

As was true on other campuses a Women's Caucus emerged to give voice to the concerns of many of United's women. One demand was to have women's concerns expressed in the search for new faculty. Another was to have a space in which women could be apart and offer support for each other. Out of this concern arose the development of a UTS Women's Resource Center. In April 1977 the Antoinette Brown Womenspace and Resource Center was dedicated. In one of the initial office spaces in the classroom wing the Center provided a private space for women, and

[8]Faculty Minutes, Nov. 13, 1974.

[9]Nov. 13, 1974 and May 9, 1979 Faculty Minutes have policy statements on Language.

resources for women were collected. This space served the women until 1986 when it was relocated to the area of the boiler room as the need for it diminished. Finally as women came to their own rightful position in the school the space was eliminated all together.

The impact of women on the Seminary was also reflected in the program and Faculty. From the time of the Spring Term of 1973 when Gayle Graham Yates offered a course on "Women in the Church" various courses were available that focused on women and issues of particular concern to them. One such course was entitled "Contemporary Feminist Ethics and Spirituality." This course raised the question of whether a class at the Seminary could be closed, in this case for women only. It reflected the change in American feminism which Alice Echols identified as the shift from radical feminism to "cultural feminism" that was a celebration of "femaleness" in its uniqueness.[10] The Faculty Senate as a consequence developed a policy on "closed classes" that permitted them upon the recommendation of the Educational Policy and Evaluation Committee and the approval of the Faculty Senate.

Another issue that came out of courses that included attention to feminist questions was the use of public spaces. In a course on Ethics a student had created as a project a large spider web, inspired by the writings of Mary Daly. The web was hung in the Library court and appeared one day without permission or explanation. When the web was removed by the maintenance staff the issue of freedom of expression was raised by the students. The brief flurry of consternation by the administration led to the development of policy statements as to the conditions under which such exhibitions might be displayed.[11]

One of the areas in which the Seminary was not able to respond to the concerns of the women students was the presence of women faculty. The presence of Patricia Wilson Kastner was a signal achievement but was also regarded as tokenism. Gayle Graham Yates was the Director of the

---

[10]Alice Echols, *Daring to be Bad: Radical Feminism in America 1967-1975*, Minneapolis, MN: University of Minnesota Press, 1990.

[11]Faculty Senate Minutes, April 9, 1980.

M.A.R.S. Program but that was on a part-time and adjunct basis. As most of the faculty were in the mid-point of their careers there was very little transition on the faculty. In 1976 when Gayle Graham Yates accepted the call to the faculty at the University of Minnesota the search was made for a new director of the M.A.R.S. Program. The search led to the coming of Mary Farrell Bednarowski.[12] In her appointment not only was the women's concern addressed but also there was the addition of a lay Roman Catholic to the Faculty. The bounds of mainline Protestantism had been broken. Bednarowski was initially appointed as an Adjunct Professor and in 1978 was made a part of the permanent Faculty as Assistant Professor of Religious Studies, though on a part-time basis. Her expertise was in American Studies with special attention to those "marginal" religious groups that brought a special critique to the major religious bodies in America.

Another important appointment in these years was that of Karen Smith Sellers. Sellers had been a M.Div. graduate from United and had also done graduate work in educational counseling.[13] Her initial appointment was an administrative action by the Academic Vice-President Thomas Campbell, designating her as Instructor in Ministry Studies and Director of Student Services in 1977. So in three years three women had been added to the faculty. All would play important roles in the life of the school in the years to come.

---

[12]Bednarowski, a native of Green Bay, Wisconsin, received her B.A. from Marquette University, her M.A. from Duquesne University and her Ph.D. from the University of Minnesota.

[13]Sellers, a native of Kutztown, Pennsylvania, had received her B.A. from Dickinson College and her M.S. from the University of Southern California.

45. Readiness for Ministry, Fall Retreat, 1974

46. Human Sexuality Course

47. White Racism Course, the Tillmans

48. Minnesota Orchestra on campus, Summer 1976

CHAPTER 15

STUDENTS AND PROGRAMS

As the Seventies progressed the changes in the student body also brought changes in the structures and programs of the school. Not only were women present in increasing numbers but the character of the students was changing. They reflected their society that was known as the "me generation." No longer was a commitment to the church and its mission a primary motivating factor for many students to come to seminary. Rather more and more students of the Seventies were concerned for their own spiritual development and came to seminary to find themselves and to answer those profound questions that the conditions of their world raised. In many ways United was a good place for them for the curriculum was predicated on the premise that teaching needed to begin with the questions the student initially brought to the seminary experience. No longer could one assume that they had been raised in the church, were answering a call to ministry and had been trained in a liberal arts undergraduate program. Increasingly the "typical" student was older, a second-career person, and had gone to a state sponsored school for the Bachelor's degree.

As the decade began one of the major questions had been the meaning and character of the Viet Nam War. Associated with that was the question whether the students were in Seminary to evade the draft that would have taken them to Viet Nam. That there was some truth to this question was reflected in the fact that after the draft was discontinued in 1974 the graduating class of 1975 at United had only eight persons who received the M.Div. Degree. It was also the case that the following year began to show the increase of women in the student body.

It was often the students who raised the issues that caused changes in the procedures and programs of the Seminary. One area of concern was participation by students in the governance of the institution. Students had often been on committees that the Faculty established. Yet their voice was seldom heard in Faculty meetings.

With Hultgren's proposals for the reorganization of the Seminary was included the concept of a Faculty Senate in which elected students would participate in the governance of the academic program. By the Fall of 1972 this reorganization was adopted by the Board of Trustees and supported by the Faculty.[1] As a consequence a dual structure developed: a Faculty Senate to deal with the official academic concerns and a Faculty that would deal with those matters exclusively pertaining to Faculty. All the committees, except the Faculty Administration Committee would have student representation. Faculty Senate meetings were to be open unless they dealt with student issues in which the student had the right to ask for a closed session. The Faculty Senate would meet once a month, and the Faculty would meet as necessary for business and once a month for discussion of theological and other issues.

The changing student body also brought other changes to the procedures and programs of the school. As the decade began the students expressed strong feelings about the traditional practices of grading by letters. An initial attempt to mitigate the seeming arbitrariness of grades was made by providing written evaluations of each student's performance along with the grades. The introduction of an optional Pass-No Credit system also permitted the students to choose a less competitive route to evaluation. The Faculty, however, had ongoing concerns about the written evaluations. Not only did they take more time and effort but the forms for evaluation were rarely deemed satisfactory and the actions of the Faculty called repeatedly for revision of the forms.

---

[1]Faculty Meeting Minutes, May 31, 1972.

In 1971 United agreed with the A.T.S. proposal that the initial professional degree for ministry become the Master of Divinity (M.Div.) rather than the Bachelor of Divinity (B.D.). This change reflected the increasing professionalization of preparation for ministry as well as student concern that one received a Bachelor Degree for three years of graduate work. In one area United maintained its concern for excellence in ministry by not following the more common practice of offering its previous graduates the new degree for a diploma fee. Rather it offered a summer program for its graduates in which they could up-date their skills and knowledge and on that basis receive the M.Div.

The curriculum also received a further change as the school calendar was changed from a three term, or quarter, system to a 4-1-4-1 pattern. This organization used two long terms of four months and two short terms of one month each, in the Winter and the Summer. Such a pattern was common among undergraduate schools and was also adopted by St. Paul Seminary.

Another area of change was the introduction into the curricular pattern of personal and professional evaluation. This evaluation took two forms at United. One dimension was psychological and vocational testing that was offered though the North Central Career Development Center. Three units of evaluation were required of each M.Div. student during the three year program of studies. This testing offered the students the opportunity to examine their place in the theological institution and in relation to the denominational structure in which they expected to serve. Often this process helped students to discern personal issues that they could pursue during their time in seminary. This was particularly crucial in the light of the many pastors who had dropped out of the ministry in the late sixties and the early seventies as well as the general ethos of the times that was highly distrustful of the "establishment."

Personal and professional evaluation was also affected by the confluence of two factors in education. In secular educational circles the Seventies were marked by the growth of concern for Performance Education or Competency Based Education. With the decline in traditional educational skills and the increasing diversity among students, ways were being sought to enhance the educational process. To bring accountability to education was one of the major goals of competency education, a goal derived from the business world. In the academic year 1974-75 Clyde Steckel and Don White received Lilly faculty grants from the A.T.S. to investigate and use the concept of competency education in a theological school. They reported back to their colleagues the fruits of their study and were granted another year of support from A.T.S.

The other factor that came out of similar concerns was the development of the Readiness for Ministry project that had been organized by Dr. Milo Brekke of the Search Institute, Inc., and others. Based on a survey of lay, clergy and executives in various denominations a set of criteria was developed which reflected those characteristics that were regarded as desirable in the ministry of the church. Each denomination would emphasize different characteristics but all shared a common set of issues. This project was also supported by the A.T.S. Thomas Campbell, Academic Vice President, was an enthusiastic supporter of this project and enlisted United in the early testing and use of this instrument. The Fall Student-Faculty Retreat of 1975 was focused on the taking of the Readiness for Ministry survey by all the students and faculty. This retreat was held at Camp Icagawhan in Wisconsin, a YMCA camp that had held fond memories for Campbell. The site became known in United's lore not only as the site of the introduction of Readiness for Ministry but as a cold, wet rainy retreat that was not fondly remembered.

Competency education and Readiness for Ministry were not easily nor quickly favored by the Faculty. Several workshops and consultations were held, including one with Neely McCarter, then Dean of Union Seminary in Richmond where competency and readiness had been incorporated into their curriculum. By 1978 a list of competencies had been developed by the Faculty and was used as the basis for evaluation in courses. However the process was never fully integrated into the program though the categories are still used at a minimal level. The cumbersome character of the process and the detail of the categories no doubt contributed to that result.

Many students were attracted to United by its emphasis upon and concern for the dialogue between Church and Society. The Harrison report of 1965 noted that United was distinct among United Church Seminaries for its many offerings in this area of the curriculum. And it has been a dimension of the school that has continued to mark its existence.

Wilson Yates, Professor of Church and Community, was instrumental in raising the consciousness of students and faculty to the problems of white racism. Out of his experience as a Southerner from Missouri and participant in the Civil Rights Movement in the 60's he introduced a Racism Seminar to the curriculum. He had been the first white student jailed in the Nashville sit-ins in 1960.[2] The Twin Cities, however, was not the South. Only 10% of the population was black, and manifestations of racism were often subtle. The riots and rampages of the 60's had not torn apart the community. Yet the issue of racism needed to be faced by the white community. In the Fall of 1971 Yates introduced a White Racism Workshop into the first year program, incorporating it into the Christianity and Culture course. In these workshops there was an intensive program of raising the awareness of the students to white racism. To achieve this goal he used the program developed by James Tillman and the Tillmans were active participants in the program.

By 1974 Yates was convinced that this awareness of white racism needed to be made available on a wider basis. On December 11 of that year he presented a funding proposal to the Bertha and Archie Walker Foundation of Minneapolis. The Walkers were members of the Hennepin Avenue Methodist Church and shared the concern for racism in the church. With that funding Yates was able to develop resources for a Church and Race Program. Not only were bibliographical resources identified but a kit was produced for use in groups and congregations to raise their awareness of the issues of white racism. Two students, Ann Brudevold and Jenny Dawson, were his assistants in this significant project and contributed to the development of the materials.

Two other programs were introduced into the curriculum of the Seminary in the Seventies. Initially James Nelson, Professor of Christian Ethics, taught a course in the Fall of 1971 on Medical Ethics and Ministry.

---

[2]Gayle Graham Yates, *Mississippi Mind: A Personal Cultural History of an American State*, Knoxville: University of Tennessee Press, 1990, p. 74.

He soon realized that a dialogue with the Medical School of the University of Minnesota would enrich not only the seminary students but also the medical students. At that time the University Medical School was not eager for such a course. Nelson was able to enlist the support of Dr. James Maddock and in January 1973 co-taught a course with him in which both seminary and medical students participated. In the Spring of 1975 the course was moved to Hennepin County General Hospital (later Hennepin County Medical Center) where Dr. Ronald E. Cranford of the University Medical School co-taught the course. With the help of Cranford the course has since been regularly offered. Cranford has become a noted authority on death with dignity and has been involved in several highly publicized court cases in this area of medical ethics.[3] In the early years hospital Chaplains Lloyd Beebe and James Anderson were also involved in the course.

Nelson was also instrumental in the offering of courses on Human Sexuality at United. The first such course, Ethics and Human Sexuality, was offered in the Spring of 1971 and was jointly taught with Yates. The following year the course was changed to Ethics and Human Sexuality: The Family, and Steckel joined Nelson and Yates in teaching the course. A significant change in the course would occur when the University of Minnesota Medical School invited United to participate in a two day intensive seminar that would involve medical school and seminary students. This seminar was predicated on the concern that the students were either not aware of or were uncomfortable with their own sexuality and therefore had difficulty dealing with their patients' sexuality. The seminar had as its goals the desensitization of the students concerning sexuality and used a battery of films depicting a wide range of sexual behaviors to accomplish this task, and the clarification of values for the participants. The Faculty approved the invitation on the basis that the Seminary would provide a context for the discussion of the ethical and theological issues.

The consequence of these actions was that there developed an annual course on Human Sexuality, offered in the Winter Term, which included not

[3]Cranford was also personally helpful to members of the Faculty as they faced terminal illnesses of parents and spouses.

only the intensive two day seminar but also a full course in which the issues of human sexuality could be examined and placed in a theological context. In an era when the norms and practices of sexuality were being questioned in society this was a critical resource in the training of ministers. The Division of Higher Education of the United Church of Christ recognized it as a unique program in the country and funded the program with a grant of $2000. By 1974 the program was joined by Northwestern Seminary and then Luther Seminary, and after their merger Luther Northwestern continued in the program. The American Lutheran Church (later the Evangelical Lutheran Church of America) also was a sponsor of the program and additional funding was received from the Lutheran Brotherhood. There were those in the Lutheran Church who questioned the program, especially the use of films that depicted explicit sexual relations.[4] Formal connection with the Medical School of the University ceased in January of 1988 but their personnel continue to participate in the leadership of the course.

The human sexuality course has often been a lightning rod for those who sought a basis for attacking the Seminary and its programs. Both the Church and society have throughout history had difficulty dealing with the human body and its functions. A veil of silence has usually been the response regarded as most appropriate. Victorian values and norms have tended to dominate any discussion of the human body and its sexuality. With the Sixties and Seventies came great changes in the way American society understood the body and human sexuality. As part of the radical movements of the time sexuality became part of the political rhetoric. The flower children of the Sixties used sexual expression to revolt against the authorities of their times. They argued that the body was a source of ecstasy and transcendental insight. The presence of the Pill gave a freedom to sexual expression in which procreation was no longer the dominant or primary goal. With the Seventies and the rise of the women's movement sexual politics became a major part of that liberation expression. The women reminded us

[4]The controversy spilled over into the local newspapers with both articles on the matter as well as letters to the editor.

that our bodies are ourselves. Therapists urged us to "get in touch with our bodies."

In the midst of this changing context the Faculty met for a discussion meeting at which James Nelson presented a paper entitled "Homosexuality and the Church." In it he argued that there is a continuum on which one can place the various responses to homosexuality in the church. These ranged from outright condemnation to an acceptance of it as part of the natural creative order. The discussion of the issue was heated and extended. The members of the Faculty illustrated the thesis by expressing a wide range of attitudes. Gunnemann represented a position that allowed for the ordination of homosexuals. But he was concerned that that not be the issue, rather the issue was seen as that of ministry and faithfulness to the Gospel. Campbell symbolized those who were willing to grant civil rights to those of a homosexual orientation but questioned whether or not such persons should be ordained into the ministry. Nelson took the stance that there was no basis for denying ordination on the basis of sexual preference or orientation. Gustafson and Merrill argued that one needed to take the socio-historical context into account. Both of them having come out of conservative contexts in which the Bible was used as a weapon they argued that one should not use it to argue for a rule ethic. Though the Bible condemns homosexual acts the biblical understanding of homosexuality is not the same understanding that present day contexts provide. And there are larger themes which need to be taken into account, such as love and justice.

Nelson's paper was first published in United's journal *Theological Markings*, then was published by *Christianity and Crisis*, and ultimately was included as a chapter in his book *Embodiment*.[5] The later publication became a cause celebre. From the right wing came responses of outrage and anger, even obscene letters. Others used it to attack the school and call it "that evil institution." For many it opened a dialogue on the role and understanding of sexuality in the Church. Unfortunately the reasoned and

---

[5]"Homosexuality: an issue for the Church," *Theological Markings* 5:2 (Winter 1975) 41-52, "Homosexuality and the Church," *Christianity and Crisis* 37:5 (April 4, 1977) 63-69, *Embodiment: an approach to sexuality and Christian theology*, Minneapolis: Augsburg, 1978.

carefully qualified statements by Nelson were often caricatured and taken out of context.

When asked about the route that had led him to take such a position, Nelson replied that there were two major factors that had influenced him in his changing understandings.[6] The first had been his participation in a Minneapolis group called the Joint Urban Mission Program (JUMP). This group had emerged as a response to the Detroit race riots and sought to be pro-active in the Twin Cities. An ecumenical group, it sought to fund grass root movements to cause social change through groups that might be too controversial for direct denominational support. One of the early grants by JUMP, of which Nelson was chair, was to a gay community house. Nelson felt he had to learn more about the gay community and to be able to interpret and defend the grant to this controversial group. For the first time in his life he was confronted by self-affirming and self-respecting and very articulate gay and lesbian people. These gay and lesbian people were deeply immersed in the Christian faith.

The other factor that caused reexamination of his stereotypes and homophobia was Nelson's involvement in the program in human sexuality with the University of Minnesota. In that process he became increasingly aware and understood that homosexuality and heterosexuality were not two sharply defined entities, but part of a continuum of human sexuality. The net result was a reexamination of the question, ethically and theologically.

The issue could not remain an intellectual debate. The ethical and theological issues arose out of the experience of real people in an ambiguous and problematic world. Soon the Seminary was to be confronted with the presence of homosexual students. By September 1, 1977, the Faculty was called upon to make a statement about its admissions policy, triggered by the fact that three women students had come "out of the closet," one by her own choice and the other two forced by others. When the Faculty Workshop, as the annual pre-school meeting was called, met on September 1, with James Nelson as Moderator, the issue was raised. The formal response was to vote that the Academic Vice President and the Moderator of the Faculty appoint

[6]Interview with James B. Nelson by ALM, in his office, April 9, 1991.

a Task Force. It was to recommend to the Faculty Senate possible positions for United in relation to those of avowed and unavowed homosexual preference and report to the Faculty Senate in November.[7]

The issue would not rest that easily and discussions around the events of the day led to a reconsideration of the issue the following day, September 2. Before lunch on the second day a statement was submitted to the Faculty but it was not acceptable. Patricia Wilson Kastner was asked to present a revision in the light of the discussion. The workshop adjourned for lunch and a Faculty Senate meeting at which student issues were decided. After that the Faculty met again and adopted the following statement:

> We, the Faculty of United Theological Seminary, affirm equal educational opportunity for all our students regardless of race, sex, or affectional preference. While aware of the issues regarding the ministry of Christians of a homosexual orientation within church structures, we do not believe that such an orientation in and of itself disqualifies a person from preparing for ministry at this seminary. As we work with churches, we have respect for their decisions about placement, and we earnestly seek to enter into dialogue with both students and churches about the relation of sexual orientation to ministry. Bearing this in mind, with regard to all factors purely internal to the seminary's life, the faculty pledges to strive for equity in its dealings with all UTS students.[8]

That action was followed by the further action that the Moderator send a letter to students, staff and administration with a copy of the Faculty Statement.

The Task Force was convened by the Moderator of the Faculty and the elected convener was Ann Brudevold, a student. The Task Force met during the year, often in Faculty homes. Much time was spent in defining the task for the group and the issues with which it wished to deal. Institutional self-study, issue raising, data collection, community education and study of and action with church judicatories were the major foci of its work.

---

[7]Faculty Workshop Minutes, September 1-2, 1977.

[8]*Ibid.* p. 4.

That the issue was hot on campus is supported by the presence of anonymous notes in the boxes of students and faculty members. The Faculty Senate as a consequence noted its abhorrence of anonymous hate mail and urged all to follow the guideline of equity in its dealings with all United students.[9]

On December 12, 1977, there was formal announcement to the Task Force that a Gay Caucus had been formed and that they would no longer participate in the Task Force. They stated that "the Task Force [is] a creation of a liberal, heterosexist, homophobic structure designed to help that structure feel that it has appropriately dealt with its own prejudices, but within which...the real issue of homophobia becomes an incidental side issue." Their vision was "for a better day when the Gay Caucus will not be necessary because Gay people will be accepted with their unique gifts into the larger community."[10]

When the Task Force presented its formal recommendations to the Faculty Senate, on April 12, 1978, the Gay Caucus not only submitted a memo to the assembled body decrying its passive stance but also some members picketed the meeting.[11] For a community that had operated on a consensual model for so many years the presence of pickets was a novel and disconcerting experience. Yet it was recalled by many for it was the most confrontive action that the Seminary had experienced through these turbulent years. The action of the Faculty Senate was perhaps typical for such situations. The various recommendations of the Task Force were referred to various persons and groups within the Seminary and they in turn were asked for reports back to the Faculty Senate.[12]

The recommendations of the Task Force moved into the mainstream of the institution. United became known as a seminary in which

---

[9]Memo to Students, Staff, Faculty from James Nelson, November 10, 1977.

[10]"Free at Last," A statement read to the meeting of the Task Force, December 12, 1977.

[11]Memo to the Faculty Senate, from the Gay Caucus, March 22, 1978, signed by Sue Ebbers, Ron Mattson, Terry Person, and Martha Winslow.

[12]Minutes of the Faculty Senate Meeting, April 12, 1978.

homosexuals had a modestly safe haven for theological study. Not that homophobic behavior did not continue, but the official policy of the school did not discriminate against those of a homosexual orientation in hiring and admissions. This was a position that was supported by Presidents and Deans and caused some loss in support from individuals and congregations. The issue of homosexuality and the church remains a critical issue until this day. There are many important moral issues on the current scene, but for the Church it stands as a particular test case. It demonstrates the variety of ways in which we deal with conflict and diversity. It manifests itself in how we do our theological work and the ways in which Scripture is invoked for moral decision making. It is comparable in many ways to the slavery issue of the nineteenth century because it is threatening to break denominations apart, causing splits in congregations and leading to defections in churches to other groups.

CHAPTER 16

NATIVE AMERICAN THEOLOGICAL ASSOCIATION

The way in which Western Europeans have encountered and interacted with the early inhabitants of the Americas has been at best ambiguous and at worse genocidal. Since 1492 the history of that relationship has not been proud chapter during human existence on this small planet. The very way in which we have labeled them, and they have understood themselves are demonstrative of that relationship. Are they Native Americans, American Indians, or The People? Are they tribes, nations, or people?

The Church has often followed in the path of the dominant society as it has interacted with the early inhabitants of the Americas. Its mission has often seemed to be a reflection of the cultural imperialism in which the Native Americans were made subservient to Western European values and understandings. Though the missionary movement has included stories of heroic and self-sacrificing actions it has also included accounts of self-serving motives and acts emerging out of gross misunderstandings. It is not surprising that by the Bicentennial of the United States in 1976 the Church had made little progress in its mission to the Native American people.

The conversations that led to the establishment of the Native American Theological Association (NATA) were prompted by a study that showed that the Native American clergy in North America were few, poorly trained and of advanced age. The questions that this study raised were first

49. Harrell Davis, Director of NATA, 1981-84

50. Norman Jackson, Director of NATA, 1985-88

51. Pow-wow for Indian Week

52. Sweat lodge for Indian Week

53. Graduation, 1983.
Left to right: Mitchel Whiterabbit, Joseph Bad Moccasin, Virgil Foote

addressed by the Council for American Indian Ministries of the United Church of Christ which in the Fall of 1974 requested United to be a center for training in ministry of American Indians. By the following Fall an independent Board had been formed and the first name of the body was "The Center for American Indian Ministries." Thomas Campbell, then Academic Vice President, took the lead as the major negotiator for United.

In 1976 NATA became a reality when the Faculty Senate voted to encourage the development of an Indian Center at United, using the colleges and universities of the upper Midwest and Cook Christian Training School in Tempe, Arizona. The Faculty was willing to enter into a contract with the Indian Center Steering Committee to offer those courses that would enable the training of Native people for ministry in the Church.[1] The organizational structure that emerged from these actions was a consortium of schools and denominational agencies. Initially the Board had representatives from the United Church of Christ, the United Methodist Church, and the Presbyterian Church (USA). The schools that were involved were United, Cook Christian Training School and the Dakota Leadership Program. A grant from the Lilly Endowment, through the Association of Theological Schools, made this development possible. An early important Indian leader on the board was the Rev. Mitchell Whiterabbit, and the executive committee was composed entirely of Native Americans.

NATA was established to strengthen Native American ministries through education for clergy, research, education and advocacy. It was also concerned to make the wider ecumenical community aware of the strengths and importance of Native American religious thought. The executive committee made the key decisions regarding policies, the supervision and guidance of the executive Director and acted on student admissions. Its major decision was to establish three tracks by which competency in ministry could be achieved by its students. The first two tracks led to the M.Div. Degree, either by full time residence (Track I) or by theological education by extension (Track II) in which one year would be spent in residence at a theological school. The third track provided for the awarding of a certificate

[1]Faculty Senate Minutes, May 12, 1976.

of competency for ministry among Native Americans. In effect the NATA program became the Native American curriculum at United, even though many of the courses, workshops and internships were taken at other member NATA institutions or judicatories.

When Howard Anderson was appointed the first full time Director of NATA on September 1, 1977, he also became an Adjunct Instructor at United. As part of the package he was given a house on the campus and an office in the Seminary buildings. The offices of NATA were located in the Minnesota Church Center in Minneapolis. It was with deep regret that the NATA Board had been unable to find a Native American person for the first Director. Anderson came from Detroit Lakes, MN where he had grown up on the edge of an Indian Reservation and had been deeply influenced by that experience. He had done his graduate work at the University of Hawaii in American Studies and focused on concerns of cross-cultural education. One of his children was an Indian. With his interests and concerns Anderson made an excellent liaison between the Native American and white dominant cultures.

The first Native American students were enrolled in United at the same time that the Director came on board. In 1976 there had been only four Indian students in seminaries in all of North America. When September of 1978 came NATA had twelve students in seminary, an increase of 300%! Of those students eight were enrolled at United Seminary. It meant that the school and the faculty had to learn new ways of teaching and dealing with students from another culture. Though United had had international students, especially from Taiwan and Europe, they had been trained in patterns that were not dissimilar from those in America.

For the Indian students seminary was a great shock. Their training and experience had led them to expect failure. They were not accustomed to having their traditions respected nor their values upheld outside their own circles. Their experiences with the educational system had often been very unsatisfactory. Despite the cultural differences they did remarkably well. This was especially true of those Indian church leaders with significant experience in ministry, who had been selected for ministry by their own community and were supported in their venture into theological education.

These students represented a wide range of experiences and backgrounds, from the North slope of Alaska to the Southwest United States. And for NATA the seminary students represented only part of the story. Some went to Cook Christian Training School, others began pre-theological studies at Huron College in South Dakota, and others studied theological education by extension. Among the seminaries where Native American students studied were United, Dubuque Theological Seminary, Luther Northwestern Seminary and eventually Garrett-Evangelical Seminary.

Among the early efforts of NATA was an ecumenical consultation held in the Black Hills (Paha Sapa in the Lakota) to acquaint Indian clergy and students with NATA and its associated institutions. A workshop on current Indian issues, including treaty rights, was held in South Dakota. Seminars were held at Huron College. Training events in conjunction with the Johnson Institute in Minneapolis focused on the issues of alcoholism. And the issues of Urban Indian Ministries were raised and addressed.

The twelve NATA seminarians, of whom eight were enrolled at United and four at three other seminaries, met in November of 1978. One of the major outcomes of this consultation was the perception that there was a serious lack of communication between the NATA students and the non-Native students. A suggestion was made that perhaps one way to help overcome the communication barrier was to have an Indian community dinner and worship to foster interchange.

At United this suggestion developed into the regularly scheduled Native American Week. These programs featured speakers, panels, Native dances, Native foods, a Pow-Wow and a pipe ceremony. Sometimes a sweat lodge was set up for the assembly. During the Native American Week speakers were also scheduled for the various classes that met during the week. These provided occasions in which Native American perspectives were presented in the context of the regular studies. This was in addition to faculty members who added materials from Native American cultural and religious backgrounds appropriate to their specific course. Such materials were added not only to honor the traditions brought by Native peoples but to also sensitize other theological students to the wealth of such traditional material. At the second Native American week gifts of tobacco and other symbolic items were given to those leaders who had contributed to the growth of NATA. Among the gifts was an Indian bola (beaded tie) with the logo of United given to President Hultgren. He and his successors have worn this gift at successive important occasions of the school's academic life.

United's faculty also contributed to NATA by developing specific materials for theological education in the Native American community. Robert Bryant developed a course dealing with comparative creation stories. Louis Gunnemann wrote a study of the history and polity of the United Church of Christ for NATA. Donald White worked on developing a course and related materials for teaching basic theology by extension. Still the resources for theological education for Native American students remain limited and undeveloped.

It was not until the Spring of 1981 that United was able to appoint its own Director of Native American Studies. Harrell D. Davis, a Cherokee from Oklahoma, had studied for his B.S. at Central State University in Oklahoma and his M.Div. at Louisville Presbyterian Theological Seminary. An ordained Presbyterian minister he came directly from seminary to his new position. He was the first NATA student to graduate from Louisville and the first NATA student appointed to a theological faculty. In him the NATA students had an excellent model of how to do theological education and lead in the Native American community.

Davis was caught in the perennial dilemma of Native people, of being between two worlds. One of his vivid images was his perception of being considered an apple, white inside and red on the outside. In his inaugural address he spoke to the issue of "Coming of Age Between Two Worlds." As he would say, "It is here in this in-between place that I find myself being confronted by problems while at the same time finding the most helpful solutions."[2] Not only was he to find himself between the traditional world and contemporary society but also as a southern Cherokee he had difficulty being accepted by the predominant Lakota and Dakota Sioux of the Great Plains.

---

[2]Harrell Davis, "Coming of Age Between Two Worlds," *Theological Markings* 11 (Spring 1982) 3-4.

The story of NATA was not a story of unmitigated success. It worked against great odds for the training of ministers in the Native American community. Much of its early success was due to the untiring enthusiasm and energy of Howard Anderson. Perhaps that was also the source of problems as the program rested too much on the shoulders of one person. Anderson resigned from the position of Director of NATA to work for the Episcopal Diocese of Minnesota, in its concerns for Native American ministries. Davis was elected in his place and United was without a faculty person for Native American Studies. The Rev. Mitchell Whiterabbit commuted from Wisconsin to help on a part time basis but was unable to provide the dynamic leadership that was needed.

United was most fortunate to obtain the leadership of Norman W. Jackson as of January 1986. Jackson, a Seneca, came from the post of executive associate to the president of the UCC, Avery D. Post. He had a joint appointment as executive director of the Council for American Indian Ministry (CAIM) of the United Church of Christ and as Director of Native American Studies at United.[3] As a mature scholar and administrator Jackson was able to give strong leadership to the Native American Studies program and challenge the faculty to own the program. He was a strong advocate for the preservation of Indian ways. In his inaugural address he challenged United to adopt a new vision, a new mission and several new programs. Particularly he was concerned that the urban situation needed to be addressed. This was not only a concern for education but a forum for raising and acting on justice questions. Jackson saw the context for both justice and education as one of genocide. A genocide that was first physical, then cultural, then spiritual and finally economic. He challenged those assembled for the Fall Convocation to see that "the task is not simply educating Indians for ministry: it is to call the Church to account; it is to

---

[3]Norman Jackson was a graduate of the University of Tulsa, earning his B.D. at Hartford Theological Seminary and his M.A. and Ed.D degrees at Indiana University. He had been on the faculty of Eden Theological Seminary from 1967-74 and served as Conference Minister of the Kansas/Oklahoma Conference of the UCC from 1974-78. He was a member of the Seneca nation.

speak a prophetic word to a preoccupied nation; and it is to use every ounce of United's resources as competently as faithfulness requires."[4]

It was perhaps inevitable that the NATA program would finally be disbanded. The centripetal forces that played upon it were strong. The denominations that had supported and encouraged the formation of NATA found their own funding sources shrinking and being stretched to their limits. They could no longer give clear and strong support for the program and found ways in which to justify their limited support. At one NATA board meeting Owanah Anderson, the national Episcopal representative, stated that, "Until Harrell Davis deigns to answer my phone calls there will be no money from the Episcopal Church." Davis defended his actions by claiming to be operating in the "Indian Way." And Davis would soon leave the directorship to pursue his own higher educational goals.

One major factor playing on NATA was the increasing growth of denominational particularism. As more schools joined the consortium that constituted NATA the options for Native American students increased. The various denominations at the same time urged their students to go to their own denominational schools to participate in the ethos and theological climate that would make them more acceptable to the denomination. Alongside that loss of ecumenical vision was the growth in each denomination of bodies that focused on the training for ministry of Native Americans. The Presbyterians formed their own Native American Theological Education Consortium a year or two after NATA and thereby siphoned off interest and involvement in NATA.

Another factor that made NATA's situation difficult was the presence of strong political forces between the various Indian groups represented in NATA. Decisions that appeared to favor one group or another would be attacked and subject to subterfuge. As long as there was a strong person in leadership these could be mitigated but often the very decisions that needed to be made for the health of NATA were subverted or not made. Native American life is not a seamless whole but a quilt of many pieces, each with its own beauty and strength, but often difficult to bring into a larger pattern

[4]Norman W. Jackson, "Fall Convocation," *Theological Markings* (Spring 1987) 1-3.

that coheres. Leadership in the Native American community does not operate according to the styles established by the dominant culture.

Perhaps the most serious factor arises out of the fact that church life in the Native American community represents only a very minuscule population. The constituency for support from the Native Americans is very small and the sources for students infinitesimal. In the United Church of Christ there are only 21 churches and 1200 members in the Dakota Association. In the Presbyterian Church (USA) there are only 24 churches and 1,300 members in the Dakota Presbytery. The United Methodist Church identifies 123 churches and 29,000 members nationwide. Most of these Native American churches are in the Southwestern or Southeastern parts of the United States. With such limited numbers one can hardly expect a single seminary to have many students when there are many schools eager to enhance their enrollment with the matriculation of Native American students.

NATA has voted itself out of existence and its files have been located at the CAIM office in Minneapolis. Norman Jackson left United and the CAIM office to become the conference minister in Hawaii.

At United the Native American Studies program continues but works under severe handicaps. There is no longer a regular faculty appointment that has responsibility for the program. The numbers of students present at any one time tends to be only one or two. However the Faculty has committed itself to being a resource for theological education in the Native American community. As part of the globalization concerns of the American Theological Schools it has focused on cross-cultural education that uses Native American resources as the basis of its study. The Library has sought to develop the materials for such study through the receipt of a grant from the Grotto Foundation to build up the collection.

Interest in theological education for the Native American people continues. Yet funding resources are limited, participant groups have their own political agendas, constituencies seek their own goals and the Christian Church has yet to find a strategy to bring justice and hope to people who have been denied access to the basic structures of the dominant culture.

From the noble experiment of NATA the Church can learn many important lessons.

CHAPTER 17

THE END OF AN ERA

When one looks at the Faculty of United during the Seventies one discerns a relatively stable group. Changes did continue with the addition of Holt H. Graham as Director of the Library and Professor of New Testament in 1974.[1] Kley, the first Librarian had resigned to take a pastorate at St. Germaine in Wisconsin and from there retired to Sheboygan, his hometown.[2] Graham had taught for many years at the Episcopal Divinity School in Virginia but had been forced to resign due to a divorce. With his personal and professional life in shambles he had taken a year of study at the Ecumenical Institute at St. John's University in Collegeville. Afterwards he taught part time at Hamline University and the College of St. Catherine until his call to United. In him the school acquired a fine New Testament scholar, a beloved teacher and a vital link to the Episcopal Church.[3]

With a strong and vibrant faculty United appeared to be entering into a new level of its ongoing existence. This was marked in part by the

---

[1]A native of the State of Washington, Graham had taken his A.B. at the University of Washington; he received his M.A. from Columbia University and his B.D., S.T.M. and Th.D. at Union Theological Seminary in New York. His scholarship and service to the church had been recognized by Seabury-Western Theological Seminary with an honorary S.T.D. He was an ordained minister in the Protestant Episcopal Church.

[2]Kley died July 8, 1985 in Sheboygan, Wisconsin.

[3]Graham retired from the faculty June 30, 1983.

invitation of Thomas Campbell to be the Sprunt Lecturer at Union Theological Seminary in Richmond, Virginia, in 1979. To prepare for these lectures Campbell took a sabbatical leave in Oxford, England. Upon his return from England the seminary community was shocked by the report that on January 27, 1979, he had been hospitalized and needed surgery for a malignant tumor in the area of his nose and left eye. This prevented his personal delivery of the Sprunt Lectures, though his colleague Wilson Yates did present Campbell's lectures at Union Theological Seminary. In the midst of his recuperation from surgery and the battling of the cancer through radiation and chemotherapy Campbell delivered a stirring chapel message on the Gospel story of the blind Bartemaeus. With his usual insightfulness he brought forth the dialectic of sight and blindness. Few left the chapel with a dry eye that day.

By July Campbell felt strong enough to travel to Manila to chair the annual meeting of the World Council of Churches Program in Theological Education. At the end of that meeting he had a severe seizure that caused a back injury and hospitalized him at Makati Medical Center in Manila for six days. From there he was transferred by medical evacuation plane to Guam for two days and finally was returned to the Twin Cities by way of Hawaii, San Francisco and Scott Air Force Base in Illinois. What had begun as a hopeful sign of recovery had ended in a nightmare of travel that was helped by the U.S. Air Force. On August 12, 1979, Campbell died in Methodist Hospital, Minneapolis, three days short of his fiftieth birthday. The seminary community was devastated. The brilliant leadership which Campbell had provided was lost. The personal relationships were sundered. It would take years before the process of grief would be worked through by those who were left behind.

Campbell had left a legacy of a sharp theological mind that could cut to the issues, an administrator who could see the personal dimensions, a theologian whose service to the Church would be invaluable. As James Nelson reported in his tribute at the memorial service held at the Seminary on September 11, Campbell's strong faith was reflected in his words of the final week, "Well, children, it's been a hard day. But we are going to make it through this together. And we're going to do it triumphantly." Surely his death marked the end of an era. Campbell had had a vital role in the development of the early curriculum and he had returned to give hope for a new day. Now the future appeared much more problematic.

President Hultgren moved quickly to appoint an interim Academic Vice President, Clyde J. Steckel. Steckel had not only been the first director of the D.Min. Program but also was serving as the Director of the M.Div. Program. With him the programs of the school could proceed. And under him two important decisions would have to be made.

The first was the search for a new Academic Vice President. The committee, appointed by the Board of Trustees, first proposed the name of Frederica Thompsett as the Academic Vice President. She was interviewed by the Faculty and was nominated for appointment. Upon further reflection Thompsett turned down the nomination and the search was renewed. Within the month the Faculty was asked to interview Clyde J. Steckel for the permanent position and he was unanimously supported by the Faculty as the candidate for Academic Vice President.[4] The transition of leadership in the school had been accomplished.

The other major decision of that academic year, 1979-80, was the establishment of the Center for the Shaping of Values. The Center was the consequence of a proposal by President Hultgren that many of the programs carried out by the school could be incorporated into a center where public issues could be debated and researched. Perhaps it goes even further back to a proposal by Louis Gunnemann in 1961 that an Institute of Church Studies be established "in order for the seminary to be the true intellectual center of the church's life." Such an institute would be a separate organization but controlled by the seminary board.[5]

In the minutes of the annual Faculty Workshop in August 1972, during the tenure of Louis Gunnemann, one finds the first reference to an Institute for Church and Society proposed to the Faculty. The matter was referred to the Faculty Administrative Committee for consideration.[6] When

[4]Minutes of the Faculty Meeting, May 7, 1980.

[5]Kley, *The First Ten Years*, p. 31.

[6]Faculty Workshop Minutes, August 30-31, 1972.

the matter appears in the records again it comes in the form of a memo to the Faculty from the Funding Proposal Committee.[7] This time consideration is made of a Center for Leadership and Organizational Development and the locus of its discussion is a Faculty Discussion meeting on February 21, 1973. The discussion led to a referral of the matter to the Office of Development for preparation and submission for funding. The faculty concurred that the proposal reflected the concern of the faculty to enhance its role in the task of professional education.

The matter had obviously become a question of not only the seminary's role in professional education but also one of funding of the institution. The precarious state of the school had led Hultgren in several directions to undergird the financial and programmatic base of the school. During the same period several discussions were held with Dubuque Theological Seminary with the goal of a possible merger. These discussions led nowhere and Dubuque would remain in a consortium with Wartburg Seminary and Aquinas Institute.

With Campbell's return as Academic Vice President in 1974 the discussions of the nature and focus of the Center continued. Yet it is significant that most of the discussions appeared to have taken place outside the normal official channels of the institution. In the minutes of the Faculty and Senate there is no reference to these discussions nor the decisions made. However the participants recall long and arduous discussions, particularly of the name of the Center. The final decision to call it the Center for the Shaping of Values represents a compromise that resulted in an ambiguous title. To many of the faculty the Center represented a funding effort to underwrite the regular program and a consolidation of previous programs in sexuality, ethics, arts, etc. For others it represented a forum in which the basic issues and values of the society could be debated in a theological context.

It was only at the end of the decade that the Center was approved as a two year pilot program with an interim director. The funding for the program was a generous gift from Mary Bigelow McMillan, an alumna of

[7]Memo dated January 24, 1973.

United and member of the Board of Trustees. With that gift the search for an interim director was launched and on May 14, 1980, Jane Boyajian Raible was called to the position.[8]

The pilot program would last for three years and in the end the evaluation of the Center called for its radical redefinition. This task was given to the Board of Trustees and it was never picked up nor developed as leadership in the school changed. It had been a painful experiment for the school as it sought to fulfill its task of theological education, not only in the training for ministry, but also in the larger community of ethical discourse. A separate structure within the school had not been a viable instrument for that goal as the Center's director had been unable to articulate a vision into which others could enter and the faculty perceived it as an additional burden to their already full lives. What it did accomplish was the financial undergirding of the school as it struggled through very difficult times.

The Director of the Center, Jane Boyajian, had been given a very difficult task. She understood the position to be one of programming and bringing links between the seminary and the larger community. In reality Boyajian had been expected to generate funding which would undergird the total institution. Her own interests in medical ethics did not coincide with the original impulse to engage the business community. Also she had expected to have greater control of the funds which had been given for the Center. In the end the task would prove to be impossible and the termination of the program extremely painful for all concerned.

Alongside these institutional dilemmas the Faculty was having to deal with personal and professional issues of its own. What had appeared as a stable residential faculty united in its commitment to theological education itself suffered various assaults and injuries. The requirement that faculty live on campus increasingly became onerous to some members. Pressures built up and exceptions to policy led to the change that faculty could opt to live off campus. Increasingly members took this option as it offered the opportunity

[8]Jane Boyajian Raible, who later dropped the last name, had earned her B.A. at Tufts University, had studied at Starr King School for Religious Leadership and Harvard University, and had received her D.Min. from San Francisco Theological Seminary. She was an ordained minister in the Unitarian-Universalist Association.

to build up equity in homes and to live a style of life not shaped by the faculty community. This led to feelings of inequity as those living off campus appeared to be financially advantaged. To remedy the problems several housing task forces were established to examine the issues and offer solutions. One significant change was that all faculty received a housing allowance and those who remained on campus paid rent and as well were given a tax sheltered annuity in place of equity in a house.

The role of the seminary as landlord to the faculty homes remained a source of irritation and contention. Increasingly it raised controversy between the faculty and the administration, especially the President, as decisions on rent and maintenance appeared to be arbitrary and not the consequence of negotiations.

In their personal lives the Faculty also experienced the stress and strains of the Seventies and their own advancing age. Several families, not only the Campbells, had to deal with cancer and death. Spouses of many years succumbed to the ravages of a disease that some wished to link to the water supply of New Brighton, a source of water that was later ascertained to have been contaminated by the U.S. Army and its arsenal in nearby Arden Hills. The Army never acknowledged responsibility but provided for new wells and a decontamination unit for the city. Various members of the faculty also experienced divorce and the break up of families of long standing. The very fabric of the school appeared to be suffering from the malaise of the times.

In the midst of these traumas in the life of United there were signs of hope and promise. By the end of the decade enrollment in all programs neared 250 persons each year. By 1979 there had been 326 M.Div. graduates since 1963, 288 men and 38 women. Seventy-three percent of them were serving parishes. In addition there had been 21 M.A.R.S. Degrees granted and 7 D.Min. Degrees.

54. Holt H. Graham, New Testament, 1974-83

55. B. Edmon Martin, Ministry Studies, 1981-

56. Mary Potter Engel, Historical Theology, 1983-91

57. Valerie DeMarinis, Theology and Psychology, 1984-86

One program, long under discussion, which came to fruition at the end of the 70's was the Doctor of Ministry degree. This was a joint offering under the aegis of the Minnesota Consortium of Theological Faculties. The program had begun as an attempt to offer professional advanced training to pastors, and the earlier offering of a Masters of Theology. The discussion of a professional doctorate had gone on both in theological faculties and in A.T.S. circles. At the biennial meeting of the A.T.S. in 1972, held in St. Paul, accrediting standards were adopted for the Doctor of Ministry degree. Among the presidents and deans of the Consortium there was agreement that the Doctor of Ministry should be the second professional degree, based on the Master of Divinity. Both the presidents and the joint graduate committee concurred that the D.Min. should be a joint consortium effort and based on a "in-ministry" program. By 1972-73 the possibility of hiring a full-time Consortium director and offering the joint professional doctorate had become the agenda of the Consortium.

Early in 1973 the presidents and deans appointed a task force to design a joint D.Min. When the task force put forth its proposal it was adopted by the Consortium and referred to the member schools for their approval. Luther, Northwestern and United were able to accept the proposal and appointed faculty members to the joint D.Min. administrative committee. Bethel, due to the nature of its governance pattern, had to have the approval of its Board of Regents. The Faculty at Bethel were aware that the Board of Regents had gone on record as approving the idea of a D.Min. Program. They were also aware that their offering a joint program with the other seminaries might raise issues with the Board. This perception was borne out when the Board received the proposal. Austin Chapman, who had just been elected to the Board, asked how the administrators could justify formal association with a liberal seminary like United? Cooperating with United would begin the process of seriously undermining Bethel's evangelical academic mission. From their perspective United had repudiated some of the cardinal tenets of historic Christian faith; it did not even have a statement of faith. Others argued that it was not an issue of substance but of perception. What if the General Conference thought that Bethel was slipping from the orthodox stance? As the matter was of crucial import in the life of the denomination the matter was postponed to a later date when the Board of Regents would meet with the other Boards of the denomination at their mid-year meeting. After many moves and contermoves Bethel did not enter the joint program but sought to offer a professional degree virtually identical to the Consortium.[9] St. Paul's and St. John's did not feel the need for nor wish to participate in a degree for which they discerned no need in their constituencies.

In retrospect Bethel's concerns were perhaps supported by the fact that United was to provide the major leadership for the D.Min. Program. Clyde Steckel would inaugurate the program while on a sabbatical leave. He was followed by Patricia Wilson Kastner. In 1975 Louis Gunnemann, upon his retirement from United, would become the director until he resigned December 31, 1980. He was followed by Lance Barker who served until 1990. The first four directors were all from United. By October 1979 the Minnesota Consortium of Theological Faculties had become incorporated as the Minnesota Consortium of Theological Schools.

As was true for many institutions in American society United reflected the crises of the day. Hultgren had succeeded in bringing organizational and developmental skills to the institution. His vision of the seminary as a place of discourse in which the church and society might interact fitted the categories of the seminary's self-understanding, yet his approach was primarily from a pragmatic point of view. The financial straits of the school were a constant burden. It moved from crisis to crisis as it sought to balance the books. Sometimes there were successes as the Center for the Shaping of Values brought support for the school and the George Dayton Foundation provided a scholarship fund of a million dollars, from which endowment scholarships were given for students preparing for ministry. Still, the north woods had been sold off and contingency plans were made if the financial exigencies should lead to cutbacks and reductions of

---

[9]Robert G. Duffett, *The History and Development of the Doctor of Ministry Degree at the Minnesota Consortium of Theological Schools: 1957-1985*, Doctoral dissertation, The University of Iowa, 1986, pp. 335-387.

staff and faculty. These emergency plans were announced to the faculty but never shared, with either the faculty or the wider community.

Faculty were initially pleased with the reorganization of the school yet found themselves no longer able to affect some the decisions that seemed to impinge on their lives. The housing issues brought divisions and some consternation. Salaries were often frozen in a time of rapid inflation. Increasingly programs were being added without more colleagues to share the load. Personal and professional strains were putting additional burdens on the Faculty. Many felt themselves becoming increasingly estranged from the inner life of the school.

Students were also changing, reflecting the changing times. An increasing focus on the self and its development appeared. Students themselves had or were undergoing divorces and changing careers. Some were dealing with recovering from alcoholism or sexual abuse. Often the faculty had to deal with persons who were in school to salvage their lives and find meaning in a seemingly meaningless world. The search for a therapeutic model of education seemed to dominate the scene.

In the midst of these crises in society and the school Dayton Hultgren was able to keep a public face of optimism and hope. When he was evaluated for his third term that non-defeatist attitude was one that recurred in many forms. He brought excellent conceptualization of institutional management but tended to act as though students and faculty should think the same way. He built constructive relationships with the judicatories of the churches and was able to interpret the mission of the school effectively. Yet the crises took their toll.

When Tom Campbell died some felt that the life also went out of Hultgren. He no longer had the support and counterbalance that he needed for those difficult times. By the Spring of 1982 the faculty felt that they needed to confront Hultgren about his style of administration and the way in which institutional decisions were made. At the annual retreat of the faculty during alternate week in March the issues were raised and discussed. It seemed to several that the points were clear and the resolution possible. At the end of one session a consensus appeared to have been reached. When the retreat resumed Hultgren announced that he was resigning. He had been called to be the president of San Francisco Theological Seminary in San Anselmo, California. For many on the faculty this sudden and unexpected news felt like a betrayal. Here they had struggled to support him and to reach a way of working together and now he was leaving.

United had come through its beginnings and into its adolescence, if one can use a metaphor. Now it was faced with new challenges as it confronted another change of leadership. The vision of an ecumenical seminary serving the church and society had been enriched in ways never expected by the founders. The world in which it sought to be faithful had changed in profound and irreversible dimensions. The next chapters will focus on the consolidation of those gains and the stabilization of the school.

PART FIVE

CONSOLIDATING THE GAINS

CHAPTER 18

TIMES OF CHANGE

The 1980's in the United States were marked by the years of President Ronald Reagan in the White House. His presidency reflected a strong shift to the right in politics and social life. Before his two terms were finished they were marked by the Iran Contra scandal and United States military incursions into Lebanon and Grenada. The New Right came to prominence and issues of sexuality, abortion, and textbook censorship raised strong opinions on both sides of the questions. Central America became the focus of strong debate in the national forum and the question of sanctuary for the refugees of the civil battles and repressive regimes of the area consumed the energies of many.

In the Middle East the government of Israel made its disastrous invasion into Lebanon and radical groups would take Americans and Europeans as hostages. Anwar Sadat was assassinated for having made peace with Israel. In India Indira Gandhi was assassinated by a radical Sikh group. South Africa continued to struggle with the issue of apartheid and Desmond Tutu, the Archbishop of South Africa, received the Nobel Peace Prize. The countries of Eastern Europe showed signs of strain and moved toward democracy as the decade ended.

The religious scene in the United States saw both the rise and fall of the Religious Right. The tele-evangelists, Jimmy Bakker and Jimmy Swaggart, fell from grace and Bakker was sentenced to jail. The Southern Baptists continued a long standing battle as the fundamentalists sought to take over the boards and institutions of the denominations. In the North the Presbyterians united with their southern counterparts to overcome generations of separation. Lutherans also cleared the way for union into the Evangelical Lutheran Church of America. The decade began with Marjory Mathews being elected the first woman bishop of a major denomination, the United Methodist Church. And the Episcopal Church in America would elect a black woman, Barbara Harris as Bishop. Yet increasingly all the major denominations were caught in the struggles of their times. Issues of sexuality and gender, of language and abortion would engross the churches. Both "liberals" and "conservatives" fought to have their voices heard and their positions recognized.

Pope Paul John II undertook journeys to the various parts of the world to demonstrate the concern of the Roman Catholic Church for all its people. The issues that were facing the world also faced that church. The Pope himself would be the object of an assassination attempt in Rome. The voices of the theologians of liberation were silenced. The scandal of the Vatican Bank rocked the institution. Women and homosexuals spoke out against the long standing positions of the church. Vocations of priests and religious would decline. No group or institution was exempt from attack or discussion.

It was in this context that Dayton Hultgren resigned and another interim President was chosen to maintain the seminary while the search for a permanent replacement was undertaken. Into the breach stepped Mary B. McMillan, known as Molly, with some reluctance but with a strong commitment to the school.[1] McMillan's formal association with the school had begun as a student, starting in the M.A.R.S. program and shifting to the M.Div. program as her call to the ministry of the church became stronger. A graduate of the class of 1978 she had been ordained and served as associate pastor at House of Hope Presbyterian Church in St. Paul. She was typical in some respects of the graduates of her time as an older person with a second

[1]Mary Bigelow McMillan, was a graduate of Vassar College and had served on the Board of Trustees of United Theological Seminary since 1977. She was Chair of the Board's Academic Affairs Committee at the time of her selection as Interim President.

58. Mary B. McMillan, Interim President, 1982-83, and Chair of Board of Trustees

59. Howard M. Mills, President, 1983-87

60. Clyde J. Steckel, Academic Vice President, 1979-89

61. Helen A. Archibald, Christian Education, 1987-91

career goal. At the same time she had prominence in the Twin Cities community as a person of stature in the civic and business circles in which she moved. McMillan had been the one to underwrite the Center for the Shaping of Values and she believed strongly in the need of the seminary to speak to and serve the larger community. It is ironic that she was the president in 1963 when the Center was evaluated and its director terminated. She understood the nature of the issues that faced the Center and agreed to the decision to redirect the energies that had gone into that venture.

Having been both a student and a trustee meant that McMillan was familiar with the school and its needs. She was an able spokesperson for the school and helped it to make the transition between presidents. The faculty trusted her and the trustees were familiar with her views on the needs of the seminary. Under her kind and gentle guidance the school was able to continue its service to the church and the community. During her tenure the seminary was in the unique position of having women as both President and Academic Vice President. Clyde Steckel was scheduled for a sabbatical during that year and was replaced for that period by Mary F. Bednarowski. Though this lasted for only six months it was reflective of United's commitment to women in the leadership of the church.

During the interim year the Trustees appointed a search committee for the third president of United, under the chair of Roger Knight. Knight was the regional director of the UCC Office of Church Life and Leadership. The candidate presented to the Board was Howard M. Mills.[2] Mills came to the presidency of United from the Office of Ministerial Preparation of the United Church of Canada. He was also a member of the World Council of Church's Programme on Theological Education and had been its moderator, following the death of Thomas Campbell.

Mills was an attractive President for United. He had a ministry which was both national and international, both denominational and inter-denominational. He brought an interest in the church that was both local

[2]Howard M. Mills was a native of Toronto, Ontario, received his B.A. from the University of Toronto, M.Div. from Emmanuel College, Toronto, and his S.T.M. and Ph.D. from Union Theological Seminary, New York. He is an ordained minister in the United Church of Canada and received dual standing in the United Church of Christ.

and ecumenical. His doctoral work at Union Seminary in New York had been in the area of Social Ethics, under the direction of John C. Bennett. A native of Toronto he exhibited a British and patrician attitude, which was open but reserved. Straightforward in his expression he was easy to work with. His sense of humor was quiet but accepting of the various pranks played by the students, including his identification with the Canadian snow goose. Perhaps his greatest weakness was an administrative style that focused on the details, and a candor about the budget that led the faculty to wonder where the money was going to come from.

As President he was an able and positive public presence, confident of himself and the seminary. An articulate spokesperson Mills was accepted well in the business and civic community. His social conscience led him to defend the stance of the seminary on unpopular issues and he often wrote pieces that appeared in the op-ed pages of the metropolitan newspaper.

One of Mills contributions to the school was his emphasis on and concern for continuing education. He accurately read the contemporary scene to see that theological education could not focus just on preparation for ministry and academic degree programs. He continued to push the faculty to find ways to develop a continuing education program. Under Mills leadership Sue Zabel was appointed as Director of Continuing Education and various programs were proposed. Unfortunately, for the faculty this represented additional work and greater responsibility and was resisted. As is true with many smaller schools additional programs are added without the resources to fully enhance their goals. Despite these problems the continuing education program was able to highlight not only those efforts that the school had already undertaken but added further elements, such as a certificate program for lay people, an Elderhostel, and programs for distribution through videotapes.

At the same time that Mills came to the presidency the faculty was enhanced by the coming of Mary Lane Potter to the chair of Historical

Theology.[3] A scholar of John Calvin, Potter was also strongly influenced by feminist and liberation perspectives. Her vocal and articulate presence was a strong influence in faculty discussions and she was a vibrant spokesperson for the issues of the day. The students found her a challenging teacher but also a compassionate friend. She had taught at Princeton Theological Seminary and Luther Northwestern Theological Seminary before coming to United.

The following year Valerie DeMarinis was added to the faculty in the area of Theology and Psychology.[4] When Steckel had assumed the position of Academic Vice President it was obvious that there needed to be additional support in the field of Theology and Psychology. The first search for such a person had led the search committee to bring four candidates to the campus for interviews with the faculty. Two women and two men were the finalists for the position. Following the interviews the faculty was unable to reach a decision on the candidates. None of them had achieved even a significant plurality. Never before had the faculty reached such an impasse. The search was canceled as a result and it was several years before the search was renewed. It was such a situation that led the faculty to ask all further search committees to present only one candidate to the faculty for the final decision.

DeMarinis brought excellent skills to the position. She had both the theoretical foundations and the clinical skills to teach effectively in the field. In addition she had a theological awareness that made the dialogue of psychology and theology a true dialogue. She quickly became a significant member of the faculty and made important contributions to its life. It was unfortunate for the school that her husband was unable to find regular employment in his field of Japanese literature and she too soon left in 1986 to teach at Pacific School of Religion in Berkeley, California where it was

---

[3]Mary Lane Potter, a native of Michigan, had her B.A. from Calvin College, and her M.A. and Ph.D. from the Divinity School of the University of Chicago. A Presbyterian layperson she would later marry Win Engel, a physician, and be known as Mary Potter Engel.

[4]Valerie DeMarinis was a native of New York. She had earned her B.A. at Brooklyn College, C.U.N.Y., the M.Div. at Princeton Theological Seminary and the Th.D. at Harvard University Divinity School. She had taught at Doshisha University in Kyoto, Japan and at Harvard University prior to her coming to United. She was a member of the United Methodist Church.

hoped he could find a position for his skills in that area. While DeMarinis was on the faculty there were four women to provide a variety of models for the women students and awaken the other faculty to the issues of women in ministry and theological education.

Other changes were also taking place in the faculty. In 1983 Holt Graham retired as Professor of New Testament and Director of Library Services. He had become a deeply beloved teacher and colleague. His gentle wit and profound commitment to the church had added an important element in the larger picture. His stature in the Episcopal Church had made a significant contribution to the ecumenical stance of the seminary. Due to financial constraints his position was not filled by a new appointment.

The following year Allan McAllaster was also to retire. His retirement took a different form as he left his administrative role as Director of Admissions and Records but continued to teach on a part-time basis as an adjunct faculty member. At his retirement party in the Spring of 1984 McAllaster became seriously ill as he presented his farewell speech and his colleague Arthur Merrill had to finish the speech for him. Fortunately his health recovered and he was able to enjoy his retirement.

Due to the changing faculty and the changing times Steckel, the Academic Vice President, came to the conclusion that it was time to review the curriculum from a comprehensive viewpoint. The "new" curriculum of 1965 was still the basis from which the educational program worked. There had been modifications and adjustments made over the years and it seemed to some that perhaps the parts no longer held together in the same way. In April 1985 a Curriculum Task Force was appointed. At the time Norman Jackson observed that it was peculiar that no member of the Biblical Field was a member of the task force. Others felt that that would not be a problem.

The Curriculum Task Force looked long and hard at the curriculum, the pedagogical principles that informed it and the theological vision that had inspired it. The theological and social climate had changed radically since the mid-Sixties when the dialogue of church and society was the reigning metaphor. In the theological arena Black theology, feminist theology, liberation theology had come into prominence. In the faculty there had been shifts from a modified neo-reformation to a more process theology orientation with some also espousing feminist and liberationist themes. The political dimensions of theology had surely come into greater focus. Yet the faculty at United could not be said to have come to a new theological consensus. Like the times the faculty reflected the diversity and plurality of the current scene.

When the Curriculum Task Force presented its revisions to the faculty two areas had received thorough examination and reformulation.[5] In those two areas there were developed two basic paradigms for the changes that were proposed. In the area of Christian Leadership the basic paradigm was one of Reflective Practitioner. Here theory and practice were to be seen in dialogue and out of that dialogue the student and/or minister was to become a practical theologian. The basic required courses were reformulated in the light of that perception and reorganized in the light of the competencies that were expected of such a reflective practioner.

In the area that had previously been called Christianity and Culture the metaphor or paradigm of dialogue had been changed to that of reflective interpreter. The courses were therefore now under the rubric of Theological and Religious Interpretation. Two major factors were influential in this shift. One was that the students who were coming to seminary did not have the background to do theological interpretation and needed to have a series of courses that would introduce them to the range and possibilities of theological interpretation. The other was that the awareness of the social location of the interpreter shaped the outcome of theological reflection and produced a variety of results. No longer could one assume a common theological perspective from which to do theological work.

To encompass these two paradigms the expression "reflective engagement" became the ruling metaphor. This shift represented a revision of the critical correlation model with a concern to make theological education applicable to the current scene. Here there was a clearer recognition that the questions and answers were given in the culture as well as in the faith tradition. What this shift accomplished was to make the

[5]The revision of the curriculum was accepted by the Senate on April 22, 1987.

educational enterprise clearer in terms of what it expected the outcomes to be. A further and important gain was to integrate the Master of Arts and the Master of Divinity programs in a manner that had not previously been achieved. All entering students now had to take the required courses in Theological and Religious Interpretation. What the revision did not accomplish was any significant change in the courses under the heading of Christian Heritage. No doubt this was in part because no Biblical professor had been involved in the process. But it could also be argued that the courses in Christian Heritage had been doing "reflective engagement," engagement with a past which shapes and forms the current theological task.

Steckel, in reflecting on the curriculum revision process, would later say that the changes were not greater due to several factors.[6] There had been no strong discontent with the curriculum since most had formulated and worked within that curriculum for some time. Further there had been no critical mass of new faculty who were seeking change or who had a compelling vision that would be accepted by their colleagues. And finally there had been no common theological perspective to which the faculty could commit itself. What shifts in the curriculum had taken place were more pedagogical than theological. The earlier concerns for integration and theological focus continued in the revised curriculum. The ecumenical vision still informed the faculty discussions and their outcomes.

During Mills tenure as President the financial situation of the seminary continued to be a major issue. One sign of the tenuous situation was the fact that often gifts were as much as 75% of the annual income of the school. The Development Office had the unenviable position of having yearly to raise unheard of amounts of gifts to keep the school operating. In a time of rapid inflation, often of double digits, it meant that increasing amounts of money were needed to maintain the institution. Just before Hultgren's resignation he had calculated that it would take 21 million dollars of endowment just to keep going on a level plain!

It also meant that the school was continually under severe economic constraints. Programs were desired by the publics of the school and faculty

[6]Interview with Clyde J. Steckel, at UTS, October 10, 1991.

were not able to fulfill those desires. Each year the budget was hopefully constructed but toward the end of the year each department was asked to go back and see where cuts could be made or economies effected. At Senate meetings the faculty were regularly reminded that funds were limited and that the expectations of a shortfall in income were real. When the monthly paycheck arrived the faculty and staff were asked to return the envelopes for reuse. Morale of the faculty and staff was at an ebb. A faculty salary erosion study showed that over the years the compensation of faculty members had fallen further and further behind their colleagues in theological education.[7]

It became clear to the President and the Development Office that without a capital campaign the situation would not improve. The question was how to undertake such a campaign? Mills had admitted that before coming to United he had never raised a cent. The Twin Cities are known for their charitable gifts and religious context. United Seminary however did not have a high profile in that context and still does not. With 80% of the population Lutherans and Catholics, the representation of "mainstream Protestantism" is very small. To show the seminary's commitment to the task and the goal of the capital campaign the decision was made to sell the faculty homes and all but eleven acres of the remaining property.

This decision was not taken without pain in the community. To sell the additional land meant that various options that had been discussed over the years would no longer be possible. The Vice President for Development, Gregory Ritter, particularly opposed the decision and resigned over the issue. Ritter had been a graduate of United and had served as a Presbyterian pastor in the area. He had joined the development staff as the Church Relations officer and had been appointed Vice President for Development when the previous incumbent had resigned. His commitment to the school was strong and deep. He felt that the moneys necessary could be raised without this serious loss of land. In keeping with the integrity of his position he felt he could no longer continue when the decision was contrary to his beliefs. Others on the Board of Trustees and on the faculty questioned the wisdom of selling the land, of divesting the school of an important asset. It

[7]Faculty Minutes, 14 October 1986.

will probably always remain an open question whether that was the correct decision.

The selling of the faculty houses also presented some other issues to the seminary. The original houses had been built to provide a community of scholars and teachers. With homes on campus it was hoped that faculty would be able to participate in the community that was the seminary and entertain students in their homes. With the coming of the Eighties this perspective no longer seemed to pertain. A variety of styles of living, both among the faculty and students, were now the rule rather than the exception. Increasingly faculty had moved off campus and often it was difficult to find tenants for the houses. There had been increasing tension between faculty and administration over the housing policies, and though several groups had worked on the issues the solutions were not generally regarded as satisfactory.

Another issue that the faculty houses raised was the question of how the alumni would react to the proposal. The alumni of Mission House Seminary and their churches had raised the money to build the initial houses. Would they regard the sale of the houses as a betrayal? It was hoped that they would see that times had changed and that the sale would now increase the endowment of the school.

In the end the decision was made by the Board of Trustees to sell the faculty houses and the land to the north and east of the school. It was hoped that the developer would use some of the land to build apartments that would house elderly, as well as offer some of the units to seminarians and faculty. The City of New Brighton would not approve multiple dwellings and the final plans included only single family houses. By December 1985 a contract of sale had been signed and on July 1986 work was begun to develop the property. The future development of the school would have to take place within the eleven acres that remained.

The sale of the land and the work of the Capital Campaign was able to raise about two and a half million dollars for endowment. With the completion of the campaign all internal and external indebtedness had been paid off. For the first time in its history United had an endowment that would play a significant role in the financial condition of the school. Such an endowment was modest compared to most institutions of higher education yet it meant that the school had some stability that had not been previously present. The financial condition of the school was still in a precarious position.

One related event to the campaign was the Tent of Meeting. This was a fabric art construction by Michelle Zackheim to symbolize the interrelatedness of Judaism, Christianity and Islam, using the form of a Bedouin tent. The Tent of Meeting became the occasion of getting the identity of the seminary out into the community as the capital campaign began. This large construction was set up as an exhibit at the Landmark Center in St. Paul. It opened on October 2, 1986, and became a location for classes, interpretive events, and the Fall Academic Convocation at which Prof. Norman Jackson was installed. Churches and the community were invited to the Tent to enter into dialogue regarding the issues of faith and society. Though the Tent of Meeting helped to get the seminary known in the community it did add to the financial burden of the school.

Mills would serve for only four years as President of United. In June 1986 he was elected General Secretary of the United Church of Canada at its annual meeting. Following that meeting he announced his resignation, effective July 1, 1987. In four short years the school, under Mills presidency, made some important transitions. In the process the institution grew up and began to reach a stability that it had not previously known. Mills had brought the Church, denominational and ecumenical, into the life of the seminary and opened up its mission through continuing education and awareness of its role in the community. One of his final acts was to help the trustees and faculty work through a revised Mission Statement that represented a reformulation of the ecumenical vision that undergirded the school.

At the same time that Mills was preparing to leave United two other resignations took place. One was the resignation of Harrell Davis as Director of NATA as he decided to pursue further education toward a graduate degree. The other was the retirement of W. Robert Strobel, Associate Professor of Christian Education. Strobel had been on part-time appointment for the past several years and decided to take retirement at the end of the school year in 1987. His leaving meant that the last direct ties with Yankton School of Theology were no longer present in the seminary. Yankton College had itself gone out of business in 1984, 102 years after its founding by Joseph Ward.

62. Benjamin T. Griffin, President, 1987- , Liturgics, 1988-

63. John W. Bodwell, III, Vice President for Development, 1990-

64. H. Wilson Yates, Dean, 1989-

65. Marilyn Salmon, New Testament Theology, 1989-

CHAPTER 19

BUILDING A FUTURE

With Mills' resignation announced a year in advance a new search committee had ample time to look for a new president. The changes in United were marked by the fact that this time there were many candidates for the position. The committee looked long and hard under the direction of Dr. Jack Rossmann, Dean of Macalester College and member of the Board of Trustees. Its first choice for the position was Benjamin T. Griffin, pastor of Trinity United Church of Christ in York, Pennsylvania from 1975-1987.[1] Griffin had also been Chair of the Board of Trustees of Lancaster Theological Seminary. His skills as minister, administrator, and trustee made him an extremely attractive candidate.

A paper he wrote on the nature of theological education was perhaps a decisive factor in his choice. In it Griffin set forth a vision that was most compatible with that at United. McMillan, who was now chair of the Board of Trustees, brought the paper to the attention of the search committee.

When Griffin arrived on the scene he quickly discovered that one of the major issues with which he had to deal was the morale of the faculty and staff. There had been serious erosion of that morale under the previous administrations. One factor was that the impression had been gained that

[1]Griffin had his B.A. from Baylor University and an M.A. from the University of Texas. His M.Div. was from Andover Newton Theological School and his D. Min. from Lancaster Theological Seminary. The son of missionary parents he was an ordained minister in the United Church of Christ.

the financial condition of the school was precarious. There had developed a dominant perspective that the school might not open the following Fall. This played itself out in some peculiar ways. One was that the control on expenditures had been problematic. Budgets were adopted that did not have a high level of reality and before each year was over the administration would come to the faculty and staff requesting savings in the various areas so that the budget might be balanced. Such an approach was demoralizing because it meant that areas were being cut not from some overall perspective but from the exigencies of the time. One consequence of this situation was Griffin's appointment of Lois Nyman as Vice President for Finance and Administration. This was the first woman to serve at that level at United.

Another aspect of this situation was that faculty and staff were being asked to do ever more without recognition of their roles nor appropriate financial reward. Though the involvement in the life of the school may have been healthy the attitudes it fostered and the perceptions it inculcated were not. It represented a penny wise and pound foolish approach to management.

Another area of serious concern was the question of the identity of the school as it approached the end of the century. United had been founded as an ecumenical theological school in the upper Midwest. With the changing times that claim no longer was a distinctive note. Other schools were also ecumenical. What does it mean to be ecumenical when every other school is becoming ecumenical? In response to this issue and other questions of identity the Board of Trustees instituted a study of the mission statement of the seminary. All parts of the school were involved in the discussions. The faculty spent several sessions debating the issues and seeking ways to express its self-understanding. In the end a new mission statement was formulated. It took several important steps forward. First it was much more theological in focus than the previous statement. Fear of misunderstanding had been replaced by a concern to express clearly the theological commitment of the seminary to the transformation of persons and society. It also declared with great forthrightness its stance in the Reformed tradition. For the first time the seminary in its ecumenical focus was able to identify its own particular contribution to the larger life of the church. And finally the new statement recognized a profound shift in theological education, the shift to a new regionalism. The old ideal of national constituencies and publics no longer worked. Students and support come primarily from the Upper Midwest region. In the light of this statement and his own standing in the United Church of Christ Griffin was able to reforge the links to elements of the constituency that had become increasingly estranged from the school.

The condition of the school became clearer under Griffin's leadership as his rhetoric and actions were consonant and reflected an open and positive approach. The budgeting process was revised to incorporate a more realistic projection of income and to shape the expenditures in the light of longer term goals. Accompanying this budgetary revision was a re-establishment of the long-range planning committee. Under the direction of Sue Zabel, who was working on her doctorate in this area, the committee examined its context and the factors impinging on the school. It held many meetings both for itself and the larger community of the school in which the issues were discussed. Out of the process that lasted several years came six strategic commitments. These became integrated into the budgeting process and thereby were not only ideal hopes but real possibilities.

One issue of increasing importance to United was that of deferred maintenance due to tight budgets and the need for more space, especially for the library. The Trustees appointed a Task Force on Physical Facilities, headed by David Hanson of the Board. Its task was to ascertain the needs of the school and the possible solutions to those needs. In the midst of that task the process was changed by an invitation from Luther Northwestern Theological Seminary to enter into conversation.

The focus of the conversation was to be the possibility of United relocating on the campus of Luther Northwestern. David Tiede, the president of Luther Northwestern, had assumed office at the same time as Griffin. Both schools were in the midst of strategic planning, including site development. Late in the fall of 1989 Tiede initiated conversations with Griffin about his concern to share the LNTS campus with other consortium schools. This would enhance the ecumenical understandings of the school and also reduce overhead costs. By January of 1990 the two presidents and the chairs of the two boards, Steve Mahle for UTS and David Nasby for LNTS, were meeting to discuss the issues involved. For United the question was primarily one of identity. How could a small school preserve its identity on the campus of the largest Lutheran seminary? Yet United expressed a strong willingness to talk.

In May the two boards took formal actions to approve the conversations. As Griffin was to say to his board, this is an "opportunity which will not come around again for many decades." One apparent option was the sharing of facilities and soon the focus became Northwestern Hall. It had its own offices, classrooms, chapel, dining area and had once even had its own library.

When the discussions became public the faculties and alumni/ae of both schools expressed strong reservations. For United the issues were those of identity and the strong tradition of social issues. For Luther Northwestern the questions tended to focus of United's theological stance which was non-confessional in character and issue oriented.

The conversations were to lead to naught. By August there had been an appraisal of Northwestern Hall which set the market value of the building at 1.8 million dollars, and the use value at 3.8 million. United was willing to pay $2 million, perhaps $2.2 million while Luther Northwestern felt it needed to have $4 million. By November of 1990 there was a seeming impasse over the price.

The goal of the conversations was not a merger between the two schools but a relocation. In the process the sharing of libraries, student housing, food services and bookstore would have provided for increased possibilities. The price for the building was more than United was willing to pay, and that for space that was not much larger than its current buildings.

The conversations came to end quite rapidly and focused too closely on real estate and money. Both schools were pressed to make decisions about their physical needs. There would be no regret that the conversations had been held. The issues of theological and social inclusivity between the two schools never reached a significant level. The economic issues finally became the breaking point.

The question remains, "What is God calling these two schools to do in these times?" If this had been the focus of the conversations the outcome might have been different. Clearly the future will call for cooperation between these two self-standing institutions. With the regionalization of theological education the interrelatedness of the task will become increasingly evident. Unfortunately misunderstanding still is extant between the two schools, the one grounded in its confessional basis and the other in its openness to the culture in which it seeks to serve.[2]

Another issue that Griffin addressed soon after his arrival was that of academic governance. Griffin had Jack Rossmann, the trustee who had led the search committee, study this aspect of the seminary's structure. Rossmann as former Dean at Macalester College had restructured the academic governance at that college. He was a logical choice and his suggestions helped to cut down the larger governance overhead that had become a burden on the faculty. The standing committees of the Senate were reduced to four and greater freedom of action was given to the directors of the academic programs. This restructuring process needs to be done periodically for faculty are prone to add committees to address the concerns of the moment. Along with these changes came the resignation of Clyde Steckel as Academic Vice President. His resignation was the consequence of his desire to return to his field of teaching.

Steckel had spent nine years in office, under very trying times. Serving under three presidents he had carried a heavy load as the person of continuity. When he assumed the office he was burdened by the fact that Tom Campbell had just died and that death would be mourned for many years afterwards. Griffin would say that mourning was still evident when he first arrived. The first Dean, Louis Gunnemann, was still alive and present on the scene, though he did not participate in the governance of the school nor involve himself in the daily life of the seminary. Steckel's own style tended to be highly responsive, a reflection of his own personality and training. Yet he had brought the school through its accreditation in 1982, virtually single-handedly and under the shadow of Hultgren's resignation. He

[2]Interview with Benjamin Griffin, in his office, January 30, 1992.

was most optimistic and trusting about those with whom he worked. At times that trust was not repaid and some of his administrative appointments would bring him great grief and distress. One of his contributions was freeing up many of the faculty to be scholars and teachers without the heavy burdens of administrative detail. As he approached retirement Steckel resigned primarily because he wanted to spend his time writing and teaching. That was his first love. He had given generously of himself to the institutional life of the seminary and brought it through difficult times. He had helped the seminary to claim its commitments to women and feminism, to Native Americans and to gays and lesbians. He would often say that his goal was a school that was inclusive, integrative and intentional. Now he was ready to take a new tack and return to teaching. In the following years he would become in many ways the successor of Louis Gunnemann as a major theologian of the United Church of Christ, contributing to both the inner and ecumenical discussions of the church. He would also succeed Louis Gunnemann as coeditor of *Prism: a theological forum for the United Church of Christ*.

The structure of academic change was again put into motion with the appointment of a search committee for a new Dean. Though the search was nationwide it soon focused on three candidates, all from within the faculty. In the end the choice of the committee was H. Wilson Yates, Professor of Religion, Society and the Arts. For some this was an unexpected choice. It would prove to be an excellent decision and the combination of Griffin and Yates would bring a high level of morale to the community and solid leadership for the school. Yates was looking for a change in his life and career, both personally and professionally. He had been teaching for twenty years and had done some innovative programming for the school. He had impeccable credentials as both a social activist and scholar. His study of theology and the arts in theological education had been a pioneering study and introduced him to the wider world of theological education.[3]

---

[3]*The Arts in Theological Education: New Possibilities for Integration*, Atlanta: Scholars Press, 1987.

Yates would prove to be a very fine Dean. A good administrator, he did not let the details get in the way of persons. A strong Dean, he could be firm yet gentle as he confronted the faculty and led them to look beyond themselves. He was a good role model for his faculty as an intellectual leader and in having high expectations for himself as well as others. He was a support to faculty as they needed time to accomplish projects or money to get research done.

His lasting contribution to United and his legacy for the years ahead will be the shaping of the faculty. Yates would take over the academic leadership just as the original faculty was beginning to retire. Some had already left, and others were in the process of detaching themselves from the school. Not only faculty but also long time staff were retiring. Among the latter one should particularly note the retirement of Alice Strobel who had started as the secretary to the Dean in 1962 and had served faithfully until 1987. When she retired she was Registrar and Director of Academic Services for the school. Her title however did not reflect her importance. She was the living memory of the institution; if you wanted to know what or when or how or whom she could answer or lead you in the right direction. She was the one who could listen and understand, but would not spread the news around. Often Alice Strobel was the one who made life at the seminary more tolerable. Alongside Alice Strobel as a stalwart of the staff was Marian Hoeft. Hoeft had begun as the secretary to President Huenemann. That was in the days when the President's office was responsible for development and public relations, for alumni affairs and institutional management, for all the matters that were outside the academic realm. Many were the nights she worked overtime to get the letters out, the mailing addressed, the proof back to the printer.

Hoeft would leave the school for several years to run a resort in northern Minnesota with her husband but she returned to serve in the front office and finally work as Administrative Assistant to the Dean. She too carried the memory of the school and worked diligently and with great commitment until her retirement in December of 1989.

It was 1989 which in many ways represented the turning of the times and the changes in the school. In February of that year the Faculty recommended to the Board of Trustees the appointment of Marilyn Salmon as Assistant Professor of New Testament, to replace Henry Gustafson.[4] Salmon had taught at the College of St. Catherine, in St. Paul, and had worked on the Gospel of Luke in her doctoral dissertation. She would make important contributions to the Jewish-Christian dialogue in the Twin Cities communities. In April the first woman was promoted to full professor: Mary Bednarowski, in Religious Studies. That distinction would last only about five minutes as Mary Potter Engel was also promoted to full professor and granted tenure at the same meeting.

In October Louis Gunnemann, the founding Dean of United, died and the seminary and church suffered a great loss. Memorial Services were held not only in the local church of which he was a member but also at the seminary. Tributes to his theological leadership and gentle human nature came from far and wide. Surely this event marked what might be called the end of the beginning.

Among the changes that came into effect at this time was the appointment of Ben Griffin as Professor of Liturgics. The faculty recognized his contributions to the educational program of the school and the importance of this field to the curriculum. In making the recommendation to the Board of Trustees Griffin became the first teaching president with professorial identification. It indeed marks his definition of the role of the President and its relationship to the rest of the faculty.

Faculty changes moved steadily onward. In 1990 Carolyn J. Pressler was appointed Assistant Professor of Old Testament to pick up the load lain down by Allan McAllaster.[5] Pressler brought a rich background, with experience as a community organizer as well as solid academic work. Her

---

[4]Salmon was a native of Minnesota, receiving her B.A. from Concordia College, Moorhead, MN, her M.Div. from Luther Northwestern Theological Seminary, and her Ph.D. from Hebrew Union College in Cincinnati, OH. She became an ordained priest in the Episcopal Church.

[5]Pressler, a native of Indiana, had received her B.A. from Kalamazoo College, her M.Div. from Wesley Theological Seminary and was finishing her doctoral work at Princeton Theological Seminary. Her ordination was in the United Methodist Church. She received her Ph.D. from Princeton in May 1991.

66. Carolyn J. Pressler, Old Testament Theology, 1990-

67. Christine M. Smith, Preaching and Worship, 1991-

68. Barbara Anne Keely,
Educational Ministries, 1991-

69. Christine Cozad Neuger,
Theology and Psychology, 1992-

70. Paul E. Capetz, Historical Theology, 1992-

dissertation focused on the laws regarding women in the Book of Deuteronomy. Her promise as a scholar and teacher in the field seems to be assured. Lance Barker resigned as Director of the D.Min. Program and in his place Wendell Debner of Luther Northwestern Theological Seminary took over, the first non-United director of the program. Barker would be able to undertake a major study of religious leadership in rural America for the Lilly Foundation as a consequence of his shift in responsibilities.

By the end of the 1990-91 academic year three faculty members had announced their intention to retire. Eugene Jaberg, Robert Bryant and Helen Archibald had all reached the stage in their lives when they wanted to lay down the responsibilities of full time teaching and administration. A major event in May 1991 recognized the great contributions they had made to the seminary and its life. Jaberg and Bryant had both been on the original faculty of United. All three faculty would continue on a part-time and adjunct basis following retirement but it did mean that a search for new faculty had to begin. The faculty had to reexamine its priorities again.

The decision was made that the initial searches would be for persons in the area of Preaching and Worship and in the area of Educational Ministries. To fill the positions the committees were fortunate to find excellent candidates. For the position in Preaching and Worship Christine Smith, who was teaching at Princeton Seminary was chosen.[6] Smith had already achieved stature in her field for her book entitled *Weaving the Sermon*, a feminist approach to preaching. For the position in Educational Ministries Barbara Anne Keely from Presbyterian School of Education in Richmond, VA was chosen.[7] Keely, a second career minister, shows great promise as a theological educator for the church.

---

[6]Smith, a native of Ohio, took her B.A. at Ohio University and her seminary training, M.Div. and M.A., at the Methodist Theological School in Ohio. Her Ph.D. was earned at the Graduate Theological Union in Berkeley, California, 1987. She had taught at Princeton Theological Seminary from 1986-1991. Smith is an ordained minister in the United Methodist Church.

[7]Keely, a native of the state of Washington, received her B.A. and M.A. from the University of Washington. Her M.Div. was earned at Princeton Theological Seminary and her Ed.D. from the Presbyterian School of Christian Education in Richmond, Virginia in 1991. She is an ordained minister in the Presbyterian Church, U.S.A.

In the midst of all these changes Mary Potter Engel shocked her colleagues with the announcement that she was resigning her position to move to South Carolina with her husband. With two small children, and a husband who was a doctor, Engel had been feeling the stress of both home and work. It was hoped that a reduced load of teaching would help to remedy the situation. This change in location meant a great loss to United. Engel was a productive and creative scholar, deeply appreciated by her students and colleagues. Her contributions to the school had been innumerable and had helped to shape the character of the seminary. She would not be easily replaced.

Her resignation did allow for another appointment. It had become evident to Dean Yates that a former student and graduate Christie Cozad Neuger was looking for another position. Neuger was teaching at Princeton in Theology and Psychology and had always been regarded as a possible addition to the faculty at United. With Steckel approaching retirement here was an opportunity to get Neuger on board early. The faculty quickly agreed that this was a good move, interviewed Neuger, and recommended her to the Board of Trustees. Her coming to United was set for the Fall of 1992, when her obligation to Princeton would terminate.

Another appointment was made in 1992 of Paul E. Capetz to the position in Historical Theology.[8] Following a full search it became evident that this new teacher at Union Theological Seminary in Virginia was the candidate for United. For the moment the faculty was at full strength again.

In two short years the composition of the faculty had changed radically and forever. Only one of the original faculty was still on full appointment as of the Fall of 1992. At the same time there were six women on full appointment. It indeed represents a true crisis, a time of opportunity as well as loss of collective memory. Into the hands of this faculty was entrusted the future of the dream that is United.

---

[8]Capetz, a native of California, received his B.A. from the University of California, Los Angeles, his M.Div. and M.A. in Religious Studies from Yale Divinity School, and is a candidate for the Ph.D. at the Divinity School of the University of Chicago. He is a minister in the Presbyterian Church, U.S.A.

EPILOGUE

As United moves into the Nineties and its fourth decade of existence there are those who decry the nature and character of theological education. A prime example of such a view is the article by Paul Wilkes entitled "The Hands that would shape our Souls."[1] In a look at theological education in America he does not find much to encourage those who look to the seminaries as the source of the leadership in the church and synagogue. What lies at the heart of the issues with which both Wilkes and the theological schools of America are attempting to deal is the question of diversity.

It is this diversity that is both the blessing and bane of theological education, and of the church itself. On the one hand Robert Bellah reminds us that individualism and pluralism are the marks of American religiosity. He argues that the churches are less and less concerned with mission and worship than with therapy and support, that the good of the individual is placed ahead of the common good. This individualism is the source of fragmentation in the society and the churches.

On the other hand Wilson Yates, in his response to Wilkes article,[2] reminds us that "theological education has had no golden age." The diversity of the student bodies in theological schools today is an enriching and

[1]Paul Wilkes, "The Hands that would shape our Souls," *The Atlantic Monthly*, December 1990, pp. 59-88.

[2]Wilson Yates, "Seminaries: Back to the Future?" *Christianity and Crisis* 51:5/6 (April 8, 1991) 122-125.

stimulating reality. Today the classroom encompasses women as well as men, people of color as well as white, married, single and divorced, homosexuals as well as heterosexuals, 50 year olds as well as those right out of college, those preparing for lay or ordained ministry as well as those who are seeking direction in their lives. Surely they raise issues with which the school and its administrators have not previously had to deal. That diversity at the same time brings a new set of possibilities and directions, not only for the educational process but for the church itself.

The very definition of ecumenical perhaps needs to be looked at again. In church circles that has meant too often some type of organic merger or institutional arrangement. In the 1950's that was the kind of ecumenism that drove those who had a vision for the seminary and its future. Even that vision looked to the nature of the church and its mission as the focus of its ecumenical task. In the context in which United came into existence the focus of theological education was on education in the Christian faith. The assumption was that the students had a Christian formation and were cognizant of ministerial practice.

United, however, has been driven by a vision that seeks the integration of theological understanding, the integration of both classical and practical fields, of theory and praxis, of action and reflection. Though the terms may change the integrative drive seeks to bring the various diversities together into a theological whole. In the oneness of God lies that mandate for theological integrity.

The diversity of the students means that the theological school has to find new ways to express it vision and commitment. The student has always been the locus of theological reflection. As the classroom has brought together a variety of persons the range of theological reflection has had to broaden. The horizon of discourse has had to be extended. This is today reflected in the emphasis on globalization that seeks to take theological education out of narrow and parochial settings. Those who envision the past as an ideal age, needing to be recaptured, forget the problems and confusions of an earlier time. What most theological schools need is more diversity. United has done relatively well with students who are women and those who have differing affectional preferences. Persons of color and international students are still few and far between. A goal of the school is not only to increase enrollment to bring in more students, but also with that increase to bring greater diversity.

With the increase in women on the faculty there is also the concern to address with greater adequacy the role and character of women in religion and ministry. This has led to the formation of a program entitled "Women's Studies: Religion, Theology and Ministry." This is the natural outgrowth of the early concerns for women's studies in 1973, as well as the focusing of various elements present in the curriculum. The inauguration of the program was March 10, 1992, with a lecture by Prof. Renita Weems Espinoza of the Divinity School of Vanderbilt University.

At the same time the preparation for the future includes a new Capital Campaign under the leadership of President Griffin and Vice-President for Development John Bodwell III. The goal of this campaign is the building of a new administrative and faculty office building, the renovation of the main building to expand the library and enhance the student services, and to build endowment for scholarships and the academic program. Part of the strategic planning of the school, this major development in the life of United reflects its commitment to the task of theological education in the world it seeks to serve.

The Spring of 1992 was marked by the achieving of accreditation from the Association of Theological Schools and the North Central Association of Schools and Colleges. The report of the team was most positive and marks the maturing of the institution into an important center for theological education.

The future continues to lure the school to faithfulness in faith, learning and service. As an institution of theological education it is called to show fidelity in the descriptive task of understanding and to be creative in the critical task as it looks at the church and society in which it lives. As a living organism it will continue to grow and change. The stories which it tells about itself reflect a self-awareness of weaknesses as well as a hopefulness toward that future. As with all faithful existence, it is Soli Deo Gloria! To God alone be the glory!

APPENDICES

APPENDIX ONE:

A NEW BEGINNING FOR CHERISHED CONTINUITIES

by Louis H. Gunnemann

When United Theological Seminary of the Twin Cities opened its doors to students in September of 1962, two traditions in American church life flowed together in a new venture in theological education. Both of these traditions had long and significantly different histories encompassing a full century of service in the westward expansion of the nation.[1]

Although the continuities in these traditions were intentionally affirmed in the formation of the new seminary, their importance emerges chiefly in relation to the ecclesial and religious climate of the latter part of that century of service. The thesis of this chapter is that the spirit and energies of modern ecumenism provided not only the vision but also an ecclesial climate favorable to the concept of merging two rather disparate traditions in theological education.

The immediate enabling event leading to the chartering of United Seminary in September of 1960 was the formation of the United Church of Christ by the union of the Evangelical and Reformed Church and the Congregational Christian Churches in 1957. That church union was in itself a landmark occasion in American church life. *The Christian Century* editorialized: "we believe the emergence of the United Church of Christ will

---

[1]Mission House Seminary was founded in 1862. The School of Theology of Yankton College had its beginning in 1878.

stand as a milestone in our spiritual history...in it American Protestantism turned a corner. A trend that had run in one direction for 300 years was reversed."[2] Reinhold Niebuhr saw this church union as offering some hope of order in America's chaotic pluralism.[3]

Although church unions were important expressions of the ecumenical spirit in mid-century, the formation of the United Church of Christ represented a significant breakthrough. It was the only union in the nation that combined diverse polity, confessional, doctrinal, ecclesial, and ethnic traditions.[4] The union of the two church bodies, one rooted in the Anglo-Saxon Puritan Reformation, the other in the German and continental Reformation, was itself a new venture in ecumenical endeavors. The theological journeys of these church bodies followed quite different paths. Their polity principles reflected diverse histories in the ordering of church life. At the same time, both church bodies embraced – although somewhat minimally – other ethnic and minority groups. On the Congregational Christian side this included German Russian people who had organized themselves into the German General Congregational Conference of Congregational Christian Churches. This Conference was the parent body of the Yankton School of Theology.

These features of the United Church of Christ provide one important key for the understanding of the events leading to the establishment of United Seminary. The same ecumenical imperative and vision that caused that church union played a crucial role in bringing together two schools with disparate traditions and histories. That ecumenical motive is attested in *A Basis of Union Between Mission House Theological Seminary and Yankton School of Theology*, adopted in 1960:

---

[2]*The Christian Century*, July 17, 1957, p. 863.

[3]"A Landmark in American Religious History," *The Messenger*, June 18, 1957, pp. 11-12.

[4][See L.H. Gunnemann, *The Shaping of the United Church of Christ*, New York: United Church Press, 1978]. In other parts of the world there were significant examples of this type of church union: the Church of South India; the Church of North India; and the United Churches in Japan and the Philippines; and the United Church of Canada are examples. Unions in the U.S.A. tended to be intra-family.

> The imperative of our faith and the compelling requirements of the world combine to lay upon the church the obligation to provide the most adequate program of theological education possible. The formation of the United Church of Christ by the denominations from which we have drawn our constituency offers an unprecedented opportunity for uniting the two into *an effective, ecumenically oriented seminary....* The seminary shall affirm its responsibility to the United Church of Christ and maintain a relationship to that body in accordance with...the constitution of the United Church. As an expression of its service to the whole Christian enterprise, the seminary, both in the structure and outreach of the ministry, shall *relate itself in effective ways to the spirit and effort of evangelical and ecumenical Protestantism."*[5]

The ecumenical significance of this statement is sharply underlined by the vastly different ecclesial, theological and religious histories of the two institutions. Because United Theological Seminary of the Twin Cities was deliberately established as a new school, the histories of the two schools in the period between 1862 and 1962 are generally overlooked. Their importance, however, cannot be disregarded without intimating that United Seminary is a rootless institution.

The background histories of the traditions merged into United Seminary provide a striking example of the influence of historical circumstance upon their common roots. It is in the interplay of German ethnicity and German pietism over a period of more than two hundred fifty years that the distinguishing characteristics of these institutional histories can be identified and understood.

Both institutions had their ecclesial roots in nineteenth-century German immigration. Although their common ethnic characteristics would suggest considerable homogeneity, the reality is quite otherwise.

On the one hand, the General Conference of Congregational Christian Churches, the parent body of Yankton School of Theology, was

---

[5]Italics added by LHG. Quoted from Section A "Principles," using portions of paragraphs 1, 3, and 4. Approval of the *Basis of Union* was achieved in three successive actions by the responsible bodies: by the Mission House Seminary trustees on June 2, 1960; by the Administrative Committee of the General Council of the Evangelical and Reformed Church on June 16, 1960; and by the General Conference of Congregational Christian churches (German) on June 22, 1960.

almost exclusively composed of German-Russian immigrants who came to the western states in the 1870s and 1880s. Their ethnic ties, which had been tested in two emigrations, first from Germany to Russia and then from Russia to America, made them sturdily independent in all matters: religious, social and economic. This independence, sustained and nurtured by ethnic insularity during the Russian sojourn, was reinforced by Pietism, a religious perspective of great importance in the eighteenth and nineteenth centuries. Pietism, of course, affected all of European Protestantism, giving the churches a spiritual counterpoint to the enervating scholasticism of the seventeenth century.

For the Germans who migrated to Russia between 1762 and 1801 the Pietist experience was a binding and driving force that knit them together in a closed community. Although having either Reformed or Lutheran background in the German homeland, their Pietist perspectives placed greater importance on the fellowship created by the work of the Spirit than upon the church. George Eisenach, eminent historian of this movement, provides a helpful interpretation:

> It is significant that the majority of the first immigrants were "Brueder" and "Schwestern," men and women converted by the power of the Holy Spirit. Fruit of the revivals that swept through their villages in the homeland and bound together here by the spirit of pietism which came to expression in the Bruederschaft (religious brotherhood), they stood ready to join almost any denomination which was not antagonistic to revivals, which granted them the freedom to hold prayer meetings and to worship in the German language.[6]

As implied in that description, the religious vitality of the Germans who migrated from Russia was less dependent upon the church than upon the common experience of the new birth and the bonds of the spirit. This meant a particular style of church life that found a hospitable home in the Congregational Churches of the western states. Autonomy of the local church made possible the maintenance of ethnic ties, but also resulted in some isolation from the mainstream church life.

---

[6]George J. Eisenach, *Pietism and the Russian Germans in the U.S.*, Berne, Indiana: Berne Publishers, 1948, p. 42.

The shared characteristics of German ethnicity and pietism, however, often reflect quite contrasting experiences. The results can be noted in the forming of a different kind of ecclesial history in the Evangelical and Reformed Church, the parent body of Mission House Theological Seminary.[7] Founders of the Mission House came directly from Germany and Switzerland, beginning in the 1840s. Grounded in the Rhineland Reformed tradition, (Calvinist, Melancthonian, and Zwinglian) their religious orientation was also pietistic. Theirs, however, was a piety nurtured not only by the Bible but also by the Heidelberg Catechism, in which the importance of regeneration and sanctification in thankful living receives major emphasis. The accent on the individual's faith and experience in German Reformed piety was balanced by the awareness that God's gracious claim in Christ brings the individual into the church, the called community. Thus these German Reformed people exhibited an ecclesial piety in which the experience of regeneration and sanctification is both affirmed and confirmed by life in the church, where Word and Sacrament are essential means of grace by the work of the Holy Spirit.

Ecclesial piety, as exhibited in the German Reformed people, naturally shared some of the major characteristics of continental pietism: the reliance on the Bible for generation of faith; the internalization of the truths of the Bible as the decisive mark of the new life; and confidence in the work of the Holy Spirit. It had its source in two writings that distinguish it from the German Lutheran Pietism of Jakob Spener and August Francke: namely Lewis Bayly, *Practice of Piety*, used first in Holland and translated into German in Zurich, and the *Heidelberg Catechism*. Nevertheless, historical circumstance led to different accents and developments. The piety of the German Reformed people was cultivated within the parishes of the state church. Therefore reliance on the order of the church's life, primarily through Word and Sacrament, countered separatist tendencies that were engendered by reliance on the intimate fellowship of small Bible study

---

[7]The German Reformed people constituted the Reformed Church in the United States and became a part of the Evangelical and Reformed Church in 1934 by union with the Evangelical Synod of North America.

groups. Moreover, these Reformed people were church unity conscious. As heirs of Calvin and Melancthon, and nurtured in the corporate piety of the Catechism, they placed the unity of the church above separatist tendencies. The devotional life of these German Reformed immigrants focused on the Bible and the Heidelberg Catechism, was carried on as much in the family circle as in small study groups. The piety of the German Russian people, in contrast, moved out of the state church ethos and order when the German homeland was left behind in their emigration to Russia. Although congregations were organized in the villages they built in Russia, the lack of an ordered structure and dearth of pastors caused these people to rely on the "Brotherhood" (Bruederschaft) in their devotional life. In come cases, according to Eisenach, the Volga Brethren (Germans who settled in the Volga region of Russia) were often at odds with church authorities and sometimes were persecuted by them.[8] An incipient anti-clericalism thus developed among some of the German Russian people. As an ever-increasing lay movement, the emphases of their common life were Bible study, prayer and fellowship. For them the authority of the Bible was no longer linked to the ecumenical creeds that symbolized the church of the centuries, nor to ecclesiastical structures, but to the experience of the new birth by the Holy Spirit.

The resultant emphases on the place of the Christian life in the world offers a summary of the differences between these two forms of piety. Eisenach wrote:

> The Brethren, in the main, despair of the power of spiritual forces to redeem the world. To be sure, they believe in the power of truth and the Holy Spirit, but they do not believe these forces are today effectively operative in the lives of men in general. *Salvation is possible only for a few...Not even the church can save the world.*[9] (Italics added)

In commenting on the experience of the German Reformed people, William Toth wrote:

---

[8]See Eisenach, *Pietism*, pp. 146 ff.

[9]Eisenach, *ibid*., p. 112.

> Something new emerged which reflected carefully screened elements from both sides (Calvin & Luther) in a uniquely different pattern. The main outlines are in the Heidelberg Catechism.... Often regarded as the "fruit and flower of the whole German and French Reformation," which stimulates the conviction that Christianity, vastly more than a system of doctrine, must be a Godward orientation of the soul of man that *culminates in the transformation of the human activity according to the design of God*. Its genius lay in the irenic spirit that cultivated the love of essentials–beyond the church the Church, and beyond the Scriptures the historic stream of faith and experience.[10] (Italics added)

These diverse emphases in the piety of the German background people of the United Church of Christ have parallels, of course, among other constituencies, especially those influenced by the Great Awakenings and the rise of evangelicalism. Nevertheless, the nineteenth century German immigrations were formative of the constituencies that established Mission House Seminary and the School of Theology of Yankton College. While rationalism (or scholastic orthodoxy) and romanticism were prominent features of the theological scene on the continent of Europe at the time of these immigrations, it was pietism that shaped the life and faith of these two German church bodies.[11]

To many American mainline church people the term "pietism" has such negative connotations that it is sometimes arbitrarily dismissed from consideration. In the preceding pages I have sought to show that an off-hand dismissal of the place of pietism in the development of United Seminary would be an error. We need now to pursue that matter in a different direction.

Pietism and Ecumenical Vision

Although popular understandings of ecumenism do not associate it in any way with Pietism, the historical evidence of the linkage is irrefutable. In fact, no accurate account of the course of the ecumenical vision in Christian

---

[10]William Toth, "European Background–Reformed," in David Dunn et al., *A History of the Evangelical and Reformed Church*, Philadelphia: Christian Education Press, 1963, Chapter I.

[11]See Claude Welch, *Protestant Thought in the Nineteenth Century*, Vol. I, Chap. 2.

history can be given without recognition of the enormous influence of Pietism, that spiritual renewal dynamic that emerged in Western Europe in the mid-seventeenth century. Sometimes called "the Spirit's revolt" against the deadening hand of Protestant scholasticism, Pietism actually transformed the religious energies of the Protestant movement. In its initial stages, and at several later periods of its development, it broke down the barriers established by a rigid and defensive confessionalism, liberating the individual Christian from the bonds of theological orthodoxy and magisterial ecclesiasticism.

Most often associated with a missionary zeal to further the conversion of all people to the Christian faith, it was nevertheless equally responsible for a new spiritual comprehension of the unity of the church. In the early nineteenth century in Europe, and in America as well, Pietism gave birth to spiritual revivals that accentuated the active and personal faith of the believer as over against the orthodox insistence on right beliefs. In so doing, ecclesiastical and creedal authority, with its well-marked boundaries dividing the church into acceptable enclaves, was countered by a spirit of freedom and zeal that embraced all believers in the cause of Christ. It is with good reason, then, that Prof. Martin Schmidt of Heidelberg could write: "Pietism regard(ed) itself as the actual incorporation of the ecumenical idea."[12]

The ecumenical spirit of Pietism exhibited its greatest vision and vigor in the many voluntary missionary enterprises that sprang up in the early 1800s. Spurred on by the Evangelical Awakenings, all of these, both in Europe and America, carried on their work without the aid of–and sometimes with the strong disapproval of–established church structures. A pervading concern for Christian unity characterized these missionary enterprises and cultivated the ground soil of the modern ecumenical movement.

---

[12]Martin Schmidt, "Ecumenical Activity on the Continent of Europe in the Seventeenth and Eighteenth Centuries," in Ruth Rouse and Stephen Neill, *A History of the Ecumenical Movement, 1517-1948*, London: SPCK, 1954, pp. 309-352.

By the 1830s, however, sectarian reactionism and self-interest began to threaten the vision. In characterizing theological developments in the middle decades of the century, Claude Welch wrote:

> The ecumenical spirit that had marked the early nineteenth century revivals in America was replaced by the party spirit, by preoccupation with the distinctiveness of the particular denomination – its theology, its polity, its rights (and likewise its own missionary and Bible societies). In part, this theological mood and strategy was concentrated on the reassertion, or preservation of biblical authority and classic theological forms. In part it represented a kind of concern about the church – its nature, status and role – that was quite new in Protestantism.[13]

The response of the ecumenically conscious voluntary organizations of mid-century to such growing denominational and sectarian self-consciousness was marked by several countering movements, three of which became the ecumenical hallmarks of the nineteenth century. The Evangelical Alliance, formed in Great Britain in 1848 by concerned lay persons, and supported by theologians such as Philip Schaff, set in motion patterns of ecumenical activity that contributed significantly to the World Missionary Conference in 1910. Prof. James Nichols of Princeton characterized the Alliance as "the explicit ecumenical agency of the benevolent empire of voluntary societies" that were the mark of Western Christianity in the nineteenth century.[14] These patterns were enhanced and strengthened by the Student Christian Movement and the World Student Christian Federation. In many respects, these movements were the outgrowth of the ecumenical activities of the Young Men's Christian Association (1844) and the Young Women's Christian Association (1855). The student involvements, having their greatest influence at the end of the nineteenth and the beginning of the twentieth centuries, were more deeply involved in ecumenical activities related directly to the churches.[15]

---

[13]*Protestant Thought in the Nineteenth Century*, Vol. 5, p. 190.

[14]*Ecumenical Testimony*, Philadelphia: Westminster, 1974, p. 178.

[15]See Ruth Rouse, "Other Aspects of the Ecumenical Movement," in *A History of the Ecumenical Movement*, pp. 599 ff.

Pietism and Ecumenism in the German Reformed Tradition

The preceding summary of the relationship between ecumenism and pietism would be incomplete without reference to the particular role of the Reformed tradition in the ecumenical consciousness of the Post-Reformation centuries. While much of that can be traced to the concerns of Calvin and Beza in Geneva, where Christian unity was a passion, it was in the development and use of the Heidelberg Catechism that Reformed theology was given an indelible ecumenical cast.[16] In the Heidelberg Catechism the unity theme, rooted in Calvin's work, was energized and made usable in the devotional life of the Reformed churches. It became the primary agent among the people of the churches, not only of Germany and Switzerland, but of Holland, Poland, Hungary and France as well.[17]

From their immersion in the Catechism Reformed people absorbed an ecclesial awareness of the church "catholic and reformed," that is, genuinely ecumenical.[18] Called "the preeminent ecumenical guide for the Christian faith,"[19] the Catechism also shaped the ecumenical vision of the German Reformed people who immigrated to the Midwest in the nineteenth century. As their daily companion in the practice of their piety, the Catechism engendered a passion for Christian unity among these people that provided a counterpoint to the isolating effects of German ethnicity.

The importance of this account of the roots of the ecumenical vision in the piety of the Reformed tradition as it was shaped by the Heidelberg Catechism, comes to a focus in the story of Mission House Theological Seminary, one of the two parent institutions of United Theological Seminary of the Twin Cities. The Mission House was established in 1862 in what was

---

[16]James Nichols, *Ecumenical Testimony*, p. 61.

[17]The Reformed tradition in its Scottish and English developments likewise carried Calvin's concern for Christian unity. That contribution to the growing ecumenism of the eighteenth and nineteenth centuries is a major part of the story of the Evangelical Alliance and related voluntary movements.

[18]Nichols, *ibid*.

[19]Hendrikus Berkhof, "The Catechism in Historical Contrast," in Bard Thompson, et al., *Essays on the Heidelberg Catechism*, Philadelphia: United Church Press, 1963, p. 91.

then the forested wilderness of eastern Wisconsin near the shores of Lake Michigan by German Reformed immigrants who had arrived only thirteen years earlier. That institution for the education and training of ordained ministers carried the seeds of Christian unity that eventually flowered into the ecumenical vision and commitment leading to the creation of United Theological Seminary one hundred years later.

It is, however, quite clear from a survey of the records of the time that founding community of the Mission House tradition had little awareness of shaping an ecumenical vision.[20] They were concerned with securing pastors for the many communities of Reformed people among the German immigrants that flooded across the upper Midwest. In that respect, they were "mission-minded" people, concerned that their fellow immigrants would have access to the same theological and spiritual tradition to which they themselves were so indebted and devoted. But it was ethnicity rather than ecumenicity that provided the energy with which they invested themselves in missionary efforts. The mark of their Calvinist piety was given in the motto they adopted for the Mission House: "Soli Deo Gloria." No more eloquent testimony can be found concerning their sense of responsibility for the Church and for Christian unity. Their contribution to what eventually became the ecumenical vision of the seminary they established can be identified and measured by their steadfast devotion to the Heidelberg Catechism – "the preeminent ecumenical guide for the Christian faith." Their immersion in the Catechism gave them an ecclesial sense that placed Christian unity above the ever-present sectarianism of expanding American denominationalism.

A fuller account of the Mission House story can be found elsewhere.[21] For the purposes of these pages it is necessary to indicate how the commitment to Christian unity became the primary impulse for ecumenical vision and commitment that emerged in that institution in the mid-twentieth

---

[20]The name *Mission House* (Das Missionshaus) was taken from similar institutions in Barmen, Germany and Basel, Switzerland, founded to train ministers and missionaries.

[21]Eugene C. Jaberg, et al., *A History of Mission House - Lakeland*, Philadelphia: Christian Education Press, 1962.

century. Between 1862 and the 1930s there is little in the institution's records to suggest latent or even an incipient ecumenical concern. The Reformed accent on Christian unity was undoubtedly reinforced by the experience and background training of the three founding ministers. Herman Muehlmeier, Jacob Bossard, and H.A. Winter, all educated in Europe, had additional study at the Mercersburg Seminary of the Reformed Church in Pennsylvania[22] before taking up their work in Wisconsin. At Mercersburg they had studied with John Williamson Nevin and Philip Schaff, two eminent theologians whose doctrine of the church, underlining organic unity, was a vigorous and profound response to the fragmentation of the church by the evangelical revivals of that time. Although there is no conclusive evidence that the theology of the Mission House founders was shaped by the Mercersburg theology, clearly the concern for Christian unity was enhanced and became a powerful thread of consistency in the Mission House tradition.

It was not until the burgeoning of the ecumenical zeal in the early twentieth century that the Mission House concern for Christian unity began to show in faculty interests and involvements. As early as the late 1920s Prof. Karl J. Ernst was in correspondence with Karl Barth of Switzerland, one of the most substantive theological architects of the modern ecumenical era. Later, Prof. Josias Friedli joined Ernst in some of the earliest translations of Barth's works into English.[23] Moreover, the unfolding of the ecumenical vision worldwide, beginning with the World Missionary Conference in 1910 and the Faith and Order and Life and Work Conferences in the 1920s and 30s, provided a new context for Christian unity concerns in the seminary.

A series of faculty retirements led to five new appointments between 1950 and 1954 that brought far reaching changes.[24] For most of its years of

---

[22]Later moved to Lancaster where it has continued under that city's name.

[23]Three volumes were published by Round Table Press (New York) between 1935 and 1937: *Come Holy Spirit*, *God's Search for Man*, and *God in Action*.

[24]In order of their appointments the five new faculty were: Theophilus F. H. Hilgeman in Church History; Walter F. Kuentzel in New Testament; Louis H. Gunnemann in Practical Theology; Frederick L. Herzog in Systematic Theology; and Brevard S. Childs in Old Testament.

educating ministers for the Reformed churches the dominant model of seminary training was one that had been shaped in European universities under the influence of Pietism. The emphases were upon the formation of the student's faith and personhood so as to make the minister a conduit and example of the faith. Added to this formation, and enhancing it with knowledge, were studies in the "theological encyclopedia," that is, studies in the Bible, dogmatics, church history and practical theology.

Although that model was not significantly changed by the new faculty it was set in a new context reflecting the theological concerns in the ecumenical era. In 1954, just a few months before the Evanston Assembly of the World Council of Churches, the new faculty, after extensive discussion, issued a statement of the foundation of theological studies at the Mission House. That statement, which appeared in all the annual catalogues of the school from 1954-1962, begins with a key declaration: "Theological studies are the integral function of the *life of the Church in the world*."[25] Succeeding paragraphs set forth the relationship of those studies to Christ, Word and Sacraments, the Bible, the Heidelberg Catechism, other confessions of the Reformation, the One Holy Catholic Church, their unity, and the general educational objectives of graduate theological education. The clarity and spirit of the entire declaration are evident in the following paragraph:

> We believe the *One Holy Catholic Church*. There is a unity of the communion of believers throughout all ages and all peoples. Jesus Christ is the foundation of this unity. Our theological studies are integrated into this communion on the basis of unity in Jesus Christ, and are therefore *intentionally ecumenical as we join in the ecumenical confessions of our faith*.[26]

The statement in its entirety, and that declaration of the church in particular, has no parallel in any previous interpretation of the seminary's self-understanding. Did it represent a change in direction? Or, was it a further development of long-heid ecumenical convictions of the founding

---

[25] *Mission House Seminary Catalogue*, 1953-54, pp. 3-8. (Italics added)

[26] Catalogue, 1953-54, p. 4. (Italics added)

German Reformed immigrants of the 1840s and 50s? The thrust of the argument in these pages implies that what emerged as an explicit ecumenical vision and commitment in the seminary in the 1950s may be likened to the blossoming of plants whose seeds had been long dormant. That inference gains greater weight from the fact that four of the five new faculty appointments were of persons who had been nurtured in the German Reformed tradition. Two of the four had studied under Ernst and Friedli when those teachers were deeply involved with Karl Barth; and another had studied with Barth in Basel.

The far-reaching changes that accompanied the efforts of the new faculty personnel at Mission House Seminary in the 1950's had other dimensions as well. Chief among them was a growing awareness that the Seminary's location on a rural campus in eastern Wisconsin was not conducive to an implementation of the faculty's conviction that, "theological studies are an integral function of *the church in the world*." The "world" confronting the seminary students was indeed undergoing radical change in the form of rural urbanization, and that was clearly only a small segment of the "world" viewed through ecumenical lens. This awareness stimulated ongoing discussion of the relationship between the vision and the immediate environment.

Pietism, Ecumenism and the German Russian Tradition

As would be expected, the linkages between ecumenism and pietism among the German Russians can be identified only by taking into account the special features of that immigrant tradition. Owing to the non-church character of the pietism that prevailed among these people, the very concept of ecumenism must be articulated in terms that take into account the emphasis of the "Brotherhood" (Bruederschaft) on the oneness of believers in Christ. The individual believer's faith in Christ, demonstrated in the new birth and in the fellowship of the Spirit, resulted in a harmony that transcended ecclesiastical lines, whether doctrinal or organizational. Thus the Brotherhood, organized to nurture the practices on which such faith depended – Bible study, prayer and fellowship – was not dependent on the church's form or teaching. Toleration and harmony, rather than ecclesiastical and theological agreement, were marks of the Spirit and, therefore, of Christian unity.

With a principal focus of all energies on the Brotherhood, the concern of the churches for a visible expression of unity was of secondary importance. In reality, then, the story of the German-Russian pietists in America is the story of the Brotherhood and less of an account of German-Russian church life. Eisenach underlined that point in reporting that although the Brotherhood constitution reads that "in no case and under no circumstance may a prayer organization regard itself as being religiously self-sufficient," many, in fact, a "vast majority did not join any church for a decade or more."[27] In time, of course, following an ancestral pattern, many did unite with Lutheran and Reformed bodies. As indicated earlier, however, the largest group of the Brethren found a church home for themselves in American Congregationalism.[28]

When the General Conference in 1927 became a part of the National Council of Congregational Churches it entered the mainstream of American denominational church life. That step, moreover, brought them into a church fellowship committed to Christian unity. It was, in fact, the first of several subsequent moves that resulted finally in the disbandment of the General Conference and the dispersion of its member congregations among conferences of the United Church of Christ.

The consequences of that dispersion cannot be told here, but it is important at this point to make reference to the affinity of the pietistic ecumenism of the German Russians to the ecumenical perspectives of one significant tradition in American Congregationalism. Eighteenth century Congregationalism, much affected by the Enlightenment, accentuated "freedom and fellowship" as the marks of the Christian community of faith. The freedom of the Christian was bonded to the fellowship of the Spirit, thus providing the essential unity of those in Christ. The influence of this perspective in American Congregational churches created a hospitable

[27]Eisenach, *Pietism and the German Russians*, p. 139.

[28]George J. Eisenach, *A History of the German Congregational Churches in the United States*, Yankton, South Dakota: Pioneer Press, 1939.

atmosphere for the German-Russian piety that also held an ecclesial view defined primarily by the fellowship of the Spirit. Ecumenism of such an ecclesial position relied heavily on toleration and harmony and concerned itself minimally with the Church as a manifestation of unity in Christ.

Although there is no documentary evidence that this affinity in ecumenical perspective was a significant factor in the events leading to the merger of Yankton School of Theology with Mission House Seminary, it is, I think, important to see it as a contributing element of change in the General Conference's understanding of its needs in the training of ministers. The formation of the United Church of Christ had underlined new notes of responsibility that the General Conference faced in the modern world. Acknowledgment of that new responsibility was exhibited in the Basis of Union for the merging schools when representatives of the Conference helped write: "The imperative of our faith and the compelling requirements of the world . . . offers an unprecedented opportunity for uniting the two into an effective, ecumenically oriented seminary." The ecumenical era had embraced the German-Russian experience in America.

In the foregoing paragraphs I have sought to identify the cherished continuities of two streams of church life that came together in the formation of United Seminary. In so doing I have traced the relationship of those continuities to the themes of the ecumenical age – the church catholic and reformed – thus underlining the importance of the Reformation heritage with which the Seminary consciously seeks to be identified. While fortuitous circumstance affects all human decisions, historical consciousness argues an intentionality that is the mark of the Christian community: confidence in the claim and call of God and a readiness to respond to the Spirit's leading. That shared confidence and readiness in the uniting schools made possible a significant venture in theological education at an opportune moment in the ecumenical era.

APPENDIX TWO:

A BASIS OF UNION BETWEEN MISSION HOUSE THEOLOGICAL SEMINARY AND YANKTON SCHOOL OF THEOLOGY

DRAWN UP BY A JOINT COMMITTEE REPRESENTING YANKTON AND MISSION HOUSE AT MINNEAPOLIS, MINNESOTA FEBRUARY 23, 1960 AND MAY 4-5, 1960

PREAMBLE

In the expectation of entering into greater service to the kingdom of Christ in the field of theological education, and in preparation for the development of a new seminary, the General Conference of Congregational Christian Churches and the Board of Trustees of Mission House Theological Seminary set forth and agree to the following statement of principles and procedures as a Basis of Union for the two schools:

A. Principles

1. The imperative of our faith and the compelling requirements of the world combine to lay upon the church the obligation to provide the most adequate program of theological education possible. The formation of the United Church of Christ by the denominations from which we have drawn

our constituency offers an unprecedented opportunity for uniting the two schools into an effective, ecumenically oriented seminary.

2. On the basis of extensive consultation and study by the responsible boards and agencies, and in the desire to continue service to the historic constituency of the schools, it is agreed that the new seminary be located in the Minneapolis - St. Paul area.

3. The seminary shall acknowledge its historic antecedents in the Congregational Christian fellowship and the Evangelical and Reformed Church, and on the basis of these shall affirm its responsibility to the United Church of Christ and maintain a relationship to that body in accordance with the provisions of the constitution for the United Church.

4. As an expression of its service to the whole Christian enterprise, the seminary, both in its structure and in the outreach of the ministry, shall relate itself in effective ways to the spirit and effort of evangelical and ecumenical Protestantism.

5. The seminary shall provide a program of theological education for the professional preparation of men and women for the whole ministry of the church in fulfillment of her mission, aiding in the preservation of values presently residing in the concerns of both schools, and taking cognizance of the special ministries demanded by rapid social changes as these affect the churches in small town and rural areas as well as in urban communities.

6. The seminary shall be established as a self-governing educational corporation with power and freedom to receive and hold property, select its teaching staff, develop and operate its program of education and service, and shall be related organically to the United Church of Christ in a manner provided by its constitution.

7. The seminary shall understand its purpose to be:

a. To serve the church in the formation of a Christian community of learning in which students may develop spiritual maturity and may be guided in a biblically oriented and professionally adequate preparation for Christian vocations;

b. To serve the church in the development of a theological center to stimulate her spiritual and intellectual life;

c. To serve the church as a vehicle for carrying on research for the enrichment of her life and mission in the world.

B. Procedures

In terms of the above principles, the organization of the new united seminary shall be accomplished in the following manner:

1. The formation of a new Board of Trustees who shall secure a charter for the seminary and shall make whatever arrangements are necessary to establish the school at the earliest possible date.

2. The new Board shall be constituted by twenty-seven persons of which at least one-third shall be ministers and one-third laymen. They shall be chosen in the following categories:

a. Nine from the General Conference constituency selected by the General Conference on nomination of its Executive Committee.

b. Nine from Mission House Seminary Board of Trustees selected by that Board.

c. Nine chosen by the above eighteen in consultation with the Superintendents of Congregational Conferences and the Presidents of Synods of the general area into which the seminary is moving, which to date includes the following conferences: Minnesota, Iowa, Kansas, Nebraska, Wisconsin, South Dakota, North Dakota, and Montana; and the following Synods: North Wisconsin, South Wisconsin, Northern, Midwest and Dakota.

3. The terms of office of members of the organizing board shall be in the following classes: (a) a two-year class (three from each of the above

categories); (b) a four-year-class (three from each of the above categories); (c) a six-year class (three from each of the above categories).

4. The power of election of the continuing Board of Trustees shall remain with the Board, subject only to veto by the General Synod of the United Church of Christ. In all subsequent elections of Board members, the principle of constituency representation shall prevail.

5. The eighteen members [2, (a) and (b)] of the new Board of Trustees shall be convened by consultation between the chairman of the Board of Education of the General Conference and the chairman of the Board of Trustees of Mission House Seminary for the purpose of selecting the additional nine members. The Board shall complete its own organization as soon as possible after its membership has been completed.

6. The new Board shall function under the general provision of the Basis of Union until a new charter has been secured and constitution ratified.

7. Both Mission House Seminary and the General Conference of Congregational Christian Churches shall pledge their present assets, including real property, invested endowments and student aid funds, or assets of any other form now being available to and used by either school, to the support of the new seminary, and shall transfer these to the new corporation when it is empowered to receive the same. The new seminary shall gain additional support from the United Seminary Appeal of the Evangelical and Reformed Church and the Christian Higher Education Fund of the Congregational Christian Churches. The resources brought to the union from the Congregational Christian and Evangelical and Reformed constituencies shall be as nearly equal as possible in value. The new seminary shall also develop its constitution and charter in a manner that shall make additional financial undergirding possible from gifts and grants from those who may be interested in supporting theological education.

8. The initial faculty of the new seminary shall be comprised of the present faculties of Mission House and Yankton, and the retired or retiring members of both faculties shall be emeriti faculty of the new seminary.

APPENDIX THREE

MEMBERS OF THE BOARD OF TRUSTEES

The Rev. Theodore R. Bader (1960-75)
The Rev. Harry W. Baumer (1960-68)
Harry T. Bernhard (1960-66)
George Burridge (1960-66)
Mrs. George Duchow (L. W. Goudie) (1960-68)
Victor H. Frank (1960-64)
Henry Gross (1960-63)
The Rev. Howard Hammelmann (1960-71)
The Rev. Carl A. Hansen (1960-61, 1968-72) Chair 1969-72
The Rev. Wilbert W. Hiller (1960-70) Temporary Chair 1960
The Rev. Ralph J. Hoffman (1960-70) Chair 1961-69
The Rev. Vernon E. Jaberg (1960-70)
The Rev. Ernest R. Klaudt (1960-70)
The Rev. Erwin Koch (1960-61)
The Rev. Carl J. Maier (1960-68)
The Rev. Jess H. Norenberg (1960-63)
The Rev. Walter Odenbach (1960-71)
Miss Florence Partridge (1960-68)
W. C. Raugust (1960-62, 1964-68)
The Rev. Henry Reifschneider (1960-70)
The Rev. Dr. Edward Sayler (1960-61) Chair 1960-61
The Rev. Fred Schneider (1960-71)

Mrs. Lawrence T. Schoen (1960-71)
The Rev. Reuben J. Schroer (1960-71)
Alvin R. Wolff (1960-72)

Prof. James M. Gustafson (1961-71)
The Rev. Wesley A. Hotchkiss (1961-74)
The Rev. Benjamin H. Kissler (1961-70)
The Rev. Samuel J. Schmeichen (1961-71)
Kent Youngdahl (1961-64)

Ludwig E. Loos (1963-72)

Robert H. Bowen (1964-70)
Christ Rau (1964-70)

Mrs. Gladys (Wright W.) Brooks (1966-74)
The Rev. James M. Butler (1966-68)
LeRoy O. Deden (1966-72)
Mrs. Richard Dougherty (1966-73)
The Rev. Edward D. Grauman (1966-68)
Gerald L. Hopkins (1966-70)
W. R. Neufeld (1966-71)
The Rev. Chester A. Pennington (1966-71)
Donald Wahl (1966-71)
Roy M. White (1966-72)
Harlan H. Wulke (1966-75)

Terrance L. Webster (1967-72)

The Rev. C. John L. Bates (1968-72)
John E. Herrnstein (1968-75)
Mrs. Mareta Kahlenberg (1968-76)
The Rev. Harold Koenig (1968-76)
William E. Mudge (1968-72)
The Rev. Clifford Perron (1968-70)

Dean McNeal (1969-72)

George D. Dayton, II (1970-75)
The Rev. Scott Libbey (1970-76, 80-85)
Bishop Philip F. McNairy (1970-76)
The Rev. Alton M. Motter (1970-72)
Alex Ostwald (1970-73)
The Rev. Charles B. Purdham (1970-76)
The Rev. Forrest L. Richeson (1970-76) Chair 1972-75
The Rev. A. Knighton Stanley (1970-73)
The Rev. Richard O. Truitt (1970-76)
Dean Louis H. Gunnemann (1970-72)
Prof. Henry A. Gustafson (1970-71)
Prof. Donald R. White (1970-71)
Mark Ketcham (1970-73)
Donald Miller (1970-71)

Mrs. Edith (Lloyd) Hatch (1971-77, 1978-82)
The Rev. Robert J. Miller (1971-73)
The Rev. Hobart Sailor (1971-77)
The Rev. Richard T. Seaman (1971-74)
The Rev. Reuben A. Sheares (1971-78)
Prof. Robert H. Bryant (1971-73)
Prof. James B. Nelson (1971-73)
Richard Gerber (1971-72)
Gary Smith (1971-72)

William N. Driscoll (1972-80) Chair 1975-78
Prof. Clyde J. Steckel (1972-73)
Lark Hapke (1972-73)
Ward Malloy (1972-73)
Tim Morrison (1972-73)

Gordon Shephard (1973-82)
Mrs. Harriet Holden (1973-78)

Dr. James A. Robinson (1973-74)
The Rev. Francis X. Pirazzini (1973-80)
Prof. Henry A. Gustafson (1973-74)
Prof. W. Robert Strobel (1973-74)
Prof. Donald R. White (1973-74)
Kenneth A. Falk (1973-74)
Sheila Henderson (1973-74)
Gary R. Lingen (1973-74)

The Rev. Howard J. Conn (1974-77)
John P. Northcott (1974-80)
Richard B. Tompkins, M.D. (1974-80)
Dean Louis H. Gunnemann (1974-75)
Prof. Arthur L. Merrill (1974-75)
Prof. H. Wilson Yates (1974-75)
Jack Cowart (1974-75)
Kenneth A. Falk (1974-75)
Howard Vogel (1974-75)

Philip M. Harder (1975-83) Chair 1978-83
Herbert D. Bissell (1975-78)
Prof. Dwight W. Culver (1975-81)
The Rev. Charles N. Duddingston (1975-78)
Mrs. Jeannette D. Kahlenberg (1975-80)
The Rev. Gregory H. Ritter (1975-78)
Prof. Holt H. Graham (1975-77)
Prof. Eugene C. Jaberg (1975-76)
Prof. Clyde J. Steckel (1975-76)
Rodger A. Kube (1975-76)
Earl P. Menchhofer (1975-76)
Thomas Stutelberg (1975-76)

Mary Lou Brackett (1976-82)
David J. Buran, M.D. (1976-83)
Charlton Dietz (1976-82)

Frank J. Hammond (1976-82)
Trudy Rogness Jensen (1976-82)
Bruce E. Kiernat (1976-82)
Prof. Allan R. McAllaster (1976-77)
Prof. H. Wilson Yates (1976-77)
Theresa M. Person (1976-77)
Diane Stelter (1976-77)

William W. George (1977-80)
Mary Bigelow McMillan (1977-82, 1983-89) Chair 1985-88
The Hon. Albert H. Quie (1977-82)
Prof. Lance R. Barker (1977-79)
Prof. James B. Nelson (1977-78)
James A. Dodge (1977-79)
Jennifer Dawson (1977-78)

Andrew Hobart (1978-81)
The Rev. Roger Knight (1978-86)
Robert McCrea (1978-86) Chair 1983-85
Harriet Stuart Spencer (1978-86)
Robert Zinn (1978-84)
Prof. Clyde J. Steckel (1978-79)
Marva Jean Hutchens (1978-80)

The Rev. Arthur A. Rouner, Jr. (1979-84)
Paul K. Schilling (1979-86)
Prof. Allan R. McAllaster (1979-80)
Prof. Karen Smith Sellers (1979-80)
Glen Herrington (1979-81)

C. E. Bayliss Griggs (1980-85)
Prof. Eugene C. Jaberg (1980-81)
Prof. Patricia Wilson-Kastner (1980-81)
Sue Zabel (1980-82)

Thomas Breckenridge (1981-90)
Marlene Whiterabbit Helgemo (1981-84)
The Rev. Murdale Leysath (1981-89)
Edward Lund (1981-87)
Margaret Tillitt (1981-85)
Prof. Jane Boyajian (1981-82)
Prof. Donald R. White (1981-83)
Sue Stull (1981-83)

Margaret Bracken (1982-87)
Virginia Brooks (1982-90)
Martha Hulings Kaemmer (1982-
Stephen H. Mahle (1982- Chair 1988-
Prof. H. Wilson Yates (1982-84)
Wilma Lawrence (1982-84)

William Hartfiel (1983-89)
Thomas Mairs (1983-86)
John Shank (1983-85)
Jack Sjoholm, Jr. (1983-87)
Lynn Truesdell, III (1983-88)
Prof. Robert H. Bryant (1983-85)
James Wilson (1983-85)

Mary Ellen Dumas (1984-88)
Dr. Edward Lindell (1984-86)
Ann Pflaum (1984-87)
Prof. Jack E. Rossmann (1984-
Barbara Roy (1984-87)
Richard Schmoker (1984-87)
Prof. Mary Farrell Bednarowski (1984-86)
Judy Bagley-Boner (1984-86)
Peter Calhoun (1984-87)

David W. Hanson (1985-

Marilyn Kingman (1985-87)
Margaret Kinney (1985-91)
Joyce McFarland (1985-86)
C. Paul Pesek (1985-87)
Louise Plank (1985-89)
Julie O'Brien Sharp (1985-86)
James Toscano, M.D. (1985-88)
The Rev. Frederick Trost (1985-
Polly Nyberg Voegeli (1985-88)
Prof. Lance R. Barker (1985-87)
Prof. H. Wilson Yates (1985-86)

Allen C. Blume (1986-90)
Sandra Casmey (1986-88)
John L. Hannaford (1986-
J. Stanley Hill (1986-91)
The Rev. Marva Jean Hutchens (1986-
Carl A. Kuhrmeyer (1986-
John Lindell (1986-89)
Lucy McCarthy (1986-88)
Prof. Henry A. Gustafson (1986-88)
Ruth Huizinga Everhart (1986-88)

Thomas B. Caswell, Jr. (1987-
Mark W. K. Heffelfinger (1987-
The Rev. David Tyler Scoates Sr.(1987-91)
Paul C. Truran (1987-
Prof. Robert H. Bryant (1987-88)
Prof. Mary Potter Engel (1987-89)
Ann Wahlers (1987-89)

William Bartel (1988-
Mark B. Dayton (1988-90)
Prof. Phebe Haugen (1988-
Oscar Howard (1988-

David Koehler (1988-
Duane W. Krohnke (1988-
Charles McGill (1988-90)
Malcolm McLean (1988-
Jonathan H. Morgan (1988-
Laura Shannon (1988-
Prof. B. Edmon Martin (1988-90)
EvaLynn Carlson (1988-90)

Chase Davies (1989-90)
William R. Kiesel (1989-
Hugh K. Schilling (1989-
Belle Scott (1989-
Prof. Helen A. Archibald (1989-91)
Charlotte Matthews (1989-90)

Keith P. Bednarowski (1990-
The Rev. Priscilla W. Braun (1990-
The Rev. Donald A. Gall (1990-91)
Danita McVay Greene (1990-
Hella Mears Hueg (1990-
Ruth Huss (1990-
The Rev. Jeffrey Stinehelfer (1990-
Prof. James B. Nelson (1990-
Sara Orem (1990-

David Haskin (1991-
Prof. Marilyn Salmon (1991-
Wanda Veldman (1991-

Emeriti/ae Trustees

Virginia Brooks
William Driscoll
Philip Harder
Edith Lyndsey Hatch
Mary Bigelow McMillan
Paul K. Schilling
Harriet Spencer Stuart

APPENDIX FOUR

FACULTY ROSTER

Ruben H. Huenemann	1960-1970 President Emeritus, May 1990 at Mission House, 1960-62
Louis H. Gunnemann	1961-1974 Dean and Ministry Studies Emeritus, June 1976 Deceased, Oct. 31, 1989 at Mission House, 1953-62
Robert H. Bryant	1962-1991 Constructive Theology Emeritus, May 1991 at Mission House, 1961-62
Paul L. Hammer	1962-1968 New Testament at Mission House, 1958-62
Theophilus F.H. Hilgeman	1962-1965 Church History Emeritus, May 1965 Deceased, Oct. 27, 1972 at Mission House, 1947-62
Eugene C. Jaberg	1962-1991 Homiletics, Communications Emeritus, May 1991 at Mission House, 1958-62
Roland G. Kley	1962-1974 Librarian Deceased, July 8, 1985 at Mission House, 1957-62
Allan R. McAllaster	1962-85 Old Testament Emeritus, May 1989 at Yankton, 1960-62

Arthur L. Merrill	1962- Old Testament 1983- Director of Library Services at Mission House, 1958-62
W. Robert Strobel	1962-87 Christian Nurture Emeritus, May 1989
Ernest Sprenger	1962-65 Never taught at UTS at Yankton, 1958-62
Thomas C. Campbell	1963-65 Church and Community 1974-79 Dean Deceased, August 12, 1979
James B. Nelson	1963- Christian Ethics
Donald R. White	1965- History and Theology
Gordon Nelson	1966-67 Interim, Church and Society
Emile J. Naef	1966-67 Human Personality Deceased, November 19, 1966
Chris M. Meadows	1967-69 Theology and Personality
H. Wilson Yates	1967- Church and Community 1989- Dean
Henry A. Gustafson	1968-89 New Testament Emeritus, May 1989
Richard L. Kozelka	1970-71 Interim President Deceased, Nov. 12, 1985
Lance R. Barker	1970- Ministry Studies
Clyde J. Steckel	1970- Theology and Psychology 1979-89 Dean
Dayton D. Hultgren	1971-82 President
Richard L. Lohr	1972-75 Vice-President, Development
Holt H. Graham	1974-83 New Testament, Director of Library Services Emeritus, May 1989
Patricia Wilson Kastner	1975-82 Church History, Theology
Mary F. Bednarowski	1976- American Studies, M.A.R.S. Director

Paul Nygren	1976-78 Vice President
Karen Smith Sellers	1977-88 Ministry Studies, M.Div. Director
Gregory H. Ritter	1979-85 Vice President for Development
Jane A. Boyajian	1980-83 Ethics, Center Director
Mitchell Whiterabbit	1980-81 Native American Studies
Harrell D. Davis	1981-84 Native American Studies
B. Edmon Martin	1981- Ministry Studies 1991- Masters Director
Mary Bigelow McMillan	1982-83 Interim President
Howard M. Mills	1983-87 President
Mary Potter Engel	1983-91 Church History, Theology
Valerie DeMarinis	1984-86 Theology and Psychology
Norman Jackson	1985-88 Native American Studies
Helen A. Archibald	1987-91 Christian Education Emerita, May 1991
Benjamin T. Griffin	1987- President 1988- Liturgics
Marilyn Salmon	1989- New Testament
Carolyn J. Pressler	1990- Old Testament
Barbara Anne Keely	1991- Educational Ministries and Contextual Studies
Christine M. Smith	1991- Preaching and Worship
Christie Cozad Neuger	1992- Theology and Psychology
Paul E. Capetz	1992- Historical Theology

APPENDIX FIVE:

GRADUATES OF UNITED

1967

Glenn N. Bender	Orville R. Krebs
Jonathan H. Bunge	John H. Krueger
Jerry A. Flueckiger	Terence L. McCreedy
Abner P. Frost	Dennis H. Peterson
Daniel E. Jonas	John C. Rinehart
Walter P. Koch	Donald L. Stoebner

1964

Reuben E. Bebler	Edward M. Robinson
Veldon Grasmick	Benjamin Talledge
Harriet Johnson	Clemence Wagstrom
Robert W. Middleton	Sheldon W. Warner

Honorary Degree

Elmer J.F. Arndt	Hugo W. Thompson

1965

Larry A. Bremer	Delbert D. Permann
Kenneth A. Dix	Ralph Sayler
R. Lynn Gaylor	Albert A. Schwenke
Ronald A. Getsay	M. Milo Sheldon
Frederick Harberg	Robert J. Tripp
Paul F. Koepke	Bruce D. Unglesbee
Philip C. Meili	Karl J. Vercouteren
Gervas W. Meinzer	

1966

Donald R. Aisenbrey	Erwin R. Miller
Gary E. DeFries	Gary Miller
Hugo Flaig	Kent A. Mosebach
Ronald D. Fruth	G. Lloyd Rediger
Jon P. Gunnemann	James M. Schatz

Gary D. Kasten
Jonathan D. Knecht
Harry D. Krebs
Larry A. Laskie
Charles H. Leck
Richard D. Scheerer
Kenneth C. Schultz
Wayne C. Schupbach
Richard K. Seaman
Donald L. Stoll

Honorary Degree

Alton M. Motter
Ferdinand Schlingensiepen

1967

Michael Adams
James Martin
Robert Randall
Larry C. Randen
Richard Stenzel
Ernest H. Strandberg
James Warn
George Woldseth

Honorary Degree

Walter E. Dobler

1968

Jon R. Almgren
William E. Carlson
Vince W. Carroll
Andrew C. J. Chao
Larry J. Davis
Allan J. Dempsey
Obid O. Hofland, Jr.
Tien Chiao Hsieh
Garret W. Karow
Dale G. Kent
Gary L. Miller
Gerald W. Montgomery
Lee A. Neuhaus
Paul H. Scheele
R. Dean Smith
Lyle W. Stork
W. Eric Walch

Honorary Degree

Chester L. Marcus

1969

Bernard A. Backman
Raymond C. Coombs
Michael F. Groh
Lanning Johnson
Herbert H. Laube
Roger E. LaWarre
Richard C. Ley
Kenneth E. Netz
Norman C. Pavey
Hobart K. Sailor
Raymond M. Schatz
Harold Schippitz, Jr.
Daniel E. Schnabel
Leonard J. Vogt
Louis E. Wollenweber

1970

Craig M. Anderson
Gene D. Bauer
Raymond E. Birkner
Bruce W. Fischer
Dale W. Frank
G. Forrest Hoppe
Dale A. Lautenschlager
David A. Rumpf
Donald R. Schultz
Gary E. Stoos
Albert H. Thompson III
Keith E. Weber

Stephen Hsieh

Honorary Degree

Andrew J. Young

1971

Gerald E. Asheim
Robert J. Blumberg
Daniel L. Busch
Pacifico G. Camarin, Jr
Benjamin C. Crosby
David R. Ecker
Earl F. Kammerud
James A. Laak
James P. Lehmann
John E. Maki
Edward G. Meads
Donald W. Miller
Walter M. Rehberg
Orville H. Sauter
Dennis R. Schaeffer
Wade J. Schemmel
Arthur Standring
Stephen J. Steiner
Hugh R. Stephenson
Jonathan Y. Yu

Master of Arts in Religious Studies

Leon L. Neve

Honorary Degree

Theophilus F. H. Hilgeman

1972

George S. Anderson
Donald E. Baumann
Donald E. Britt
Carl L. Canaday
Marilyn K. Creel
Steven J. Daniels
Kenton C. Fletcher
John W. Fruth
Richard J. Gerber
Richard D. Grobe
Max B. Hayden
Thietje A. Hunt
Carl E. Jensen
George O. Jorenby
William K. Kaseman
Kim L. Katterheinrich
Jerry H. Kruse
C. Richard McNeill
Gary W. Meade
Robert H. Meyer
Jonathan L. Neuse
Robert D. Paulson
Eldon E. Schmidt
Venton H. Scott
Terry C. Tessari
Donald H. Tolzmann
Donald L. Yegerlehner
Robert J. Zeimes

Master of Arts in Religious Studies

Susan M. Ecker
Donna M. Wolff

Master of Theology

John A. Esau
Walter P. Koch

1973

Martha A. Baumer
Steven A. Boots
Shing-Long Lin
Charles Paskvan

Wallace B. Cason
Gregory J. Flint
Otis H. Godfrey III
Lyle B. Greiner
Eric M. Hucke
Mark R. Johnson
Gilbert H. Kinnunen
Rodney E. Rawson
Richard W. Reinwald
Rodney C. Slessor
Alcyd N. Soderfelt
Martin E. Strom
David B. Williams

Master of Arts in Religious Studies

Jean Daugherty
Joyce H. Rosene

Master of Theology

James A. Sorenson

1974

Gregory T. Anderson
John D. Butson
Kermit W. Dancy
Dean P. Fletcher
C. Thomas French
James L. Harmon
Raymond J. Larson
Gary R. Lingen
R. Jeffrey Lupient
Timothy A. Morrison
John R. Pearson
David R. Plumb
Richard E. Poppen
Gregory H. Ritter
Philip G. Schairbaum
Arthur W. Stark
Nelson C. Stone
Robert L. Thaden
David A. Tillyer
Keith A. Tussing
Richard A. Wierwille
Ross S. Wyman

Master of Arts in Religious Studies

Glenn D. Geissinger
Ronald W. Petrich
Harry C. Piper, Jr.
Glendoris Rash

Master of Theology

Thomas R. Breckenridge
David B. Williams
Norman C. Pavey

1975

Kristina Pearson Campbell
Paul C. Genter
Ronald J. Hillstrom
Larry W. Mens
Mary Moreland Hendrickson
Ronald L. Weber
Keith R. Weiland
Ronald R. White

Master of Arts in Religious Studies

Bruce M. Brown
Marjie H. Hawthorne

Master of Theology

Ji Duk Dho
Richard J. Gerber
Paul L. C. Hallett
Ronald A. Rising

1976

Daniel P. Almquist
Richard E. Townsend-Anderson
Don L. Arnold
Wayne H. Brass
Keith J. Brudevold
Sam L. Chollar, Jr.
E. Mark Clemens
Peggy L. Cooper
Alison M. D. Crellin
Charlie Ellis
Donavon P. Eslinger
Kenneth A. Falk
Ronald J. Fletcher
Mathias Geiger
Lark J. Hapke
James M. Harwood
Sally L. Hill
David J. Hodak
Mark E. Jaberg
Marnie A. Kildow
Wayne T. Lura, Sr.
Ward B. Malloy
Richard G. Maser
Patrick F. McKinney
Roger J. Mealiff
Gerrit Molenaar, Jr.
Mary Ann Murray
Mark H. Parsons
Richard L. Pratt, Jr.
John A. Rehnberg, Jr.
John F. Saville
Karen Smith Sellers
Stanley L. Smith
Paul L. Stambaugh
William D. Thurlby
John J. Tschudy, Jr.

Master of Theology

Robert R. Robinson

1977

Verda L. W. Aegerter
Kristin P. Anderson
Anita I. Brander
Wayne C. Drueck
John W. Haddorff
William P. Handy
Sheila C. Henderson
Ned L. Hintzman
Dennis D. Hollinger-Lant
John M. Kelley
Alan S. McCalister
Catherine J. W. McDonald
Ronald N. Meyer
Daniel L. Mott
Douglas E. Nielsen
Michael E. Obenhauer
Marjorie E. Peterson
Roger J. Ring
Joyce H. Rosene
Andrew J. Rosulek
Gary W. Smith
Richard K. Stelter
Randall K. Taber
Terry L. Tilton
Elwyn G. Tinklenberg
Dale C. Trana
Kenneth M. Trana
Lloyd O. Werthmann

Master of Arts in Religious Studies

Marilyn Gustafson Asp
Mark R. Roggenkamp
Thomas F. Hill

Doctor of Ministry

Max B. Hayden
Howard W. Krueger

1978

Joseph R. Alfred
Kathy S. Arnold
Ralph L. Kershner
Katherine A. Mahle

Timothy J. Berg
Susan N. Blons
J. Hollis Bredeweg
William R. Brylinger
Jo H. Campe
James M. Clausen
David E. Crum
Mary Carolyn F. Dorfman
Susan K. Ebbers
Kevin M. Gowdy
David W. Holling
Kenton V. Johnson
Wayne B. McKinney
Mary B. McMillan
F. Dale Parson
Marcella (Peg) Pfab
Muriel Pool
Gary B. Reierson
William G. Schurter
Gifford M. Smith, Jr.
Dane R. Sommer
William F. Swan
Jeremiah Yu

Master of Arts in Religious Studies

Ann E. Millin Brudevold
Howard J. Vogel

Doctor of Ministry

Traverce W. Harrison

1979

Lance A. Bentley
Walter J. Boris
Constance O. Carothers
Lynda N. Christman
Dennis R. Clinefelter
Jennifer C. Dawson
James A. Dodge
Jon C. Fleming
Gretchen W. Fogo
Kenneth A. Giere, Jr.
Ken Grundon
Karl D. Gustafson
Michael K. Hansen
Beth D. Kastner
Willam W. Klossner
Rodger A. Kube
Lanny L. Kuester
Richard A. Jackson
Daniel Larson
Nathan A. Miller
Margaret Z. Morris
Wilys Claire Nelson
Sheryl E. L. Peterson
Richard W. Runge
Robert J. Shaffer
Diane Stelter-Tuttle
Edgar B. Storey
Diane I. Wachtler
Martha A. Winslow

Master of Arts in Religious Studies

Mentor C. Addicks, Jr.
Robert W. David
Juda M. M. Kimbio
Theresa M. Person
Mary Ellen Shaw

Doctor of Ministry

Leonard K. Haggin, Jr.
Jonathan R. Leonard
George R. Robie
R. Deane Postlethwaite

1980

Phyllis H. Averill
Bruce M. Brown
Margaret K. Brudos
Marva Jean Hutchins
Bonnie Jones-Witthuhn
Margery L. Lisle

Edna Mae Carlson
Larry R. Christianson
Curtiss S. DeMars-Johnson
Christofer Duff
Jeff Dybdahl
Robert W. Fitzmeier
Kathleen Goodwill
Ronald O. Greene
Randall M. Hachfeld
Sandra S. Herrmann
James F. Martin
Mary Ellen Mayer
Helen McEvoy-Freese
Christie Cozad Neuger
Estella S. Pettit
Glenn S. Pickering
Philip W. Reller
Katharine S. Reynolds
Nancy B. Rohde
Catherine L. Zelle

NATA Certificates

Gene A. Klein
Norman Nauska

Master of Arts in Religious Studies

Jane E. Delger
Anne A. Hage
Steven D. Newcom
Christina M. Potyondy
Robert J. Smith

Doctor of Ministry

Paul F. Koepke
Larry J. Kuntz
Ronald E. Mattson
Roger A. Parks
Delbert D. Permann
Dwight D. Snesrud

1981

Robert C. Anderson
Joy M. Bailey
Carla J. Bailey-Turner
Bebe L. Baldwin
Katherine H. Bostrom
Melinda L. Chambers
Betty H. Clark
Anita O. Cummings
Kenneth V. Daniel
Virgil J. Foote
Sandra E. Graham
Carol E. Hanson
Katherine L. Harding
Fred M. Huskey
Mary Jane G. Knapp
Mary M. Lundgren
Joanne C. Perrin
Gladys P. Priest
Gloria A. Rusch
Carolyn M. Saunders
Karl F. Schiltz
James C. Swenson
Doris E. Underdahl
Mark A. Voll
Raymond J. Wreford
Brenda K. Yeager

Master of Arts in Religious Studies

Randina J. Cragg
Michael N. Flanagin
Evelyn M. Holthus
Susan M. Wilhelm

Doctor of Ministry

James L. Harmon
Christin M. Lore-Kelly
Peter K. Nord
Robert H. Tucker

1982

Donald L. Adams
Leola Allen
John D. Carson
Peggy Chemberlin
C. Arlene Denzer
Cheryl L. Downey
Duane Ernst
Katherine Gibson
Dawn L. Gillette
Larry Hakes
Glen N. Herrington
Linda M. Hustad
Betty Lundeen
JoBeth Marshall
Cora L. Noble
Mark Nordell
William Rishel
Margaret Lynn Scott
Lyta G. Seddig
Margaret E. Shepherd
Shirley Cox Stoos
John Swisher
Mary Tappe
Gregory Young
Sue Zabel

Master of Arts in Religious Studies

Catherine L. Bakken
Jacqolyn L. Cherne
Randy L. Christiansen
Katharine G. Colby-Newton
Thoma Daniel
Jeanne J. Felder
James R. Kyle
Mary A. Meeker
Norma K. Mossman
William D. Peterson
Jo Anne Smith Rohricht
Florence B. Rusterholz
Laurel A. Stiebler

Doctor of Ministry

Josephine A. Barnes
Bruce W. Fischer
S. Thomas Shifflet

1983

Jeffrey A. Aderman
Joseph C. Bad Moccasin
Jean L. Boese-Rosenstein
Karen K. Boston
Priscilla W. Braun
Sheryl L. Braun-Grundon
Henry D. Campbell
Joanne E. Cassiday
Gary C. Cavender
Jeffrey B. Childs
William R. Colby-Newton
Thomas R. Degnitz
Harold L. EagleBull
William Englund
Wesley D. Fox, Jr.
Nancy R. Kapp
Steven O. Langehough
Mary J. Leisman
Carole S. Lloyd
Mary K. Lunau
Mark I. Magnuson
Kevin M. Maloney
Gary N. McLean
Gene E. Miller
Doris L. Potter
Barry J. Rempp
Elton A. Ryberg
Betty A. Schilling
Barbara E. Schmidt
Gloria L. Stevens
Sheryl L. Stowman
Susan R. Stull
Rosanna M. Walker
Michael Lee Wuehler

Master of Arts in Religious Studies

Katherine B. Lufkin Day
Lee F. Ducette
Bruce Jones
Carol A. Lewis-Newberg
Carolyn S. Nelson
Patricia E. Noble Olson
Lynn C. W. Rossow
Robbyn R. Shiell
Jean T. Wieczorek

Doctor of Ministry

Tyrone L. Burkette
Alan J. Hagstrom
Marion D. Pocker

1984

David A. Barr
Cathy Ann Beaty
Marilyn J. Beckstrom
Audrey D. Benjamin
Scott A. Boese-Rosenstein
Laurie M. Bushbaum
Joseph W. Carpenter
Debra L. Clausen
Donald H. Crissinger-Clark
Janet S. Crissinger-Clark
Nancy J. Deever
Douglas J. Federhart
Roseann Giguere, CSJ
James A. Graham
Daniel J. Herman
Paul A. Howard
Norma Rae Hunt
Ralph O. Johnson
Mary Keen-Antonneau
Wilma J. Lawrence
Lonnie L. Logan
Lynn H. McLean
Janet C. Morey
Susan M. Moss
Richard L. Nichols
Daniel S. Ondich-Batson
Jody L. Ondich-Batson
Jeffrey B. Palmer
Timothy R. Perkins
Mark P. Schowalter
Stuart A. Taylor
Susan M. Taylor
Gary A. Titusdahl
Joanne M. Williamsen

Master of Arts in Religious Studies

Sarah Burton Marshall
Alice F. J. Gallegos
Sandra L. Johnson
Joan M. S. Klink
Mancy L. Lakoskey
Jeanne D. Lischer
Craig A. Moen
Ann M. Pederson
Meredith L. Robinson

Doctor of Ministry

Norman C. Pavey
John F. Roschen

1985

John E. Aeschbury
Teryl K. Akkerman
Eric D. Burnard
Myra A. Carroll-Pezzella
Richard E. Close
Barbara M. de Souza
John F. Dumke
Dee D. Dunn
Ilo J. Madden
Kathleen F. Main
Amanda Merlin-Molstad
Brian A. Miller
Ronald L. Miller
Karen L. Nichols
Hilda A. Parks
Ruth M. Phelps

Barbara L. Edson-Meyer
Richard W. Fylling
James T. Guckenberg
Judith Hambleton
Patrick Handlson
Susan Allers Hatlie
Carol S. Henderson
Terri D. Horn
Jaclyn J. Hoy
James A. Kledis
Julie A. Mall
Cynthia D. Sautter
Carolyn L. Schunter
Carole Shelby
David D. Sickelka
Gene R. Sipprell
Gail A. Van Buren
Lois E. Vetvick
Richard Weaver
Jim Wilson
John R. Yoakam
Lyndon R. Zabel

Master of Arts in Religious Studies

John R. Gutterman, Jr.
Patricia A. McAuliffe
Margaret N. Molinari
Madeleine L. Wiegrefe
Elizabeth Ann Paulson
Jeanette Pettit
Jeanne M.S. Strickland

Doctor of Ministry

James W. Battle
Robert E. Hoeft
Sunday Makinde
Burrell A. Pennings
George L. Sublette

NATA Certificate

Kathleen Nanette Foote

1986

Sandra K. Anderson
Cheryl A. Awtry
Judith E. Bagley-Boner
Patricia F. Berg
Mary E. Bissell
Jill S. Bobholz
Alida M. CeCoster
James A. Faunce-Zimmerman
Susan Faunce-Zimmerman
Cheryl K. Gelner
Cindy M. Gregorson
Evonne M. Kundert-Grosskopf
Carol J. Heckman
Brenda Barnes Jamieson
Stuart Barnes Jamieson
Daniel M. Jensen
Linda P. Johnson
Martha G. Kincaid
Katherine Laine
Lois Ann Laughlin
Joan Lovrien
Michael A. Moore
Judy A. Mulock
Sandra B. Muschewske
Kathryn A. Nelson
Susan R. Preshaw
Ann T. Rabe
Nancy C. Rosenthal
Doris I. Ruben
Frederick C. Sauer
Judith A. Strausz
Jeffrey G. Wartgow

Master of Arts in Religious Studies

Jacqueline M. Goheen
Pamela C. Joern
JoAnn P. O'Reilly
Betty S. Wentworth

Doctor of Ministry

Kristina Campbell
Carl C. Caskey
Lee F. Ducette
Robert J. Galston
Albert O. Grendler
Gary B. Reierson
Robert A. Kunz
Ira S. Williams, Jr.

1987

Pamela E. Barbour
Heather L. Bjork
Peter J. Calhoun
Shirley J. H. Duncanson
Ruth M. Egerer
Gregory H. Garman
Susan Burns Gausman
Sandra Stuart Gray
Allan D. Henden
Jeanny V. House
Jean E. Greenwood
Gregory K. Kapphahn
Deborah Lind Kastanek
Kenneth G. Leischner
Catherine A. McDonald
Kent A. Peterson
Jean E. Rollins
Marilyn J. T. Stone
Richard A. Yramategui
Kathleen W. Zielinski

Master of Arts in Religious Studies

Susan J. Carter
Solveig M. N. Dale
Laura French
Anita C. Hill
Martha G. Wilson
Ruth Larsen
Julie C. Larson
Elizabeth Liebenstein
Ann M. Minnick
Meg A. Riley

Doctor of Ministry

Donald D. Budd
Grace D. Hanson
Gerald R. Wick

NATA Certificate

Darlene Perkins

Honorary Degree

Howard M. Mills

1988

Mary Ann Brown
Samuel J. Buehrer
Katherine M. Burbo
Terry J. Erickson
Jerald A. Fenske
Marylee C. Fithian
Michelle M. Lyons Hanson
Sandra Hareld
Jonathan D. Holmer
Felix H. Hoover
David M. Long-Higgins
Beth A. Long-Higgins
David J. Mampel
Patricia A. Ondarko
Byron K. Perrine
Theresa M. Roos
Judith S. Roska
Stephen P. Savides
Joseph T. Schulte
Isaac Y.-C. Shin
Margaret C. Snyder
Marcial Vasquez

Master of Arts in Religious Studies

Sarah Amos
Howard O. Christenson
Nancy A. Moore

Master of Arts in Theology

Samuel G. Crecelius
JeMae L. Gulliksen
Victoria L. Kessler
Marijane G. Schaefer
David C. Turyagumanawe
Marie E. Vanderbark

Doctor of Ministry

Obid O. Hofland, Jr.
Alva F. Hohl, Jr.
Gerald D. Iwerks
Donald L. McBride
James Porter
Marie Schwann, CSJ

Honorary Doctorate

James M. Savides

1989

Hilary J. Barrett
Leland D. Boss
Karen Chatfield Bruns
Sarah E. Campbell
Mary Helen Cedarholm
Molly M. Cox
Bverly J. Crow
Trri Lee Cuppett
Karen E. Dimon
Lynda S. Ellis
Ruth H. Everhart
John R. Guttemann, Jr.
Katherine A. Hawker
David G. Johnson
Marty J. Jones
Judith A. Kim
Susan E. Lincoln
Donald P. Olsen
Elizabeth Raasch-Gilman
Karen S. Schulte
Noah S. Smith
Andrea L. Stoeckl
Penny L. VanderBerg
Ann P. Wahlers
Gary Walpole
Kay S. Welsch
Ric J. Wilberg
Ronald L. Ziemer

Master of Arts in Religious Studies

Jean S. Mohrig
Sara J. Roberson
Paulette L. Speed
David J. Tidball
Howard G. Wilson

Master of Arts in Theology

Dale C. Dobias
Jillian D. Lay

Doctor of Ministry

Joseph L. Arackal
Ronald A. Erickson
Rosario de Lugo-Batlle
David C. Turyagumanawe

NATA Certificate

Richard S. Charging Eagle

Honorary Degree

Mary Bigelow McMillan

1990

Nancy L. Anderson
David P. Bahr
Mary L. P. Beckman
Robert W. Bellin
Virginia Bergman
Rufus R. Campbell
EvaLyn A. Carlson
Mark L. Farrar
Leonetta B. Green
J. Paige Harmon
Philip A. Harper
Glen A. Holland
Sharon I. F. Johnson
Victoria L. Kessler
Donna Kjonaas
Jungja Haynes Lee
Elizabeth Liebenstein
Kay O. Lindahl
Jeanne D. Lischer
Sandra P. Longfellow
Curtis D. Miller
Jean M. Ottensmann
Mary H. Parker
John R. Praetorius
Helen W. Quintela
Ricky K. Rask
Cynthia L. J. Shepherd
Dale A. Swan
Lark Verzalik

Master of Arts in Religious Studies

Nancy S. Baltins
Bonnie J. Johnson
Joan M. Lilja

Master of Arts in Theology

Arlene C. Dahl
Cheryl S. McKinley
Judith N. Scoville
Sally J. W. Wills

Master of Arts in Religious Leadership

James R. Kikaffunda

Doctor of Ministry

Bruce M. Brown
Harold R. Case
Wendell R. Debner
Gerusa S. dos Santos
Michael L. Papesh
Mary C. Seidel

Honorary Degree

Vivian Jones

1991

Glenn W. Aber
Scott D. Carlson
Rosemary T. Condon
Melinda L. Feller
Karla M. Forsyth
Judith H. Hoover
Nancy J. Horvath
Brian A. Knoderer
Karen W. Mackey
Michelle H. Mathews
Jane C. Nelson
Raymond A. Robinson
Joan Pauly Schneider
John R. Strunk
Deborah M. Walkes
Jack Wieczorek

Scott A. Larson
Barbara J. Wolf

Master of Arts in Religious Studies

Scott C. Morrison
Mary W. Wallace

Master of Arts in Theology

A. Marjorie Erickson
Michael A. Olson
Mary D. Vincent
Kelly N. Waterman
Sheila F. Weidendorf
Linda H. Willette
Donald H. Young

Master of Arts in Religious Leadership

Ann M. Johnson

Doctor of Ministry

James E. Cook
James R. Kikaffunda
Virginia L. Pharr

APPENDIX SIX:

SUPPORT STAFF ROSTER

Allen, Betty	Library Assistant
Anderson, Diane	Library Assistant
Anderson, Doris	Kitchen
Aro, Dorothy	Secretary, Finance
Aronson, Leone	Bookkeeper
Bacon, Virginia	Secretary, President
Babin, Pam	Kitchen
Barz, Emma	Cook
Barz, Ronald	Maintenance Engineer
Batholomew, Donna	Cook
Beightol, Dorothy	Secretary, Faculty
Belohlavek, Betty	Secretary
Bodwell, III, John W.	Vice President for Development
Brandt, Mary Lou (Kley)	Secretary; Library Assistant
Briggs, Evelyn	Secretary, President
Burck, Katherine	Director, Public Relations
Bursell, Donna	Library, Secretary
Bye, Jean	Mail records
Campbell, Carolyn	Secretary, Admissions
Campbell, Treeva	Secretary
Carlson, Edna Mae	Coordinator of Clergy and Lay Relations
Christiansen, Sally	Library assistant
Clark, Windy	Secretary, Accounting
Clifford, Karla	Administrative Secretary, Development
Clinchy, John	Administrative Assistant, AVP
Crannell, Sylvia	Secretary, Development
Crow, Beverly	Admissions Counselor, Community Life
Dahlgren, Ed	Business manager
Dahlin, Dick	Custodian
Day, Katherine	Library Assistant

Dawson, Jennifer	Library Assistant
Dehn, Rob	Custodian
Densine, Jim	Custodian
DeWitt, Joe	Custodian
Dierker, Peter	Business Manager
Dille, Donna (Zigas)	Administrative Assistant, Dean
Dobias, Dale	Librarian, Technical Services
Eastlund, Pam	Development cashier
Ebbers, Sue	Library Assistant, Librarian
Flynn, Mary	Kitchen
Fowler, Dolores	Kitchen
Frieden, Helen	Kitchen
Fudali, Maryonne	Secretary, Development
Gagnon, Judy (Dahlin)	Administrative Assistant, Center
Galligan, Kathy	Library Assistant
Garman, Greg	Admissions Interpreter
Gaylord, Helen	Business Administrator
Gerber, Richard	Program Interpreter
Green, Charles	Vice President for Development
Groh, Michael	Program Interpreter
Grosskopf, Terry	Chef
Gruetzmacher, Mary	Kitchen
Harper, Sharon	Secretary, Development
Harris, Rodney	Caretaker
Hassel, Kris	Secretary
Hedican, Dawn	Kitchen
Heinl, John	Interim Director of Development
Hendricks, Dwight	Director, Deferred Giving
Hoeft, Marian	Secretary, President; Secretary, Front Office Manager; Administrative Asst, AVP
Holler, Karen	Receptionist; Secretary, Development; Administrative Secretary, President
Hollinger-Lant, Dennis	Program Interpreter
Hong, Norma	Secretary, President
Hutchison, Virginia	Secretary
Jaeger, Carolyn	Administrative Secretary
Johnsen, Gladys	Director, Recruitment
Johnson, Liz	Chef
Johnson, Jody	Secretary, Development
Karsten, Nancy	Admissions Intern
Keen-Antonneau, Mary	Pre-Admissions Intern

Keller, Vi	Secretary, Faculty; Receptionist
Kemp, Sharon	Library Assistant
Kewatt, Pat	Maintenance
Kingstedt, Marlowe	Director of Deferred Giving
Kley, Tom	Director of Building and Grounds
Krefting, Margaret	Library Assistant
Kruse, Harriet	Librarian
Kruse, Karyn	Library Assistant
LaDoux, Millie	Secretary, Receptionist
Landmann, Joanne	Development Cashier
Laskie, Janice	Library Assistant
Law, Judith	Director Financial Aid, Registrar
Lewandowski, Sue	Cook, Food Service Director
Lischer, Jeanne	Pre-Admissions Intern
Long-Higgins, David	Admissions Counselor
Lupient, Jeffrey	Program Interpreter
Madison, Albert	Business Administrator
Magnuson, Delores	Secretary, President
Manthey, Janice	Bookkeeper
Marsh, Beth	Secretary, Faculty
Marx, Doris	Secretary
Mattson, Ronald	Food Service Manager
Matushak, Bernadine	Secretary
Meads, Ted	Program Interpreter
Merrill, Jean	Library Assistant
Miller, Curtis	Admissions Counselor
Miller, Diane	Secretary
Miller, Nathan	Program Interpreter
Murray, Mary Anne	Coordinator, Reading Program
Mutch, Virginia	Secretary, President
Neal, Evelyn	Library Assistant
Neal, Clifford	Maintenance Engineer
Nelson, Barbara	Secretary
Nelson, Christine	Library Assistant
Nelson, Mary Ann	Secretary, Ministry Studies; Office Coordinator
Newcom, Steven	Intern, Center for the Shaping of Values
Nyman, Connie	Bookeeper; Director of Financial Aid; Director of Accounting
Nyman, Karen	Administrative Secretary
Nyman, Lois	Business Manager; Vice President for Financial Affairs and Administration
Olson, Donald	Admissions Counselor
Osgood, Don	Building and Grounds

Pahl, Marilyn	Kitchen
Parson, Dale	Program Interpreter
Pearson, Kristina	Program Interpreter
Pentz, Ruth	Kitchen
Perna, Mayme	Library Assistant
Perna, Vernon	Maintenance Engineer
Peters, Donna Lou	Administrative Secretary, Academic
Pharr, Virginia	Acting Director of Admissions
Ranney, Gail	Secretary, President
Richardson, Bea	Cook
Riley, Agnes	Secretary, Development
Rinas, Don	Custodian
Robinson, Raymond	Admissions Counselor
Romano, June	Cook
Rossin, Ruth (Wahlberg)	Secretary
Ruzin, Linda	Kitchen
Scarcella, Karla	Secretary, Development
Schmidt, Michelle (Turneau)	Bookkeeper; Director of Financial Affairs and Personnel; Business Manager; Director of Financial Aid
Schoffelman, Shirley	Administrative Assistant, AVP
Schupbach, Janet	Secretary
Severson, Hazel	Kitchen
Smith, Jean	Library and Bookstore
Spado, Barbara	Secretary, Development
Steltzer, Gladie	Secretary
Stiebler, Laurel	Program Interpreter
Stoos, Gary	Director of Development
Strobel, Alice	Academic Secretary; Administrative Assistant, Dean; Director of Records and Registrar
Swanson, Stella	Kitchen
Swanson, Vera	Secretary, Faculty
Tabbert, Deborah	Secretary
Taber, Chris (Tschudy)	Secretary
Tate, Harris	Heating Engineer
Taylor, Anne	Secretary, Faculty
Tesch, Sandy	Secretary, Business Office
Thayer, Donald	Director, Financial Aid; Registrar
Thorp, Nathan	Custodian
Turner, Paul	Assistant to the President, Development
Tussing, Keith	Director, Alumni and Pre-Admissions

Usher, Joann	Administrative Secretary, President; Director of Business Administration; Assistant to the President; Director, Annual Fund
Vollbrecht, Mae	Secretary, Gifts
Vollbrecht, Robert	Cook
Wahlers, Ann	Secretary
Weiss, Janet	Librarian, Cataloger
White, Becky	Accounting Clerk, Bookkeeper
Whitney, Howard	Business Manager
Wilcoxon, Clair	Assistant Librarian
Wills, Jack	Volunteer Development Associate
Withrow, Betty	Kitchen
Wolff, Mary Lee	Campaign Office; Bookstore Manager
Zabel, Sue	Director, Continuing Ed.; Director of Admissions and Planning
Zelle, Trina	Program Interpreter
Zigas, Jack	Maintenance; Director of Physical Plant

BIBLIOGRAPHY

Anon. *A Short History of the Congregational Christian Council of Theological Schools*. Mimeographed, n.d.

Betsworth, Roger G., *The Radical Movements of the 1960's*. ATLA Monograph Series, No. 14. Metuchen, NJ: Scarecrow Press.

Bridston, Keith R. and Dwight Culver, *Pre-Seminary Education: Report of the Lilly Endowment Study*. Minneapolis, MN: Augsburg Publishing House, 1965.

Duffett, Robert, *The History and Development of the Doctor of Ministry Degree at the Minnesota Consortium of Theological Schools: 1957-1985*. Unpublished Ph.D. dissertation, The University of Iowa, 1986.

Dunn, David, et al. *A History of the Evangelical and Reformed Church*. Philadelphia: Christian Education Press, 1961.

Durand, George, *Joseph Ward of Dakota*. Boston: Pilgrim Press, 1913.

Eisenach, George, J., *A History of the German Congregational Churches in the United States*. Yankton: Pioneer Press, 1938.

_____, *Pietism and the Russian Germans in the United States*. Berne, IN: Berne Publishers, 1948.

Evangelical and Reformed Church, *General Synod, Minutes*, 1938-61.

Good, James, I., *History of the Reformed Church in the U.S. in the Nineteenth Century*. Philadelphia: Reformed Church Publication House, 1899.

Gunnemann, Louis H., *The Shaping of the United Church of Christ*. New York: United Church Press, 1977.

_____, Correspondence. Archives of United Theological Seminary.

Harrison, Paul M., *Theological Education and the United Church of Christ*. Mimeographed, 1967.

Jaberg, Eugene C., et al. *A History of Mission House-Lakeland*. Philadelphia: Christian Education Press, 1962.

Kley, Roland G., *United Theological Seminary: The First Ten Years*. New Brighton: United Theological Seminary, 1972.

Koch, Fred C., *The Volga Germans - In Russia and the Americas*. University Park, PA: Pennsylvania State University Press, 1977.

Meier, Heinrich, A., ed., *Das Missionshaus der Deutch-Reformierten Synode*. Cleveland, OH: Deutsches Verlagshaus der Reformierten Kirche, 1897.

Merrill, Arthur L., Personal Papers. Archives of United Theological Seminary.

Neibuhr, H. Richard, et al. *The Advancement of Theological Education*. New York: Harper and Bros., 1957.

Pusey, Nathan and Charles Taylor, *Ministry for Tomorrow: Report of the Special Committee on Theological Education*, New York: Seabury Press, 1967.

United Church of Christ, *General Synod, Minutes*. 1957-1991.

United Theological Seminary. *Announcements*, 1960-1992.

______. *Board of Trustees, Minutes*, 1960-1992.

______. *Faculty and Faculty Senate, Minutes*, April 14, 1961- .

______. *Self-Study Report*, 1966.

______. *Self-Study Report*, 1975.

______. *Self-Study Report*, 1982.

______. *Self-Study Report*, 1992.

INDEX

J

K

L

M

N

Y